Edmund Burke

Speech of Edmund Burke on moving his resolutions for conciliation with the colonies

March 22, 1775

Edmund Burke

Speech of Edmund Burke on moving his resolutions for conciliation with the colonies
March 22, 1775

ISBN/EAN: 9783337150129

Printed in Europe, USA, Canada, Australia, Japan

Cover: Foto ©ninafisch / pixelio.de

More available books at **www.hansebooks.com**

SPEECH

OF

EDMUND BURKE, Esq.

ON

MOVING HIS RESOLUTIONS

FOR

CONCILIATION with the COLONIES,

MARCH 22, 1775.

THE SECOND EDITION.

LONDON:
Printed for J. DODSLEY, in PALL-MALL.
MDCCLXXV.

SPEECH

OF

EDMUND BURKE, Esq.

I HOPE, Sir, that, notwithstanding the austerity of the Chair, your good-nature will incline you to some degree of indulgence towards human frailty. You will not think it unnatural, that those who have an object depending, which strongly engages their hopes and fears, should be somewhat inclined to superstition. As I came into the house full of anxiety about the event of my motion, I found to my infinite surprize, that the grand penal Bill, by which we had passed sentence on the trade and sustenance of America, is to be returned to us from the other House*. I do confess, I could not help looking on this event as a fortunate omen. I look upon it as a sort of providential favour; by which we are put once more in possession of our deliberative capacity, upon a business so very questionable in its nature, so very uncertain in its issue. By the return of this Bill, which seemed to have taken its flight for ever, we are at this very instant nearly as free to chuse a plan for our American Government, as we were on the first day of the Session. If, Sir, we incline to the side of conciliation, we are not at all embarrassed (unless we please to make ourselves so) by any incongruous mixture of coercion and restraint. We are therefore called upon, as it were by a superior warning voice, again to attend to America; to attend to the whole of it together; and to review the subject with an unusual degree of care and calmness.

Surely it is an awful subject; or there is none so on this side of the grave. When I first had the honour of a seat in this House, the affairs of that Continent pressed themselves upon us, as the most important and most delicate object of parliamentary attention. My little share in this

---

* *The Act to restrain the Trade and Commerce of the Provinces of Massachuset's Bay and New Hampshire, and Colonies of Connecticut and Rhode Island, and Providence Plantation, in North America, to Great Britain, Ireland, and the British Islands in the West Indies; and to prohibit such Provinces and Colonies from carrying on any Fishery on the Banks of Newfoundland, and other places therein mentioned, under certain Conditions and Limitations.*

great

great deliberation oppreſſed me. I found myſelf a partaker in a very high truſt; and having no ſort of reaſon to rely on the ſtrength of my natural abilities for the proper execution of that truſt, I was obliged to take more than common pains, to inſtruct myſelf in every thing which relates to our Colonies. I was not leſs under the neceſſity of forming ſome fixed ideas, concerning the general policy of the Britiſh Empire. Something of this ſort ſeemed to be indiſpenſable; in order, amidſt ſo vaſt a fluctuation of paſſions and opinions, to concenter my thoughts; to ballaſt my conduct; to preſerve me from being blown about by every wind of faſhionable doctrine. I really did not think it ſafe, or manly, to have freſh principles to ſeek upon every freſh mail which ſhould arrive from America.

At that period, I had the fortune to find myſelf in perfect concurrence with a large majority in this Houſe. Bowing under that high authority, and penetrated with the ſharpneſs and ſtrength of that early impreſſion, I have continued ever ſince, without the leaſt deviation, in my original ſentiments. Whether this be owing to an obſtinate perſeverance in error, or to a religious adherence to what appears to me truth and reaſon, it is in your equity to judge.

Sir, Parliament having an enlarged view of objects, made, during this interval, more frequent changes in their ſentiments and their conduct, than

than could be juſtified in a particular perſon upon the contracted ſcale of private information. But though I do not hazard any thing approaching to a cenſure on the motives of former parliaments to all thoſe alterations, one fact is undoubted; that under them the ſtate of America has been kept in continual agitation. Every thing adminiſtered as remedy to the public complaint, if it did not produce, was at leaſt followed by, an heightening of the diſtemper; until, by a variety of experiments, that important Country has been brought into her preſent ſituation;—a ſituation, which I will not miſcall, which I dare not name; which I ſcarcely know how to comprehend in the terms of any deſcription.

In this poſture, Sir, things ſtood at the beginning of the ſeſſion. About that time, a worthy member * of great parliamentary experience, who, in the year 1766, filled the chair of the American committee with much ability, took me aſide; and, lamenting the preſent aſpect of our politicks, told me, things were come to ſuch a paſs, that our former methods of proceeding in the houſe would be no longer tolerated. That the public tribunal (never too indulgent to a long and unſucceſsful oppoſition) would now ſcrutinize our conduct with unuſual ſeverity. That the very viciſſitudes and ſhiftings of miniſterial meaſures, inſtead of convicting their authors

* Mr. Roſe Fuller.

of inconstancy and want of system, would be taken as an occasion of charging us with a predetermined discontent, which nothing could satisfy; whilst we accused every measure of vigour as cruel, and every proposal of lenity as weak and irresolute. The publick, he said, would not have patience to see us play the game out with our adversaries: we must produce our hand. It would be expected, that those who for many years had been active in such affairs should shew, that they had formed some clear and decided idea of the principles of Colony Government; and were capable of drawing out something like a platform of the ground, which might be laid for future and permanent tranquillity.

I felt the truth of what my Hon. Friend represented; but I felt my situation too. His application might have been made with far greater propriety to many other gentlemen. No man was indeed ever better disposed, or worse qualified, for such an undertaking than myself. Though I gave so far into his opinion, that I immediately threw my thoughts into a sort of parliamentary form, I was by no means equally ready to produce them. It generally argues some degree of natural impotence of mind, or some want of knowledge of the world, to hazard Plans of Government, except from a seat of Authority. Propositions are made, not only ineffectually, but somewhat disreputably, when the minds of men are not properly disposed for their reception; and for my part, I am not ambitious of ridicule; not absolutely a candidate for disgrace.

Besides, Sir, to speak the plain truth, I have in general no very exalted opinion of the virtue of Paper Government; nor of any Politicks, in which the plan is to be wholly separated from the execution. But when I saw, that anger and violence prevailed every day more and more; and that things were hastening towards an incurable alienation of our Colonies; I confess, my caution gave way. I felt this, as one of those few moments in which decorum yields to an higher duty. Public calamity is a mighty leveller; and there are occasions when any, even the slightest, chance of doing good, must be laid hold on, even by the most inconsiderable person.

To restore order and repose to an Empire so great and so distracted as ours, is, merely in the attempt, an undertaking that would ennoble the flights of the highest genius, and obtain pardon for the efforts of the meanest understanding. Struggling a good while with these thoughts, by degrees I felt myself more firm. I derived, at length, some confidence from what in other circumstances usually produces timidity. I grew less anxious, even from the idea of my own insignificance. For, judging of what you are, by what you ought to be, I persuaded myself, that you would not reject a reasonable proposition, because it had nothing but its reason to recommend it.

it. On the other hand, being totally deſtitute of all ſhadow of influence, natural or adventitious, I was very ſure, that, if my propoſition were futile or dangerous; if it were weakly conceived, or improperly timed, there was nothing exterior to it, of power to awe, dazzle, or delude you. You will ſee it juſt as it is; and you will treat it juſt as it deſerves.

The propoſition is Peace. Not Peace through the medium of War; not Peace to be hunted through the labyrinth of intricate and endleſs negociations; not Peace to ariſe out of univerſal diſcord, fomented, from principle, in all parts of the Empire; not Peace to depend on the Juridical Determination of perplexing queſtions; or the preciſe marking the ſhadowy boundaries of a complex Government. It is ſimple Peace; ſought in its natural courſe, and its ordinary haunts.—It is Peace ſought in the Spirit of Peace; and laid in principles purely pacific. I propoſe, by removing the Ground of the difference, and by reſtoring the *former unſuſpecting confidence of the Colonies in the Mother Country*, to give permanent ſatisfaction to your people; and (far from a ſcheme of ruling by diſcord) to reconcile them to each other in the ſame act, and by the bond of the very ſame intereſt, which reconciles them to Britiſh Government.

My idea is nothing more. Refined policy ever has been the parent of confuſion; and ever

ever will be so, as long as the world endures. Plain good intention, which is as easily discovered at the first view, as fraud is surely detected at last, is, let me say, of no mean force in the Government of Mankind. Genuine Simplicity of heart is an healing and cementing principle. My Plan, therefore, being formed upon the most simple grounds imaginable, may disappoint some people, when they hear it. It has nothing to recommend it to the pruriency of curious ears. There is nothing at all new and captivating in it. It has nothing of the Splendor of the Project, which has been lately laid upon your Table by the Noble Lord in the Blue Ribband*. It does not propose to fill your Lobby with squabbling Colony Agents, who will require the interposition of your Mace, at every instant, to keep the peace amongst them. It does not institute a

---

* "That when the Governor, Council, or Assembly, or General Court, of any of his Majesty's Provinces or Colonies in America, shall *propose* to make provision, *according to the condition, circumstances*, and *situation*, of such Province or Colony, for contributing their *proportion* to the *Common Defence* (such *proportion* to be raised under the Authority of the General Court, or General Assembly, of such Province or Colony, and disposable by Parliament) and shall *engage* to make Provision also for the support of the Civil Government, and the Administration of Justice, in such Province or Colony, it will be proper, *if such Proposal shall be approved by his Majesty, and the two Houses of Parliament*, and for so long as such Provision shall be made accordingly, to forbear, *in respect of such Province or Colony*, to levy any Duty, Tax, or Assessment, or to impose any further Duty, Tax, or Assessment, except such Duties as it may be expedient to continue to levy or impose, for the Regulation of Commerce; the Nett Produce of the Duties last mentioned to be carried to the account of such Province or Colony respectively." Resolution moved by Lord North in the Committee; and agreed to by the House, 27 Feb. 1775.

magnificent

magnificent Auction of Finance, where captivated provinces come to general ransom by bidding against each other, until you knock down the hammer, and determine a proportion of payments, beyond all the powers of Algebra to equalize and settle.

The plan, which I shall presume to suggest, derives, however, one great advantage from the proposition and registry of that Noble Lord's Project. The idea of conciliation is admissible. First, the House, in accepting the resolution moved by the Noble Lord, has admitted, notwithstanding the menacing front of our Address, notwithstanding our heavy Bill of Pains and Penalties—that we do not think ourselves precluded from all ideas of free Grace and Bounty.

The House has gone farther; it has declared conciliation admissible, *previous* to any submission on the part of America. It has even shot a good deal beyond that mark, and has admitted, that the complaints of our former mode of exerting the Right of Taxation were not wholly unfounded. That right thus exerted is allowed to have had something reprehensible in it; something unwise, or something grievous: since, in the midst of our heat and resentment, we, of ourselves, have proposed a capital alteration; and, in order to get rid of what seemed so very exceptionable, have instituted a mode that is altogether new; one that is, indeed, wholly alien
from

from all the ancient methods and forms of Parliament.

The *principle* of this proceeding is large enough for my purpose. The means proposed by the Noble Lord for carrying his ideas into execution, I think indeed, are very indifferently suited to the end; and this I shall endeavour to shew you before I sit down. But, for the present, I take my ground on the admitted principle. I mean to give peace. Peace implies reconciliation; and where there has been a material dispute, reconciliation does in a manner always imply concession on the one part or on the other. In this state of things I make no difficulty in affirming, that the proposal ought to originate from us. Great and acknowledged force is not impaired, either in effect or in opinion, by an unwillingness to exert itself. The superior power may offer peace with honour and with safety. Such an offer from such a power will be attributed to magnanimity. But the concessions of the weak are the concessions of fear. When such a one is disarmed, he is wholly at the mercy of his superior; and he loses for ever that time and those chances, which, as they happen to all men, are the strength and resources of all inferior power.

The capital leading questions on which you must this day decide, are these two. First, whether you ought to concede; and secondly, what your concession ought to be. On the first of these

these questions we have gained (as I have just taken the liberty of observing to you) some ground. But I am sensible that a good deal more is still to be done. Indeed, Sir, to enable us to determine both on the one and the other of these great questions with a firm and precise judgement, I think it may be necessary to consider distinctly the true nature and the peculiar circumstances of the object which we have before us. Because after all our struggle, whether we will or not, we must govern America, according to that nature, and to those circumstances; and not according to our own imaginations; not according to abstract ideas of right; by no means according to mere general theories of government, the resort to which appears to me, in our present situation, no better than arrant trifling. I shall therefore endeavour, with your leave, to lay before you some of the most material of these circumstances in as full and as clear a manner as I am able to state them.

The first thing that we have to consider with regard to the nature of the object is—the number of people in the Colonies. I have taken for some years a good deal of pains on that point. I can by no calculation justify myself in placing the number below Two Millions of inhabitants of our own European blood and colour; besides at least 500,000 others, who form no inconsiderable part of the strength and opulence of the whole. This, Sir, is, I believe, about the true number.

There

There is no occasion to exaggerate, where plain truth is of so much weight and importance. But whether I put the present numbers too high or too low, is a matter of little moment. Such is the strength with which population shoots in that part of the world, that state the numbers as high as we will, whilst the dispute continues, the exaggeration ends. Whilst we are discussing any given magnitude, they are grown to it. Whilst we spend our time in deliberating on the mode of governing Two Millions, we shall find we have Millions more to manage. Your children do not grow faster from infancy to manhood, than they spread from families to communities, and from villages to nations.

I put this consideration of the present and the growing numbers in the front of our deliberation; because, Sir, this consideration will make it evident to a blunter discernment than yours, that no partial, narrow, contracted, pinched, occasional system will be at all suitable to such an object. It will shew you, that it is not to be considered as one of those *Minima* which are out of the eye and consideration of the law; not a paltry excrescence of the state; not a mean dependant, who may be neglected with little damage, and provoked with little danger. It will prove, that some degree of care and caution is required in the handling such an object; it will shew, that you ought not, in reason, to trifle with so large a mass of the interests and feelings of the human race.

race. You could at no time do so without guilt; and be assured you will not be able to do it long with impunity.

But the population of this country, the great and growing population, though a very important consideration, will lose much of its weight, if not combined with other circumstances. The commerce of your Colonies is out of all proportion beyond the numbers of the people. This ground of their commerce indeed has been trod some days ago, and with great ability, by a distinguished * person, at your bar. This gentleman, after Thirty-five years—it is so long since he first appeared at the same place to plead for the commerce of Great Britain—has come again before you to plead the same cause, without any other effect of time, than, that to the fire of imagination and extent of erudition, which even then marked him as one of the first literary characters of his age, he has added a consummate knowledge in the commercial interest of his country, formed by a long course of enlightened and discriminating experience.

Sir, I should be inexcusable in coming after such a person with any detail; if a great part of the members who now fill the House had not the misfortune to be absent, when he appeared at your bar. Besides, Sir, I propose to take the matter at periods of time somewhat different

* Mr. Glover.

from

from his. There is, if I miftake not, a point of view, from whence if you will look at this fubject, it is impoffible that it fhould not make an impreffion upon you.

I have in my hand two accounts; one a comparative ftate of the export trade of England to its Colonies, as it ftood in the year 1704, and as it ftood in the year 1772. The other a ftate of the export trade of this country to its Colonies alone, as it ftood in 1772, compared with the whole trade of England to all parts of the world (the Colonies included) in the year 1704. They are from good vouchers; the latter period from the accounts on your table, the earlier from an original manufcript of Davenant, who firft eftablifhed the Infpector General's office, which has been ever fince his time fo abundant a fource of parliamentary information.

The export trade to the Colonies confifts of three great branches. The African, which, terminating almoft wholly in the Colonies, muft be put to the account of their commerce; the Weft Indian; and the North American. All thefe are fo interwoven, that the attempt to feparate them, would tear to pieces the contexture of the whole; and if not entirely deftroy, would very much depreciate the value of all the parts. I therefore confider thefe three denominations to be, what in effect they are, one trade.

The

The trade to the Colonies, taken on the export side, at the beginning of this century, that is, in the year 1704, stood thus:

Exports to North America, and the
 West Indies, - - - - - - £483,265
   To Africa, - - - - - - 86,665
            ———
            569,930

In the year 1772, which I take as a middle year between the highest and lowest of those lately laid on your table, the account was as follows:

To North America, and the West
 Indies, - - - - - £4,791,734
To Africa, - - - - - - - 866,398

To which if you add the export trade from Scotland, which had in 1704 no existence, - - - } 364,000
            ———
            6,024,171

From Five Hundred and odd Thousand, it has grown to Six Millions. It has increased no less than twelve-fold. This is the state of the Colony trade, as compared with itself at these two

two periods, within this century;—and this is matter for meditation. But this is not all. Examine my second account. See how the export trade to the Colonies alone in 1772 stood in the other point of view, that is, as compared to the whole trade of England in 1704.

The whole export trade of England, including that to the Colonies, in 1704, - - - - - - £ 6,509,000

Export to the Colonies alone, in 1772, - - - - - - 6,024,000

Difference, 485,000

The trade with America alone is now within less than 500,000 *l.* of being equal to what this great commercial nation, England, carried on at the beginning of this century with the whole world! If I had taken the largest year of those on your table, it would rather have exceeded. But, it will be said, is not this American trade an unnatural protuberance, that has drawn the juices from the rest of the body? The reverse. It is the very food that has nourished every other part into its present magnitude. Our general trade has been greatly augmented; and augmented more or less in almost every part to which it ever extended; but with this material difference; that of the Six Millions which in the beginning of the century constituted the whole mass of our export commerce, the Colony trade was but one twelfth

twelfth part; it is now (as a part of Sixteen Millions) confiderably more than a third of the whole. This is the relative proportion of the importance of the Colonies at thefe two periods: and all reafoning concerning our mode of treating them muft have this proportion as its bafis; or it is a reafoning weak, rotten, and fophiftical.

Mr. Speaker, I cannot prevail on myfelf to hurry over this great confideration. It is good for us to be here. We ftand where we have an immenfe view of what is, and what is paft. Clouds indeed, and darknefs, reft upon the future. Let us however, before we defcend from this noble eminence, reflect that this growth of our national profperity has happened within the fhort period of the life of man. It has happened within Sixty-eight years. There are thofe alive whofe memory might touch the two extremities. For inftance, my Lord Bathurft might remember all the ftages of the progrefs. He was in 1704 of an age, at leaft to be made to comprehend fuch things. He was then old enough *acta parentum jam legere, et quæ fit poterit cognofcere virtus*— Suppofe, Sir, that the angel of this aufpicious youth, forefeeing the many virtues, which made him one of the moft amiable, as he is one of the moft fortunate men of his age, had opened to him in vifion, that, when, in the fourth generation, the third Prince of the Houfe of Brunfwick had fat Twelve years on the throne of that nation, which (by the happy iffue of
moderate

derate and healing councils) was to be made Great Britain, he should see his son, Lord Chancellor of England, turn back the current of hereditary dignity to its fountain, and raise him to an higher rank of Peerage, whilst he enriched the family with a new one — If amidst these bright and happy scenes of domestic honour and prosperity, that angel should have drawn up the curtain, and unfolded the rising glories of his country, and whilst he was gazing with admiration on the then commercial grandeur of England, The Genius should point out to him a little speck, scarce visible in the mass of the national interest, a small seminal principle, rather than a formed body, and should tell him — " Young man,
" There is America—which at this day serves
" for little more than to amuse you with stories
" of savage men, and uncouth manners; yet
" shall, before you taste of death, shew itself
" equal to the whole of that commerce which
" now attracts the envy of the world. What-
" ever England has been growing to by a pro-
" gressive increase of improvement, brought in
" by varieties of people, by succession of civiliz-
" ing conquests and civilizing settlements in a
" series of Seventeen Hundred years, you shall
" see as much added to her by America in the
" course of a single life!" If this state of his country had been foretold to him, would it not require all the sanguine credulity of youth, and all the fervid glow of enthusiasm, to make him believe it? Fortunate man, he has lived to see it!

it! Fortunate indeed, if he lives to see nothing that shall vary the prospect; and cloud the setting of his day!

Excuse me, Sir, if turning from such thoughts I resume this comparative view once more. You have seen it on a large scale; look at it on a small one. I will point out to your attention a particular instance of it in the single province of Pensylvania. In the year 1704 that province called for 11,459 *l.* in value of your commodities, native and foreign. This was the whole. What did it demand in 1772? Why nearly Fifty times as much; for in that year the export to Pensylvania was 507,909 *l.* nearly equal to the export to all the Colonies together in the first period.

I choose, Sir, to enter into these minute and particular details; because generalities, which in all other cases are apt to heighten and raise the subject, have here a tendency to sink it. When we speak of the commerce with our Colonies, fiction lags after truth; invention is unfruitful, and imagination cold and barren.

So far, Sir, as to the importance of the object in the view of its commerce, as concerned in the exports from England. If I were to detail the imports, I could shew how many enjoyments they procure, which deceive the burthen of life; how many materials which invigorate the springs of

national

national industry, and extend and animate every part of our foreign and domestic commerce. This would be a curious subject indeed—but I must prescribe bounds to myself in a matter so vast and various.

I pass therefore to the Colonies in another point of view, their agriculture. This they have prosecuted with such a spirit, that, besides feeding plentifully their own growing multitude, their annual export of grain, comprehending rice, has some years ago exceeded a Million in value. Of their last harvest, I am persuaded, they will export much more. At the beginning of the century, some of these Colonies imported corn from the mother country. For some time past, the old world has been fed from the new. The scarcity which you have felt would have been a desolating famine; if this child of your old age, with a true filial piety, with a Roman charity, had not put the full breast of its youthful exuberance to the mouth of its exhausted parent.

As to the wealth which the Colonies have drawn from the sea by their fisheries, you had all that matter fully opened at your bar. You surely thought those acquisitions of value; for they seemed even to excite your envy; and yet the spirit, by which that enterprizing employment has been exercised, ought rather, in my opinion, to have raised your esteem and admiration. And pray,

pray, Sir, what in the world is equal to it? Pass by the other parts, and look at the manner in which the people of New England have of late carried on the Whale Fishery. Whilst we follow them among the tumbling mountains of ice, and behold them penetrating into the deepest frozen recesses of Hudson's Bay, and Davis's Streights, whilst we are looking for them beneath the Arctic circle, we hear that they have pierced into the opposite region of polar cold, that they are at the Antipodes, and engaged under the frozen serpent of the south. Falkland Island, which seemed too remote and romantic an object for the grasp of national ambition, is but a stage and resting-place in the progress of their victorious industry. Nor is the equinoctial heat more discouraging to them, than the accumulated winter of both the poles. We know that whilst some of them draw the line and strike the harpoon on the coast of Africa, others run the longitude, and pursue their gigantic game along the coast of Brazil. No sea but what is vexed by their fisheries. No climate that is not witness to their toils. Neither the perseverance of Holland, nor the activity of France, nor the dextrous and firm sagacity of English enterprize, ever carried this most perilous mode of hardy industry to the extent to which it has been pushed by this recent people; a people who are still, as it were, but in the gristle, and not yet hardened into the bone of manhood. When I contemplate these things;

things; when I know that the Colonies in general owe little or nothing to any care of ours, and that they are not squeezed into this happy form by the constraints of watchful and suspicious government, but that through a wise and salutary neglect, a generous nature has been suffered to take her own way to perfection: when I reflect upon these effects, when I see how profitable they have been to us, I feel all the pride of power sink, and all presumption in the wisdom of human contrivances melt, and die away within me. My rigour relents. I pardon something to the spirit of Liberty.

I am sensible, Sir, that all which I have asserted in my detail, is admitted in the gross; but that quite a different conclusion is drawn from it. America, Gentlemen say, is a noble object. It is an object well worth fighting for. Certainly it is, if fighting a people be the best way of gaining them. Gentlemen in this respect will be led to their choice of means by their complexions and their habits. Those who understand the military art, will of course have some predilection for it. Those who wield the thunder of the state, may have more confidence in the efficacy of arms. But I confess, possibly for want of this knowledge, my opinion is much more in favour of prudent management, than of force; considering force not as an odious, but a feeble instrument, for preserving a people so numerous, so active, so growing, so spirited as this,

this, in a profitable and subordinate connexion with us.

First, Sir, permit me to observe, that the use of force alone is but *temporary*. It may subdue for a moment; but it does not remove the necessity of subduing again: and a nation is not governed, which is perpetually to be conquered.

My next objection is its *uncertainty*. Terror is not always the effect of force; and an armament is not a victory. If you do not succeed, you are without resource; for, conciliation failing, force remains; but, force failing, no further hope of reconciliation is left. Power and authority are sometimes bought by kindness; but they can never be begged as alms, by an impoverished and defeated violence.

A further objection to force is, that you *impair the object* by your very endeavours to preserve it. The thing you fought for, is not the thing which you recover; but depreciated, sunk, wasted, and consumed in the contest. Nothing less will content me, than *whole America*. I do not choose to consume its strength along with our own; because in all parts it is the British strength that I consume. I do not choose to be caught by a foreign enemy at the end of this exhausting conflict; and still less in the midst of it. I may escape; but I can make no insurance against such an event. Let me add, that I do not

not choose wholly to break the American spirit, because it is the spirit that has made the country.

Lastly, we have no sort of *experience* in favour of force as an instrument in the rule of our Colonies. Their growth and their utility has been owing to methods altogether different. Our ancient indulgence has been said to be pursued to a fault. It may be so. But we know, if feeling is evidence, that our fault was more tolerable than our attempt to mend it; and our sin far more salutary than our penitence.

These, Sir, are my reasons for not entertaining that high opinion of untried force, by which many Gentlemen, for whose sentiments in other particulars I have great respect, seem to be so greatly captivated. But there is still behind a third consideration concerning this object, which serves to determine my opinion on the sort of policy which ought to be pursued in the management of America, even more than its Population and its Commerce, I mean its *Temper and Character.*

In this Character of the Americans, a love of Freedom is the predominating feature, which marks and distinguishes the whole: and as an ardent is always a jealous affection, your Colonies become suspicious, restive, and untractable, whenever they see the least attempt to wrest from them by force, or shuffle from them by chicane,

chicane, what they think the only advantage worth living for. This fierce spirit of Liberty is stronger in the English Colonies probably than in any other people of the earth; and this from a great variety of powerful causes; which, to understand the true temper of their minds, and the direction which this spirit takes, it will not be amiss to lay open somewhat more largely.

First, the people of the Colonies are descendents of Englishmen. England, Sir, is a nation, which still I hope respects, and formerly adored, her freedom. The Colonists emigrated from you, when this part of your character was most predominant; and they took this bias and direction the moment they parted from your hands. They are therefore not only devoted to Liberty, but to Liberty according to English ideas, and on English principles. Abstract Liberty, like other mere abstractions, is not to be found. Liberty inheres in some sensible object; and every nation has formed to itself some favourite point, which by way of eminence becomes the criterion of their happiness. It happened, you know, Sir, that the great contests for freedom in this country were from the earliest times chiefly upon the question of Taxing. Most of the contests in the ancient commonwealths turned primarily on the right of election of magistrates; or on the balance among the several orders of the state. The question of money was not with them so immediate. But in England it was otherwise.

wife. On this point of Taxes the ablest pens, and most eloquent tongues have been exercised; the greatest spirits have acted and suffered. In order to give the fullest satisfaction concerning the importance of this point, it was not only necessary for those who in argument defended the excellence of the English constitution, to insist on this privilege of granting money as a dry point of fact, and to prove, that the right had been acknowledged in ancient parchments, and blind usages, to reside in a certain body called an House of Commons. They went much further; they attempted to prove, and they succeeded, that in theory it ought to be so, from the particular nature of a House of Commons, as an immediate representative of the people; whether the old records had delivered this oracle or not. They took infinite pains to inculcate, as a fundamental principle, that, in all monarchies, the people must in effect themselves mediately or immediately possess the power of granting their own money, or no shadow of liberty could subsist. The Colonies draw from you as with their life-blood, these ideas and principles. Their love of liberty, as with you, fixed and attached on this specific point of taxing. Liberty might be safe, or might be endangered in twenty other particulars, without their being much pleased or alarmed. Here they felt its pulse; and as they found that beat, they thought themselves sick or sound. I do not say whether they were right or wrong in applying

your

your general arguments to their own cafe. It is not eafy indeed to make a monopoly of theorems and corollaries. The fact is, that they did thus apply thofe general arguments; and your mode of governing them, whether through lenity or indolence, through wifdom or miftake, confirmed them in the imagination, that they, as well as you, had an intereft in thefe common principles.

They were further confirmed in this pleafing error by the form of their provincial legiflative affemblies. Their governments are popular in an high degree; fome are merely popular; in all, the popular reprefentative is the moft weighty; and this fhare of the people in their ordinary government never fails to infpire them with lofty fentiments, and with a ftrong averfion from whatever tends to deprive them of their chief importance.

If any thing were wanting to this neceffary operation of the form of government, Religion would have given it a complete effect. Religion, always a principle of energy, in this new people, is no way worn out or impaired; and their mode of profeffing it is alfo one main caufe of this free fpirit. The people are proteftants; and of that kind, which is the moft adverfe to all implicit fubmiffion of mind and opinion. This is a perfuafion not only favourable to liberty, but built upon it. I do not think, Sir, that the reafon of

this

this averseness in the dissenting churches from all that looks like absolute Government is so much to be sought in their religious tenets, as in their history. Every one knows, that the Roman Catholick religion is at least coeval with most of the governments where it prevails; that it has generally gone hand in hand with them; and received great favour and every kind of support from authority. The Church of England too was formed from her cradle under the nursing care of regular government. But the dissenting interests have sprung up in direct opposition to all the ordinary powers of the world; and could justify that opposition only on a strong claim to natural liberty. Their very existence depended on the powerful and unremitted assertion of that claim. All protestantism, even the most cold and passive, is a sort of dissent. But the religion most prevalent in our Northern Colonies is a refinement on the principle of resistance; it is the diffidence of dissent; and the protestantism of the protestant religion. This religion, under a variety of denominations, agreeing in nothing but in the communion of the spirit of liberty, is predominant in most of the Northern provinces; where the Church of England, notwithstanding its legal rights, is in reality no more than a sort of private sect, not composing most probably the tenth of the people. The Colonists left England when this spirit was high; and in the emigrants was the highest of all: and even that stream of foreigners, which

has

has been conſtantly flowing into theſe Colonies, has, for the greateſt part, been compoſed of diſſenters from the eſtabliſhments of their ſeveral countries, and have brought with them a temper and character far from alien to that of the people with whom they mixed.

Sir, I can perceive by their manner, that ſome Gentlemen object to the latitude of this deſcription; becauſe in the Southern Colonies the Church of England forms a large body, and has a regular eſtabliſhment. It is certainly true. There is however a circumſtance attending theſe Colonies, which in my opinion, fully counterbalances this difference, and makes the ſpirit of liberty ſtill more high and haughty than in thoſe to the Northward. It is that in Virginia and the Carolinas, they have a vaſt multitude of ſlaves. Where this is the caſe in any part of the world, thoſe who are free, are by far the moſt proud and jealous of their freedom. Freedom is to them not only an enjoyment, but a kind of rank and privilege. Not ſeeing there, that freedom, as in countries where it is a common bleſſing, and as broad and general as the air, may be united with much abject toil, with great miſery, with all the exterior of ſervitude, Liberty looks amongſt them, like ſomething that is more noble and liberal. I do not mean, Sir, to commend the ſuperior morality of this ſentiment, which has at leaſt as much pride as virtue in it; but I cannot alter the nature of of man. The fact is so; and these people of the Southern Colonies are much more strongly, and with an higher and more stubborn spirit, attached to liberty than those to the Northward. Such were all the ancient common wealths; such were our Gothick ancestors; such in our days were the Poles; and such will be all masters of slaves, who are not slaves themselves. In such a people the haughtiness of domination combines with the spirit of freedom, fortifies it, and renders it invincible.

Permit me, Sir, to add another circumstance in our Colonies, which contributes no mean part towards the growth and effect of this untractable spirit. I mean their education. In no country perhaps in the world is the law so general a study. The profession itself is numerous and powerful; and in most provinces it takes the lead. The greater number of the Deputies sent to the Congress were Lawyers. But all who read, and most do read, endeavour to obtain some smattering in that science. I have been told by an eminent Bookseller, that in no branch of his business, after tracts of popular devotion, were so many books as those on the Law exported to the Plantations. The Colonists have now fallen into the way of printing them for their own use. I hear that they have sold nearly as many of Blackstone's Commentaries in America as in England. General Gage marks out this disposition very particularly in a letter on your table.

table. He states, that all the people in his government are lawyers, or smatterers in law; and that in Boston they have been enabled, by successful chicane, wholly to evade many parts of one of your capital penal constitutions. The smartness of debate will say, that this knowledge ought to teach them more clearly the rights of legislature, their obligations to obedience, and the penalties of rebellion. All this is mighty well. But my * honourable and learned friend on the floor, who condescends to mark what I say for animadversion, will disdain that ground. He has heard as well as I, that when great honours and great emoluments do not win over this knowledge to the service of the state, it is a formidable adversary to government. If the spirit be not tamed and broken by these happy methods, it is stubborn and litigious. *Abeunt studia in mores.* This study renders men acute, inquisitive, dextrous, prompt in attack, ready in defence, full of resources. In other countries, the people, more simple and of a less mercurial cast, judge of an ill principle in government only by an actual grievance; here they anticipate the evil, and judge of the pressure of the grievance by the badness of the principle. They augur misgovernment at a distance; and snuff the approach of tyranny in every tainted breeze.

The last cause of this disobedient spirit in the Colonies is hardly less powerful than the rest, as

* The Attorney General.

it is not merely moral, but laid deep in the natural constitution of things. Three thousand miles of ocean lie between you and them. No contrivance can prevent the effect of this distance, in weakening Government. Seas roll, and months pass, between the order and the execution; and the want of a speedy explanation of a single point is enough to defeat an whole system. You have, indeed, winged ministers of vengeance, who carry your bolts in their pounces to the remotest verge of the sea. But there a power steps in, that limits the arrogance of rageing passions and furious elements, and says, "So far shalt thou go, and no farther." Who are you, that should fret and rage, and bite the chains of Nature?—Nothing worse happens to you, than does to all Nations, who have extensive Empire; and it happens in all the forms into which Empire can be thrown. In large bodies, the circulation of power must be less vigorous at the extremities. Nature has said it. The Turk cannot govern Ægypt, and Arabia, and Curdistan, as he governs Thrace; nor has he the same dominion in Crimea and Algiers, which he has at Brusa and Smyrna. Despotism itself is obliged to truck and huckster. The Sultan gets such obedience as he can. He governs with a loose rein, that he may govern at all; and the whole of the force and vigour of his authority in his centre, is derived from a prudent relaxation in all his borders. Spain, in her provinces, is, perhaps, not so well obeyed, as you

are

are in yours. She complies too; she submits; she watches times. This is the immutable condition; the eternal Law, of extensive and detached Empire.

Then, Sir, from these six capital sources; of Descent; of Form of Government; of Religion in the Northern Provinces; of Manners in the Southern; of Education; of the Remoteness of Situation from the First Mover of Government, from all these causes a fierce Spirit of Liberty has grown up. It has grown with the growth of the people in your Colonies, and encreased with the encrease of their wealth; a Spirit, that unhappily meeting with an exercise of Power in England, which, however lawful, is not reconcileable to any ideas of Liberty, much less with theirs, has kindled this flame, that is ready to consume us.

I do not mean to commend either the Spirit in this excess, or the moral causes which produce it. Perhaps a more smooth and accommodating Spirit of Freedom in them would be more acceptable to us. Perhaps ideas of Liberty might be desired, more reconcileable with an arbitrary and boundless authority. Perhaps we might wish the Colonists to be persuaded, that their Liberty is more secure when held in trust for them by us (as their guardians during a perpetual minority) than with any part of it in their own hands. But the question is, not whether their spirit deserves praise or blame;—what, in the name of God, shall we do with it? You have before you the object; such as it is, with all its glories, with all its imperfections on its head. You see the magnitude; the importance; the temper; the habits; the disorders. By all these considerations, we are strongly urged to determine something concerning it. We are called upon to fix some rule and line for our future conduct, which may give a little stability to our politics, and prevent the return of such unhappy deliberations as the present. Every such return will bring the matter before us in a still more untractable form. For, what astonishing and incredible things have we not seen already? What monsters have not been generated from this unnatural contention? Whilst every principle of authority and resistance has been pushed, upon both sides, as far as it would go, there is nothing so solid and certain, either in reasoning or in practice, that has been not shaken. Until very lately, all authority in America seemed to be nothing but an emanation from yours. Even the popular part of the Colony Constitution derived all its activity, and its first vital movement, from the pleasure of the Crown. We thought, Sir, that the utmost which the discontented Colonists could do, was to disturb authority; we never dreamt they could of themselves supply it; knowing in general what an operose business it is, to establish a Goverment absolutely new. But having, for our purposes in this contention, resolved, that none but an

obedient

obedient Assembly should sit, the humours of the people there, finding all passage through the legal channel stopped, with great violence broke out another way. Some provinces have tried their experiment, as we have tried ours; and theirs has succeeded. They have formed a Government sufficient for its purposes, without the bustle of a Revolution, or the troublesome formality of an Election. Evident necessity, and tacit consent, have done the business in an instant. So well they have done it, that Lord Dunmore (the account is among the fragments on your table) tells you, that the new institution is infinitely better obeyed than the antient Government ever was in its most fortunate periods. Obedience is what makes Government, and not the names by which it is called; not the name of Governor, as formerly, or Committee, as at present. This new Government has originated directly from the people; and was not transmitted through any of the ordinary artificial media of a positive constitution. It was not a manufacture ready formed, and transmitted to them in that condition from England. The evil arising from hence is this; that the Colonists having once found the possibility of enjoying the advantages of order, in the midst of a struggle for Liberty, such struggles will not henceforward seem so terrible to the settled and sober part of mankind, as they had appeared before the trial.

Pursuing the same plan of punishing by the denial of the exercise of Government to still greater lengths, we wholly abrogated the antient Government of Massachuset. We were confident, that the first feeling, if not the very prospect of anarchy, would instantly enforce a compleat submission. The experiment was tried. A new, strange, unexpected face of things appeared. Anarchy is found tolerable. A vast province has now subsisted, and subsisted in a considerable degree of health and vigour, for near a twelvemonth, without Governor, without public Council, without Judges, without executive Magistrates. How long it will continue in this state, or what may arise out of this unheard-of situation, how can the wisest of us conjecture? Our late experience has taught us, that many of those fundamental principles, formerly believed infallible, are either not of the importance they were imagined to be; or that we have not at all adverted to some other far more important, and far more powerful principles, which entirely over-rule those we had considered as omnipotent. I am much against any further experiments, which tend to put to the proof any more of these allowed opinions, which contribute so much to the public tranquillity. In effect, we suffer as much at home, by this loosening of all ties, and this concussion of all established opinions, as we do abroad. For, in order to prove, that the Americans have no right to their Liberties, we are every day endeavouring to subvert the maxims,

which

which preserve the whole Spirit of our own. To prove that the Americans ought not to be free, we are obliged to depreciate the value of Freedom itself; and we never seem to gain a paltry advantage over them in debate, without attacking some of those principles, or deriding some of those feelings, for which our ancestors have shed their blood.

But, Sir, in wishing to put an end to pernicious experiments, I do not mean to preclude the fullest enquiry. Far from it. Far from deciding on a sudden or partial view, I would patiently go round and round the subject, and survey it minutely in every possible aspect. Sir, if I were capable of engaging you to an equal attention, I would state, that, as far as I am capable of discerning, there are but three ways of proceeding relative to this stubborn Spirit, which prevails in your Colonies, and disturbs your Government. These are—To change that Spirit, as inconvenient, by removing the Causes. To prosecute it as criminal. Or, to comply with it as necessary. I would not be guilty of an imperfect enumeration; I can think of but these three. Another has indeed been started, that of giving up the Colonies; but it met so slight a reception, that I do not think myself obliged to dwell a great while upon it. It is nothing but a little sally of anger; like the frowardness of peevish children; who, when they cannot get all they would have, are resolved to take nothing.

The firſt of theſe plans, to change the Spirit as inconvenient, by removing the cauſes, I think is the moſt like a ſyſtematick proceeding. It is radical in its principle; but it is attended with great difficulties, ſome of them little ſhort, as I conceive, of impoſſibilities. This will appear by examining into the Plans which have been propoſed.

As the growing population in the Colonies is evidently one cauſe of their reſiſtance, it was laſt ſeſſion mentioned in both Houſes, by men of weight, and received not without applauſe, that, in order to check this evil, it would be proper for the crown to make no further grants of land. But to this ſcheme, there are two objections. The firſt, that there is already ſo much unſettled land in private hands, as to afford room for an immenſe future population, although the crown not only withheld its grants, but annihilated its ſoil. If this be the caſe, then the only effect of this avarice of deſolation, this hoarding of a royal wilderneſs, would be to raiſe the value of the poſſeſſions in the hands of the great private monopoliſts, without any adequate check to the growing and alarming miſchief of population.

But, if you ſtopped your grants, what would be the conſequence? The people would occupy without grants. They have already ſo occupied
in

in many places. You cannot ſtation garriſons in every part of theſe deſerts. If you drive the people from one place, they will carry on their annual Tillage, and remove with their flocks and herds to another. Many of the people in the back ſettlements are already little attached to particular ſituations. Already they have topped the Apalachian mountains. From thence they behold before them an immenſe plain, one vaſt, rich, level meadow; a ſquare of five hundred miles. Over this they would wander, without a poſſibility of reſtraint; they would change their manners with the habits of their life; would ſoon forget a government, by which they were diſowned; would become Hordes of Engliſh Tartars; and, pouring down upon your unfortified frontiers a fierce and irreſiſtible cavalry, become maſters of your Governors and your Counſellors, your collectors and comptrollers, and of all the Slaves that adhered to them. Such would, and, in no long time, muſt be, the effect of attempting to forbid as a crime, and to ſuppreſs as an evil, the Command and Bleſſing of Providence, "Encreaſe and Multiply." Such would be the happy reſult of an endeavour to keep as a lair of wild beaſts, that earth, which God, by an expreſs Charter, has given to the children of men. Far different, and ſurely much wiſer, has been our policy hitherto. Hitherto we have invited our people by every kind of bounty, to fixed eſtabliſhments. We have invited the huſbandman, to look to authority for his title. We have taught him piously to believe in the mysterious virtue of wax and parchment. We have thrown each tract of land, as it was peopled, into districts; that the ruling power should never be wholly out of sight. We have settled all we could; and we have carefully attended every settlement with government.

Adhering, Sir, as I do, to this policy, as well as for the reasons I have just given, I think this new project of hedging-in population to be neither prudent nor practicable.

To impoverish the Colonies in general, and in particular to arrest the noble course of their marine enterprizes, would be a more easy task. I freely confess it. We have shewn a disposition to a system of this kind; a disposition even to continue the restraint after the offence; looking on ourselves as rivals to our Colonies, and persuaded that of course we must gain all that they shall lose. Much mischief we may certainly do. The power inadequate to all other things is often more than sufficient for this. I do not look on the direct and immediate power of the Colonies to resist our violence, as very formidable. In this, however, I may be mistaken. But when I consider, that we have Colonies for no purpose but to be serviceable to us, it seems to my poor understanding a little preposterous, to make them unserviceable, in order to keep them obedient. It is, in truth, nothing more than the old,

old, and, as I thought, exploded problem of tyranny, which propofes to beggar its fubjects into fubmiffion. But, remember, when you have compleated your fyftem of impoverifhment, that Nature ftill proceeds in her ordinary courfe; that difcontent will encreafe with mifery; and that there are critical moments in the fortune of all ftates, when they, who are too weak to contribute to your profperity, may be ftrong enough to complete your ruin. *Spoliatis arma fuperfunt.*

The temper and character which prevail in our Colonies, are, I am afraid, unalterable by any human art. We cannot, I fear, falfify the pedigree of this fierce people, and perfuade them that they are not fprung from a nation, in whofe veins the blood of freedom circulates. The language in which they would hear you tell them this tale, would detect the impofition; your fpeech would betray you. An Englifhman is the unfitteft perfon on earth, to argue another Englifhman into flavery.

I think it is nearly as little in our power to change their republican Religion, as their free defcent; or to fubftitute the Roman Catholick, as a penalty; or the Church of England, as an improvement. The mode of inquifition and dragooning, is going out of fafhion in the old world; and I fhould not confide much to their efficacy in the new. The education of the

Americans is also on the same unalterable bottom with their religion. You cannot persuade them to burn their books of curious science; to banish their lawyers from their courts of law; or to quench the lights of their assemblies, by refusing to choose those persons who are best read in their privileges. It would be no less impracticable to think of wholly annihilating the popular assemblies, in which these lawyers sit. The army, by which we must govern in their place, would be far more chargeable to us; not quite so effectual; and perhaps, in the end, full as difficult to be kept in obedience.

With regard to the high aristocratick spirit of Virginia and the southern Colonies, it has been proposed, I know, to reduce it, by declaring a general enfranchisement of their slaves. This project has had its advocates and panegyrists; yet I never could argue myself into any opinion of it. Slaves are often much attached to their masters. A general wild offer of liberty, would not always be accepted. History furnishes few instances of it. It is sometimes as hard to persuade slaves to be free, as it is to compel freemen to be slaves; and in this auspicious scheme, we should have both these pleasing tasks on our hands at once. But when we talk of enfranchisement, do we not perceive that the American master may enfranchise too; and arm servile hands in defence of freedom? A measure to which other people have had recourse more than once,

once, and not without succeſs, in a deſperate ſituation of their affairs.

Slaves as theſe unfortunate black people are, and dull as all men are from ſlavery, muſt they not a little ſuſpect the offer of freedom from that very nation which has ſold them to their preſent maſters? From that nation, one of whoſe cauſes of quarrel with thoſe maſters, is their refuſal to deal any more in that inhuman traffick? An offer of freedom from England, would come rather oddly, ſhipped to them in an African veſſel, which is refuſed an entry into the ports of Virginia or Carolina, with a cargo of three hundred Angola negroes. It would be curious to ſee the Guinea captain attempting at the ſame inſtant to publiſh his proclamation of liberty, and to advertiſe his ſale of ſlaves.

But let us ſuppoſe all theſe moral difficulties got over. The Ocean remains. You cannot pump this dry; and as long as it continues in its preſent bed, ſo long all the cauſes which weaken authority by diſtance will continue. " Ye gods, " annihilate but ſpace and time, and make two " lovers happy!"—was a pious and paſſionate prayer;—but juſt as reaſonable, as many of the ſerious wiſhes of very grave and ſolemn politicians.

If then, Sir, it ſeems almoſt deſperate to think of any alterative courſe, for changing the moral

caufes

caufes (and not quite eafy to remove the natural), which produce prejudices irreconcileable to the late exercife of our authority; but that the fpirit infallibly will continue; and, continuing, will produce fuch effects, as now embarrafs us; the fecond mode under confideration is, to profecute that fpirit in its overt acts, as *criminal*.

At this propofition, I muft paufe a moment. The thing feems a great deal too big for my ideas of jurifprudence. It fhould feem, to my way of conceiving fuch matters, that there is a very wide difference in reafon and policy, between the mode of proceeding on the irregular conduct of fcattered individuals, or even of bands of men, who difturb order within the ftate, and the civil diffenfions which may, from time to time, on great queftions, agitate the feveral communities which compofe a great Empire. It looks to me to be narrow and pedantic, to apply the ordinary ideas of criminal juftice to this great public conteft. I do not know the method of drawing up an indictment againft an whole people. I cannot infult and ridicule the feelings of Millions of my fellow-creatures, as Sir Edward Coke infulted one excellent individual (Sir Walter Rawleigh) at the bar. I am not ripe to pafs fentence on the graveft public bodies, entrufted with magiftracies of great authority and dignity, and charged with the fafety of their fellow-citizens, upon the very fame title that I am. I really think, that for wife men, this is not judicious;

judicious; for sober men, not decent; for minds tinctured with humanity, not mild and merciful.

Perhaps, Sir, I am mistaken in my idea of an Empire, as distinguished from a single State or Kingdom. But my idea of it is this; that an Empire is the aggregate of many States, under one common head; whether this head be a monarch, or a presiding republic. It does, in such constitutions, frequently happen (and nothing but the dismal, cold, dead uniformity of servitude can prevent its happening) that the subordinate parts have many local privileges and immunities. Between these privileges, and the supreme common authority, the line may be extremely nice. Of course disputes, often too, very bitter disputes, and much ill blood, will arise. But though every privilege is an exemption (in the case) from the ordinary exercise of the supreme authority, it is no denial of it. The claim of a privilege seems rather, *ex vi termini*, to imply a superior power. For to talk of the privileges of a State or of a person, who has no superior, is hardly any better than speaking nonsense. Now, in such unfortunate quarrels, among the component parts of a great political union of communities, I can scarcely conceive any thing more compleatly imprudent, than for the Head of the Empire to insist, that, if any privilege is pleaded against his will, or his acts, that his whole authority is denied; instantly to proclaim rebellion, to beat to arms,

and

and to put the offending provinces under the ban. Will not this, Sir, very soon teach the provinces to make no distinctions on their part? Will it not teach them that the Government, against which a claim of Liberty is tantamont to high-treason, is a Government to which submission is equivalent to slavery? It may not always be quite convenient to impress dependent communities with such an idea.

We are, indeed, in all disputes with the Colonies, by the necessity of things, the judge. It is true, Sir. But, I confess, that the character of judge in my own cause, is a thing that frightens me. Instead of filling me with pride, I am exceedingly humbled by it. I cannot proceed with a stern, assured, judicial confidence, until I find myself in something more like a judicial character. I must have these hesitations as long as I am compelled to recollect, that, in my little reading upon such contests as these, the sense of mankind has, at least, as often decided against the superior as the subordinate power. Sir, let me add too, that the opinion of my having some abstract right in my favour, would not put me much at my ease in passing sentence; unless I could be sure, that there were no rights which, in their exercise under certain circumstances, were not the most odious of all wrongs, and the most vexatious of all injustice. Sir, these considerations have great weight with me, when I find things so circumstanced; that

I see

I see the same party, at once a civil litigant against me in a point of right; and a culprit before me, while I sit as a criminal judge, on acts of his, whose moral quality is to be decided upon the merits of that very litigation. Men are every now and then put, by the complexity of human affairs, into strange situations; but Justice is the same, let the Judge be in what situation he will.

There is, Sir, also a circumstance which convinces me, that this mode of criminal proceeding is not (at least in the present stage of our contest) altogether expedient; which is nothing less than the conduct of those very persons who have seemed to adopt that mode, by lately declaring a rebellion in Massachuset's Bay, as they had formerly addressed to have Traitors brought hither under an act of Henry the Eighth, for Trial. For though rebellion is declared, it is not proceeded against as such; nor have any steps been taken towards the apprehension or conviction of any individual offender, either on our late or our former address; but modes of public coercion have been adopted, and such as have much more resemblance to a sort of qualified hostility towards an independant power than the punishment of rebellious subjects. All this seems rather inconsistent; but it shews how difficult it is to apply these juridical ideas to our present case.

In

In this situation, let us seriously and coolly ponder. What is it we have got by all our menaces, which have been many and ferocious? What advantage have we derived from the penal laws we have passed, and which, for the time, have been severe and numerous? What advances have we made towards our object, by the sending of a force, which, by land and sea, is no contemptible strength? Has the disorder abated? Nothing less.—When I see things in this situation, after such confident hopes, bold promises, and active exertions, I cannot, for my life, avoid a suspicion, that the plan itself is not correctly right.

If then the removal of the causes of this Spirit of American Liberty be, for the greater part, or rather entirely, impracticable; if the ideas of Criminal Process be inapplicable, or, if applicable, are in the highest degree inexpedient, what way yet remains? No way is open, but the third and last—to comply with the American Spirit as necessary; or, if you please, to submit to it, as a necessary Evil.

If we adopt this mode; if we mean to conciliate and concede; let us see of what nature the concession ought to be? To ascertain the nature of our concession, we must look at their complaint. The Colonies complain, that they have not the characteristic Mark and Seal of British

British Freedom. They complain, that they are taxed in a Parliament, in which they are not reprefented. If you mean to fatisfy them at all, you muft fatisfy them with regard to this complaint. If you mean to pleafe any people, you muft give them the boon which they afk; not what you may think better for them, but of a kind totally different. Such an act may be a wife regulation, but it is no conceffion: whereas our prefent theme is the mode of giving fatisfaction.

Sir, I think you muft perceive, that I am refolved this day to have nothing at all to do with the queftion of the right of taxation. Some gentlemen ftartle—but it is true: I put it totally out of the queftion. It is lefs than nothing in my confideration. I do not indeed wonder, nor will you, Sir, that gentlemen of profound learning are fond of difplaying it on this profound fubject. But my confideration is narrow, confined, and wholly limited to the Policy of the queftion. I do not examine, whether the giving away a man's money be a power excepted and referved out of the general truft of Government; and how far all mankind, in all forms of Polity, are intitled to an exercife of that Right by the Charter of Nature. Or whether, on the contrary, a Right of Taxation is neceffarily involved in the general principle of Legiflation, and infeparable from the ordinary Supreme Power? Thefe are deep queftions, where great names militate

militate againſt each other; where reaſon is perplexed; and an appeal to authorities only thickens the confuſion. For high and reverend authorities lift up their heads on both ſides; and there is no ſure footing in the middle. This point is the *great Serbonian bog, betwixt Damiata and Mount Caſius old, where armies whole have ſunk*. I do not intend to be overwhelmed in that bog, though in ſuch reſpectable company. The queſtion with me is, not whether you have a right to render your people miſerable; but whether it is not your intereſt to make them happy? It is not, what a lawyer tells me, I *may* do; but what humanity, reaſon, and juſtice, tell me, I ought to do. Is a politic act the worſe for being a generous one? Is no conceſſion proper, but that which is made from your want of right to keep what you grant? Or does it leſſen the grace or dignity of relaxing in the exerciſe of an odious claim, becauſe you have your evidence-room full of Titles, and your magazines ſtuffed with arms to enforce them? What ſignify all thoſe titles, and all thoſe arms? Of what avail are they, when the reaſon of the thing tells me, that the aſſertion of my title is the loſs of my ſuit; and that I could do nothing but wound myſelf by the uſe of my own weapons?

Such is ſtedfaſtly my opinion of the abſolute neceſſity of keeping up the concord of this empire by a Unity of Spirit, though in a diverſity of operations, that, if I were ſure the Coloniſts
had,

had, at their leaving this country, sealed a regular compact of servitude; that they had solemnly abjured all the rights of citizens; that they had made a vow to renounce all Ideas of Liberty for them and their posterity, to all generations; yet I should hold myself obliged to conform to the temper I found universally prevalent in my own day, and to govern two million of men, impatient of Servitude, on the principles of Freedom. I am not determining a point of law; I am restoring tranquillity; and the general character and situation of a people must determine what sort of government is fitted for them. That point nothing else can or ought to determine.

My idea therefore, without considering whether we yield as matter of right, or grant as matter of favour, is *to admit the people of our Colonies into an interest in the constitution*; and, by recording that admission in the Journals of Parliament, to give them as strong an assurance as the nature of the thing will admit, that we mean for ever to adhere to that solemn declaration of systematic indulgence.

Some years ago, the repeal of a revenue act, upon its understood principle, might have served to shew, that we intended an unconditional abatement of the exercise of a Taxing Power. Such a measure was then sufficient to remove all suspicion; and to give perfect content. But unfortunate events, since that time, may make something further necessary; and not more necessary for the satisfaction of the Colonies, than for the dignity and consistency of our own future proceedings.

I have taken a very incorrect measure of the disposition of the House, if this proposal in itself would be received with dislike. I think, Sir, we have few American Financiers. But our misfortune is, we are too acute; we are too exquisite in our conjectures of the future, for men oppressed with such great and present evils. The more moderate among the opposers of Parliamentary Concession freely confess, that they hope no good from Taxation; but they apprehend the Colonists have further views; and if this point were conceded, they would instantly attack the Trade-laws. These Gentlemen are convinced, that this was the intention from the beginning; and the quarrel of the Americans with Taxation was no more than a cloke and cover to this design. Such has been the language even of a * Gentleman of real moderation, and of a natural temper well adjusted to fair and equal Government. I am, however, Sir, not a little surprized at this kind of discourse, whenever I hear it; and I am the more surprized, on account of the arguments which I constantly find in company with it, and which are often

* Mr. Rice.

urged

urged from the same mouths, and on the same day.

For instance, when we alledge, that it is against reason to tax a people under so many restraints in trade as the Americans, the * Noble Lord in the blue ribband shall tell you, that the restraints on trade are futile and useless; of no advantage to us, and of no burthen to those on whom they are imposed; that the trade to America is not secured by the acts of navigation, but by the natural and irresistible advantage of a commercial preference.

Such is the merit of the trade laws in this posture of the debate. But when strong internal circumstances are urged against the taxes; when the scheme is dissected; when experience and the nature of things are brought to prove, and do prove, the utter impossibility of obtaining an effective revenue from the Colonies; when these things are pressed, or rather press themselves, so as to drive the advocates of Colony taxes to a clear admission of the futility of the scheme; then, Sir, the sleeping trade laws revive from their trance; and this useless taxation is to be kept sacred, not for its own sake, but as a counter-guard and security of the laws of trade.

Then, Sir, you keep up revenue laws which are mischievous, in order to preserve trade laws

* Lord North.

that are useless. Such is the wisdom of our plan in both its members. They are separately given up as of no value; and yet one is always to be defended for the sake of the other. But I cannot agree with the Noble Lord, nor with the pamphlet from whence he seems to have borrowed these ideas, concerning the inutility of the trade laws. For without idolizing them, I am sure they are still, in many ways, of great use to us; and in former times, they have been of the greatest. They do confine, and they do greatly narrow, the market for the Americans. But my perfect conviction of this, does not help me in the least to discern how the revenue laws form any security whatsoever to the commercial regulations; or that these commercial regulations are the true ground of the quarrel; or, that the giving way in any one instance of authority, is to lose all that may remain unconceded.

One fact is clear and indisputable. The public and avowed origin of this quarrel, was on taxation. This quarrel has indeed brought on new disputes on new questions; but certainly the least bitter, and the fewest of all, on the trade laws. To judge which of the two be the real radical cause of quarrel, we have to see whether the commercial dispute did, in order of time, precede the dispute on taxation? There is not a shadow of evidence for it. Next, to enable us to judge whether at this moment a dislike to the Trade Laws be the real cause of quarrel, it is absolutely

necessary

necessary to put the taxes out of the question by a repeal. See how the Americans act in this position, and then you will be able to discern correctly what is the true object of the controversy, or whether any controversy at all will remain? Unless you consent to remove this cause of difference, it is impossible, with decency, to assert that the dispute is not upon what it is avowed to be. And I would, Sir, recommend to your serious consideration, whether it be prudent to form a rule for punishing people, not on their own acts, but on your conjectures? Surely it is preposterous at the very best. It is not justifying your anger, by their misconduct; but it is converting your ill-will into their delinquency.

But the Colonies will go further.—Alas! alas! when will this speculating against fact and reason end? What will quiet these panic fears which we entertain of the hostile effect of a conciliatory conduct? Is it true, that no case can exist, in which it is proper for the sovereign to accede to the desires of his discontented subjects? Is there any thing peculiar in this case, to make a rule for itself? Is all authority of course lost, when it is not pushed to the extreme? Is it a certain maxim, that, the fewer causes of dissatisfaction are left by government, the more the subject will be inclined to resist and rebel?

All these objections being in fact no more than suspicions, conjectures, divinations; formed in defiance

defiance of fact and experience; they did not, Sir, discourage me from entertaining the idea of a conciliatory conceffion, founded on the principles which I have juft ftated.

In forming a plan for this purpofe, I endeavoured to put myfelf in that frame of mind, which was the moſt natural, and the moſt reaſonable; and which was certainly the moſt probable means of ſecuring me from all error. I ſet out with a perfect diftruft of my own abilities; a total renunciation of every ſpeculation of my own; and with a profound reverence for the wifdom of our anceftors, who have left us the inheritance of fo happy a conftitution, and fo flouriſhing an empire; and what is a thouſand times more valuable, the treaſury of the maxims and principles which formed the one, and obtained the other.

During the reigns of the kings of Spain of the Auftrian family, whenever they were at a lofs in the Spaniſh councils, it was common for their ſtateſmen to ſay, that they ought to conſult the genius of Philip the Second. The genius of Philip the Second might miſlead them; and the iſſue of their affairs ſhewed, that they had not choſen the moſt perfect ſtandard. But, Sir, I am ſure that I ſhall not be miſled, when, in a caſe of conftitutional difficulty, I conſult the genius of the Engliſh conftitution. Conſulting at that oracle (it was with all due humility and piety)

I found

I found four capital examples in a similar case before me: those of Ireland, Wales, Chester, and Durham.

Ireland, before the English conquest, though never governed by a despotick power, had no Parliament. How far the English Parliament itself was at that time modelled according to the present form, is disputed among antiquarians. But we have all the reason in the world to be assured, that a form of Parliament, such as England then enjoyed, she instantly communicated to Ireland; and we are equally sure that almost every successive improvement in constitutional liberty, as fast as it was made here, was transmitted thither. The feudal Baronage, and the feudal Knighthood, the roots of our primitive constitution, were early transplanted into that soil; and grew and flourished there. Magna Charta, if it did not give us originally the House of Commons, gave us at least an House of Commons of weight and consequence. But your ancestors did not churlishly sit down alone to the feast of Magna Charta. Ireland was made immediately a partaker. This benefit of English laws and liberties, I confess, was not at first extended to *all* Ireland. Mark the consequence. English authority and English liberties had exactly the same boundaries. Your standard could never be advanced an inch before your privileges. Sir John Davis shews beyond a doubt, that the refusal of a general communication of these rights,

was

was the true cause why Ireland was five hundred years in subduing; and after the vain projects of a Military Government, attempted in the reign of Queen Elizabeth, it was soon discovered, that nothing could make that country English, in civility and allegiance, but your laws and your forms of legiſlature. It was not English arms, but the English constitution, that conquered Ireland. From that time, Ireland has ever had a general Parliament, as ſhe had before a partial Parliament. You changed the people; you altered the religion; but you never touched the form or the vital ſubſtance of free government in that kingdom. You depoſed kings; you reſtored them; you altered the ſucceſſion to theirs, as well as to your own crown; but you never altered their conſtitution; the principle of which was reſpected by uſurpation; reſtored with the reſtoration of Monarchy, and eſtabliſhed, I truſt, for ever, by the glorious Revolution. This has made Ireland the great and flouriſhing kingdom that it is; and from a diſgrace and a burthen intolerable to this nation, has rendered her a principal part of our ſtrength and ornament. This country cannot be ſaid to have ever formally taxed her. The irregular things done in the confuſion of mighty troubles, and on the hinge of great revolutions, even if all were done that is ſaid to have been done, form no example. If they have any effect in argument, they make an exception to prove the rule. None of your own liberties could ſtand a moment, if the caſual deviations

tions from them, at such times, were suffered to be used as proofs of their nullity. By the lucrative amount of such casual breaches in the constitution, judge what the stated and fixed rule of supply has been in that Kingdom. Your Irish pensioners would starve, if they had no other fund to live on than taxes granted by English authority. Turn your eyes to those popular grants from whence all your great supplies are come; and learn to respect that only source of public wealth in the British empire.

My next example is Wales. This country was said to be reduced by Henry the Third. It was said more truly to be so by Edward the First. But though then conquered, it was not looked upon as any part of the realm of England. Its old constitution, whatever that might have been, was destroyed; and no good one was substituted in its place. The care of that tract was put into the hands of Lords Marchers—a form of Government of a very singular kind; a strange heterogeneous monster, something between Hostility and Government; perhaps it has a sort of resemblance, according to the modes of those times, to that of commander in chief at present, to whom all civil power is granted as secondary. The manners of the Welsh nation followed the Genius of the Government: The people were ferocious, restive, savage, and uncultivated; sometimes composed, never pacified. Wales within itself, was in perpetual disorder; and it kept the

frontier

frontier of England in perpetual alarm. Benefits from it to the state, there were none. Wales was only known to England, by incursion and invasion.

Sir, during that state of things, Parliament was not idle. They attempted to subdue the fierce spirit of the Welsh by all sorts of rigorous laws. They prohibited by statute the sending all sorts of arms into Wales, as you prohibit by proclamation (with something more of doubt on the legality) the sending arms to America. They disarmed the Welsh by statute, as you attempted (bu still with more question on the legality) to disarm New England by an instruction. They made an act to drag offenders from Wales into England for trial, as you have done (but with more hardship) with regard to America. By another act, where one of the parties was an Englishman, they ordained, that his trial should be always by English. They made acts to restrain trade, as you do; and they prevented the Welsh from the use of fairs and markets, as you do the Americans from fisheries and foreign ports. In short, when the statute-book was not quite so much swelled as it is now, you find no less than fifteen acts of penal regulation on the subject of Wales.

Here we rub our hands—A fine body of precedents for the authority of Parliament and the use of it!—I admit it fully; and pray add likewise likewife to thefe precedents, that all the while, Wales rid this kingdom like an *incubus*; that it was an unprofitable and oppreffive burthen; and that an Englifhman travelling in that country, could not go fix yards from the high road without being murdered.

The march of the human mind is flow. Sir, it was, not, until after Two Hundred years, difcovered, that by an eternal law, Providence had decreed vexation to violence; and poverty to rapine. Your anceftors did however at length open their eyes to the ill hufbandry of injuftice. They found that the tyranny of a free people could of all tyrannies the leaft be endured; and that laws made againft an whole nation were not the moft effectual methods for fecuring its obedience. Accordingly, in the Twenty-feventh year of Henry VIII. the courfe was entirely altered. With a preamble ftating the entire and perfect rights of the crown of England, it gave to the Welfh all the rights and privileges of Englifh fubjects. A political order was eftablifhed; the military power gave way to the civil; the marches were turned into counties. But that a nation fhould have a right to Englifh liberties, and yet no fhare at all in the fundamental fecurity of thefe liberties, the grant of their own property, feemed a thing fo incongruous; that Eight years after, that is, in the Thirty-fifth of that reign, a complete and not ill proportioned reprefentation by counties and boroughs was beftowed upon Wales,

Wales, by act of Parliament. From that moment, as by a charm, the tumults subsided; obedience was restored; peace, order, and civilization, followed in the train of liberty—When the day-star of the English constitution had arisen in their hearts, all was harmony within and without—

> *Simul alba nautis*
> *Stella refulsit,*
> *Defluit saxis agitatus humor:*
> *Concidunt venti, fugiuntque nubes:*
> *Et minax (quòd sic voluere) ponto*
> *Unda recumbit.*

The very same year the county palatine of Chester received the same relief from its oppressions, and the same remedy to its disorders. Before this time Chester was little less distempered than Wales. The inhabitants, without rights themselves, were the fittest to destroy the rights of others; and from thence Richard II. drew the standing army of Archers, with which for a time he oppressed England. The people of Chester applied to Parliament in a petition penned as I shall read to you:

To the King our Sovereign Lord, in most humble wise shewn unto your Excellent Majesty, the inhabitants of your Grace's county palatine of Chester; That where the said county palatine of Chester is and hath been always hitherto exempt, excluded and separated

separated out and from your high court of parliament, to have any knights and burgesses within the said court; by reason whereof the said inhabitants have hitherto sustained manifold disherisons, losses and damages, as well in their lands, goods, and bodies, as in the good, civil, and politick governance and maintenance of the commonwealth of their said country: (2.) *And for as much as the said inhabitants have always hitherto been bound by the acts and statutes made and ordained by your said highness, and your most noble progenitors, by authority of the said court, as far forth as other counties, cities, and boroughs have been, that have had their knights and burgesses within your said court of parliament, and yet have had neither knight ne burgess there for the said county palatine; the said inhabitants, for lack thereof, have been oftentimes touched and grieved with acts and statutes made within the said court, as well derogatory unto the most antient jurisdictions, liberties, and privileges of your said county palatine, as prejudicial unto the common wealth, quietness, rest, and peace of your grace's most bounden subjects inhabiting within the same.*

What did Parliament with this audacious address?—reject it as a libel? Treat it as an affront to government? Spurn it as a derogation from the rights of legislature? Did they toss it over the table? Did they burn it by the hands of the common hangman?— They took the petition of grievance, all rugged as it was, without softening or temperament, unpurged of the original

bitterness

bitternefs and indignation of complaint; they made it the very preamble to their act of redrefs; and confecrated its principle to all ages in the fanctuary of legiflation.

Here is my third example. It was attended with the fuccefs of the two former. Chefter, civilized as well as Wales, has demonftrated that freedom and not fervitude is the cure of anarchy; as religion, and not atheifm, is the true remedy for fuperftition. Sir, this pattern of Chefter was followed in the reign of Charles II. with regard to the county palatine of Durham, which is my fourth example. This county had long lain out of the pale of free legiflation. So fcrupuloufly was the example of Chefter followed, that the ftyle of the preamble is nearly the fame with that of the Chefter act; and without affecting the abftract extent of the authority of Parliament, it recognizes the equity of not fuffering any confiderable diftrict in which the Britifh fubjects may act as a body, to be taxed without their own voice in the grant.

Now if the doctrines of policy contained in thefe preambles, and the force of thefe examples in the acts of Parliament, avail any thing, what can be faid againft applying them with regard to America? Are not the people of America as much Englifhmen as the Welfh? The preamble of the act of Henry VIII. fays, the Welfh fpeak a language no way refembling that of his

Majefty's

Majesty's English subjects. Are the Americans not as numerous? If we may trust the learned and accurate Judge Barrington's account of North Wales, and take that as a standard to measure the rest, there is no comparison. The people cannot amount to above 200,000; not a tenth part of the number in the Colonies. Is America in rebellion? Wales was hardly ever free from it. Have you attempted to govern America by penal statutes? You made Fifteen for Wales. But your legislative authority is perfect with regard to America; was it less perfect in Wales, Chester, and Durham? But America is virtually represented. What! does the electric force of virtual representation more easily pass over the Atlantic, than pervade Wales, which lies in your neighbourhood; or than Chester and Durham, surrounded by abundance of representation that is actual and palpable? But, Sir, your ancestors thought this sort of virtual representation, however ample, to be totally insufficient for the freedom of the inhabitants of territories that are so near, and comparatively so inconsiderable. How then can I think it sufficient for those which are infinitely greater, and infinitely more remote?

You will now, Sir, perhaps imagine, that I am on the point of proposing to you a scheme for a representation of the Colonies in Parliament. Perhaps I might be inclined to entertain some such thought; but a great flood stops me in my course. *Opposuit natura*—I cannot remove the eternal barriers of the creation. The thing in that mode, I do not know to be poſſible. As I meddle with no theory, I do not abſolutely aſſert the impracticability of ſuch a repreſentation. But I do not ſee my way to it; and thoſe who have been more confident, have not been more ſuccefsful. However, the arm of public benevolence is not ſhortened; and there are often ſeveral means to the ſame end. What nature has disjoined in one way, wiſdom may unite in another. When we cannot give the benefit as we would wiſh, let us not refuſe it altogether. If we cannot give the principal, let us find a ſubſtitute. But how? Where? What ſubſtitute?

Fortunately I am not obliged for the ways and means of this ſubſtitute to tax my own unproductive invention. I am not even obliged to go to the rich treaſury of the fertile framers of imaginary common wealths; not to the Republick of Plato, not to the Utopia of More; not to the Oceana of Harrington. It is before me—It is at my feet, *and the rude ſwain treads daily on it with his clouted ſhoon*. I only wiſh you to recognize, for the theory, the ancient conſtitutional policy of this kingdom with regard to repreſentation, as that policy has been declared in acts of parliament; and, as to the practice, to return to that mode which an uniform experience has marked out to you, as beſt; and in which you walked with ſecurity, advantage, and honour, until the year 1763.

My

My resolutions therefore mean to establish the equity and justice of a taxation of America, by *grant*, and not by *imposition*. To mark the *legal competency* of the Colony assemblies for the support of their government in peace, and for public aids in time of war. To acknowledge that this legal competency has had *a dutiful and beneficial exercise*; and that experience has shewn the *benefit of their grants*, and the *futility of parliamentary taxation as a method of supply*.

These solid truths compose six fundamental propositions. There are three more resolutions corollary to these. If you admit the first set, you can hardly reject the others. But if you admit the first, I shall be far from sollicitous whether you accept or refuse the last. I think these six massive pillars will be of strength sufficient to support the temple of British concord. I have no more doubt than I entertain of my existence, that, if you admitted these, you would command an immediate peace; and with but tolerable future management, a lasting obedience in America. I am not arrogant in this confident assurance. The propositions are all mere matters of fact; and if they are such facts as draw irresistible conclusions even in the stating, this is the power of truth, and not any management of mine.

Sir, I shall open the whole plan to you together, with such observations on the motions as may tend to illustrate them where they may want explanation. The first is a resolution — "*That the Colonies and Plantations of Great Britain in North America, consisting of Fourteen separate Governments, and containing Two Millions and upwards of free inhabitants, have not had the liberty and privilege of electing and sending any Knights and Burgesses, or others to represent them in the high Court of Parliament.*" — This is a plain matter of fact, necessary to be laid down, and (excepting the description) it is laid down in the language of the constitution; it is taken nearly *verbatim* from acts of Parliament.

The second is like unto the first — "*That the said Colonies and Plantations have been liable to, and bounden by, several subsidies, payments, rates, and taxes, given and granted by Parliament, though the said Colonies and Plantations have not their Knights and Burgesses, in the said high Court of Parliament, of their own election, to represent the condition of their country; by lack whereof they have been oftentimes touched and grieved by subsidies given, granted, and assented to, in the said court, in a manner prejudicial to the common wealth, quietness, rest, and peace of the subjects inhabiting within the same.*"

Is

Is this description too hot, or too cold, too strong, or too weak? Does it arrogate too much to the supreme legislature? Does it lean too much to the claims of the people? If it runs into any of these errors, the fault is not mine. It is the language of your own ancient acts of Parliament. *Non meus hic sermo, sed quæ præcepit Ofellus, rusticus, abnormis sapiens.* It is the genuine produce of the ancient rustic, manly, home-bred sense of this country—I did not dare to rub off a particle of the venerable rust that rather adorns and preserves, than destroys the metal. It would be a profanation to touch with a tool the stones which construct the sacred altar of peace. I would not violate with modern polish the ingenuous and noble roughness of these truly constitutional materials. Above all things, I was resolved not to be guilty of tampering, the odious vice of restless and unstable minds. I put my foot in the tracks of our forefathers; where I can neither wander nor stumble. Determining to fix articles of peace, I was resolved not to be wise beyond what was written; I was resolved to use nothing else than the form of sound words; to let others abound in their own sense; and carefully to abstain from all expressions of my own. What the law has said, I say. In all things else I am silent. I have no organ but for her words. This, if it be not ingenious, I am sure is safe.

There are indeed words expressive of grievance in this second resolution, which those who are resolved always to be in the right, will deny to contain matter of fact, as applied to the present case; although Parliament thought them true, with regard to the counties of Chester and Durham. They will deny that the Americans were ever "touched and grieved" with the taxes. If they consider nothing in taxes but their weight as pecuniary impositions, there might be some pretence for this denial. But men may be sorely touched and deeply grieved in their privileges, as well as in their purses. Men may lose little in property, by the act which takes away all their freedom. When a man is robbed of a trifle on the highway, it is not the Two-pence lost that constitutes the capital outrage. This is not confined to privileges. Even ancient indulgences withdrawn, without offence on the part of those who enjoyed such favours, operate as grievances. But were the Americans then not touched and grieved by the taxes, in some measure, merely as taxes? If so, why were they almost all, either wholly repealed or exceedingly reduced? Were they not touched and grieved, even by the regulating Duties of the Sixth of George II? Else why were the duties first reduced to one Third in 1764, and afterwards to a Third of that Third in the year 1766? Were they not touched and grieved by the Stamp Act? I shall say they were, until that tax is revived. Were they not touched and

and grieved by the duties of 1767, which were likewise repealed, and which, Lord Hillsborough tells you (for the ministry) were laid contrary to the true principle of commerce? Is not the aſſurance given by that noble perſon to the Colonies of a reſolution to lay no more taxes on them, an admiſſion that taxes would touch and grieve them? Is not the reſolution of the noble Lord in the blue ribband, now ſtanding on your Journals, the ſtrongeſt of all proofs that parliamentary ſubſidies really touched and grieved them? Elſe, why all theſe changes, modifications, repeals, aſſurances, and reſolutions?

The next propoſition is—"*That, from the diſtance of the ſaid Colonies, and from other circumſtances, no method hath hitherto been deviſed for procuring a repreſentation in Parliament for the ſaid Colonies.*" This is an aſſertion of a fact. I go no further on the paper; though in my private judgement, an uſeful repreſentation is impoſſible; I am ſure it is not deſired by them; nor ought it perhaps by us; but I abſtain from opinions.

The fourth reſolution is—"*That each of the ſaid Colonies hath within itſelf a body, choſen in part, or in the whole, by the freemen, freeholders, or other free inhabitants thereof, commonly called the General Aſſembly, or General Court, with powers legally to raiſe, levy, and aſſeſs, according to the ſeveral uſage of ſuch Colonies,*

"*duties*

" *duties and taxes towards defraying all sorts of*
" *public services.*"

This competence in the Colony assemblies is certain. It is proved by the whole tenour of their acts of supply in all the assemblies, in which the constant style of granting is, " an aid to his Majesty;" and acts granting to the Crown have regularly for near a century passed the public offices without dispute. Those who have been pleased paradoxically to deny this right, holding that none but the British parliament can grant to the Crown, are wished to look to what is done, not only in the Colonies, but in Ireland, in one uniform unbroken tenour every session. Sir, I am surprized, that this doctrine should come from some of the law servants of the Crown. I say, that if the Crown could be responsible, his Majesty—but certainly the ministers, and even these law officers themselves, through whose hands the acts pass, biennially in Ireland, or annually in the Colonies, are in an habitual course of committing impeachable offences. What habitual offenders have been all Presidents of the Council, all Secretaries of State, all First Lords of Trade, all Attornies and all Sollicitors General! However, they are safe; as no one impeaches them; and there is no ground of charge against them, except in their own unfounded theories.

The fifth refolution is alfo a refolution of fact — "*That the said General Assemblies, General Courts, or other bodies legally qualified as aforesaid, have at sundry times freely granted several large subsidies and public aids for his Majesty's service, according to their abilities, when required thereto by letter from one of his Majesty's principal Secretaries of State; and that their right to grant the same, and their chearfulness and sufficiency in the said grants, have been at sundry times acknowledged by Parliament.*" To say nothing of their great expences in the Indian wars; and not to take their exertion in foreign ones, so high as the supplies in the year 1695; not to go back to their public contributions in the year 1710; I shall begin to travel only where the Journals give me light; resolving to deal in nothing but fact, authenticated by parliamentary record; and to build myself wholly on that solid basis.

On the 4th of April 1748*, a Committee of this House came to the following Resolution:

" Resolved,
" *That it is the opinion of this Committee*, that it is just and reasonable *that the several Provinces and Colonies of Massachuset's Bay, New Hampshire, Connecticut, and Rhode Island, be reimbursed the expences they have been at in*

---
* Journals of the House, Vol. XXV.

" *taking*

" *taking and securing to the crown of Great Bri-*
" *tain, the Island of Cape Breton, and its depen-*
" *dencies.*"

These expences were immense for such Colonies. They were above 200,000 *l.* sterling; money first raised and advanced on their public credit.

On the 28th of January 1756*, a message from the King came to us, to this effect—" *His* " *Majesty, being sensible of the zeal and vigour with* " *which his faithful subjects of certain Colonies in* " *North America have exerted themselves in defence* " *of His Majesty's just rights and possessions, recom-* " *mends it to this House to take the same into their* " *consideration, and to enable His Majesty to give* " *them such assistance as may be a* proper reward " and encouragement."

On the 3d of February 1756†, the House came to a suitable resolution, expressed in words nearly the same as those of the message: but with the further addition, that the money then voted was as an *encouragement* to the Colonies to exert themselves with vigour. It will not be necessary to go through all the testimonies which your own records have given to the truth of my resolutions. I will only refer you to the places in the Journals:

* Journals of the House, Vol. XXVII.   † Ibid.

Vol. XXVII.—16th and 19th May 1757.
Vol. XXVIII.—June 1ft, 1758—April 26th and 30th, 1759—March 26th and 31ft, and April 28th, 1760—Jan. 9th and 20th, 1761.
Vol. XXIX.—Jan. 22d and 26th, 1762—March 14th and 17th, 1763.

Sir, here is the repeated acknowledgement of Parliament, that the Colonies not only gave, but gave to fatiety. This nation has formally acknowledged two things; firft, that the Colonies had gone beyond their abilities, Parliament having thought it neceffary to reimburfe them; fecondly, that they had acted legally and laudably in their grants of money, and their maintenance of troops, fince the compenfation is exprefsly given as reward and encouragement. Reward is not beftowed for acts that are unlawful; and encouragement is not held out to things that deferve reprehenfion. My refolution therefore does nothing more than collect into one propofition, what is fcattered through your Journals. I give you nothing but your own; and you cannot refufe in the grofs, what you have fo often acknowledged in detail. The admiffion of this, which will be fo honourable to them and to you, will, indeed, be mortal to all the miferable ftories, by which the paffions of the mifguided people have been engaged in an unhappy fyftem. The people heard, indeed, from the beginning of
thefe

these disputes, one thing continually dinned in their ears, that reason and justice demanded, that the Americans, who paid no Taxes, should be compelled to contribute. How did that fact of their paying nothing, stand, when the Taxing System began? When Mr. Grenville began to form his system of American Revenue, he stated in this House, that the Colonies were then in debt two millions six hundred thousand pounds sterling money; and was of opinion they would discharge that debt in four years. On this state, those untaxed people were actually subject to the payment of taxes to the amount of six hundred and fifty thousand a year. In fact, however, Mr. Grenville was mistaken. The funds given for sinking the debt did not prove quite so ample as both the Colonies and he expected. The calculation was too sanguine: the reduction was not compleated till some years after, and at different times in different Colonies. However, the Taxes after the war, continued too great to bear any addition, with prudence or propriety; and when the burthens imposed in consequence of former requisitions were discharged, our tone became too high to resort again to requisition. No Colony, since that time, ever has had any requisition whatsoever made to it.

We see the sense of the Crown, and the sense of Parliament, on the productive nature of a *Revenue by Grant*. Now search the same Journals for the produce of the *Revenue by Imposition*—

Where

Where is it?—let us know the volume and the page?—what is the grofs, what is the nett produce?—to what fervice is it applied?—how have you appropriated its furplus?—What, can none of the many fkilful Index-makers, that we are now employing, find any trace of it?—Well, let them and that reft together.—But are the Journals, which fay nothing of the Revenue, as filent on the difcontent?—Oh no! a child may find it. It is the melancholy burthen and blot of every page.

I think then I am, from thofe Journals, juftified in the fixth and laft refolution, which is—
" *That it hath been found by experience, that the*
" *manner of granting the faid fupplies and aids,*
" *by the faid General Affemblies, hath been more*
" *agreeable to the faid Colonies, and more benefi-*
" *cial, and conducive to the public fervice, than*
" *the mode of giving and granting aids in Parlia-*
" *ment, to be raifed and paid in the faid Colonies.*"
This makes the whole of the fundamental part of the plan. The conclufion is irrefiftible. You cannot fay, that you were driven by any neceffity, to an exercife of the utmoft Rights of Legiflature. You cannot affert, that you took on yourfelves the tafk of impofing Colony Taxes, from the want of another legal body, that is competent to the purpofe of fupplying the Exigencies of the State without wounding the prejudices of the people. Neither is it true that the body fo qualified, and having that competence, had neglected the duty.

The question now, on all this accumulated matter, is;—whether you will chuse to abide by a profitable experience, or a mischievous theory; whether you chuse to build on imagination or fact; whether you prefer enjoyment or hope; satisfaction in your subjects, or discontent?

If these propositions are accepted, every thing which has been made to enforce a contrary system, must, I take it for granted, fall along with it. On that ground, I have drawn the following resolution, which, when it comes to be moved, will naturally be divided in a proper manner: " *That it may be proper to repeal an act,*
" *made in the seventh year of the reign of his pre-*
" *sent Majesty, intituled,* An act for granting cer-
" tain duties in the British Colonies and Plantations
" in America; *for allowing a drawback of the*
" *duties of customs upon the exportation from this*
" *Kingdom, of coffee and cocoa-nuts of the produce*
" *of the said Colonies or Plantations; for discon-*
" *tinuing the drawbacks payable on China earthen-*
" *ware exported to America; and for more effectu-*
" *ally preventing the clandestine running of goods in*
" *the said Colonies and Plantations.—And that it*
" *may be proper to repeal an act, made in the four-*
" *teenth year of the reign of his present Majesty,*
" *intituled,* An act to discontinue, in such manner,
" and for such time, as are therein mentioned, the
" landing and discharging, lading or shipping, of
" goods, wares, and merchandize, at the town and
" *within*

"within the harbour of Boston, in the Province of
"Massachuset's Bay, in North America.—And
"that it may be proper to repeal an act, made in
"the fourteenth year of the reign of his present
"Majesty, intituled, An act for the impartial ad-
"ministration of justice, in the cases of persons ques-
"tioned for any acts done by them, in the execution
"of the law, or for the suppression of riots and tu-
"mults, in the province of Massachuset's Bay in
"New England.—And that it may be proper to
"repeal an act, made in the fourteenth year of the
"reign of his present Majesty, intituled, An act for
"the better regulating the Government of the pro-
"vince of the Massachuset's Bay in New England.
"—And also that it may be proper to explain and
"amend an act, made in the thirty-fifth year of the
"reign of King Henry the Eighth, intituled, An
"act for the Trial of Treasons committed out of the
"King's Dominions."

I wish, Sir, to repeal the Boston Port Bill, because (independently of the dangerous precedent
of suspending the rights of the subject during the
King's pleasure) it was passed, as I apprehend,
with less regularity, and on more partial principles, than it ought. The corporation of Boston
was not heard, before it was condemned. Other
towns, full as guilty as she was, have not had
their ports blocked up. Even the Restraining
Bill of the present Session does not go to the
length of the Boston Port Act. The same ideas
of prudence, which induced you not to extend

equal

equal punishment to equal guilt, even when you were punishing, induce me, who mean not to chastise, but to reconcile, to be satisfied with the punishment already partially inflicted.

Ideas of prudence, and accommodation to circumstances, prevent you from taking away the Charters of Connecticut and Rhode-island, as you have taken away that of Massachuset's Colony, though the Crown has far less power in the two former provinces than it enjoyed in the latter; and though the abuses have been full as great, and as flagrant, in the exempted as in the punished. The same reasons of prudence and accommodation have weight with me in restoring the Charter of Massachuset's Bay. Besides, Sir, the Act which changes the Charter of Massachuset's is in many particulars so exceptionable, that, if I did not wish absolutely to repeal, I would by all means desire to alter it; as several of its provisions tend to the subversion of all public and private justice. Such, among others, is the power in the Governor to change the sheriff at his pleasure; and to make a new returning officer for every special cause. It is shameful to behold such a regulation standing among English Laws.

The act for bringing persons accused of committing murder under the orders of Government to England for Trial, is but temporary. That act has calculated the probable duration of our quarrel

quarrel with the Colonies; and is accommodated to that fuppofed duration. I would haften the happy moment of reconciliation; and therefore muft, on my principle, get rid of that moft juftly obnoxious act.

The act of Henry the Eighth, for the Trial of Treafons, I do not mean to take away, but to confine it to its proper bounds and original intention; to make it exprefsly for Trial of Treafons (and the greateft Treafons may be committed) in places where the jurifdiction of the Crown does not extend.

Having guarded the privileges of Local Legiflature, I would next fecure to the Colonies a fair and unbiaffed Judicature; for which purpofe, Sir, I propofe the following refolution: " *That,*
" *from the time when the General Affembly or*
" *General Court of any Colony or Plantation in*
" *North America, fhall have appointed by act of*
" *Affembly, duly confirmed, a fettled falary to the*
" *offices of the Chief Juftice and other Judges of*
" *the Superior Court, it may be proper, that the*
" *faid Chief Juftice and other Judges of the Superior*
" *Courts of fuch Colony, fhall hold his and their*
" *office and offices during their good behaviour;*
" *and fhall not be removed therefrom, but when*
" *the faid removal fhall be adjudged by his Majefty in Council, upon a hearing on complaint*
" *from the General Affembly, or on a complaint*

G " *from*

" *from the Governor, or Council, or the House*
" *of Representatives severally, of the Colony in*
" *which the said Chief Justice and other Judges*
" *have exercised the said offices.*"

The next resolution relates to the Courts of Admiralty.

It is this. " *That it may be proper to regulate*
" *the Courts of Admiralty, or Vice Admiralty, au-*
" *thorized by the 15th Chap. of the 4th of George*
" *the Third, in such a manner as to make the same*
" *more commodious to those who sue, or are sued, in*
" *the said Courts, and to provide for the more decent*
" *maintenance of the Judges in the same.*"

These Courts I do not wish to take away; they are in themselves proper establishments. This Court is one of the capital securities of the Act of Navigation. The extent of its jurisdiction, indeed, has been encreased; but this is altogether as proper, and is, indeed, on many accounts, more eligible, where new powers were wanted, than a Court absolutely new. But Courts incommodiously situated, in effect, deny justice; and a Court, partaking in the fruits of its own condemnation, is a robber. The congress complain, and complain justly, of this grievance*.

---

* The Solicitor-general informed Mr. B. when the resolutions were separately moved, that the grievance of the judges partaking of the profits of the seizure had been redressed by office; accordingly the resolution was amended.

These are the three consequential propositions. I have thought of two or three more; but they come rather too near detail, and to the province of executive Government, which I wish Parliament always to superintend, never to assume. If the first six are granted, congruity will carry the latter three. If not, the things that remain unrepealed, will be, I hope, rather unseemly incumbrances on the building, than very materially detrimental to its strength and stability.

Here, Sir, I should close; but that I plainly perceive some objections remain, which I ought, if possible, to remove. The first will be, that, in resorting to the doctrine of our ancestors, as contained in the preamble to the Chester act, I prove too much; that the grievance from a want of representation, stated in that preamble, goes to the whole of Legislation as well as to Taxation. And that the Colonies grounding themselves upon that doctrine, will apply it to all parts of Legistative Authority.

To this objection, with all possible deference and humility, and wishing as little as any man living to impair the smallest particle of our supreme authority, I answer, that *the words are the words of Parliament, and not mine*; and, that all false and inconclusive inferences, drawn from them, are not mine; for I heartily disclaim any such

such inference. I have chosen the words of an act of Parliament, which Mr. Grenville, surely a tolerably zealous and very judicious advocate for the sovereignty of Parliament, formerly moved to have read at your table, in confirmation of his tenets. It is true that Lord Chatham considered these preambles as declaring strongly in favour of his opinions. He was a no less powerful advocate for the privileges of the Americans. Ought I not from hence to presume, that these preambles are as favourable as possible to both, when properly understood; favourable both to the rights of Parliament, and to the privilege of the dependencies of this crown? But, Sir, the object of grievance in my resolution, I have not taken from the Chester, but from the Durham act, which confines the hardship of want of representation, to the case of subsidies; and which therefore falls in exactly with the case of the Colonies. But whether the unrepresented counties were *de jure*, or *de facto*, bound, the preambles do not accurately distinguish; nor indeed was it necessary; for, whether *de jure*, or *de facto*, the Legislature thought the exercise of the power of taxing, as of right, or as of fact without right, equally a grievance and equally oppressive.

I do not know, that the Colonies have, in any general way, or in any cool hour, gone much beyond the demand of immunity in relation to taxes. It is not fair to judge of the temper or dispositions

dispositions of any man, or any set of men, when they are composed and at rest, from their conduct, or their expressions, in a state of disturbance and irritation. It is besides a very great mistake to imagine, that mankind follow up practically any speculative principle, either of government or of freedom, as far as it will go in argument and logical illation. We Englishmen, stop very short of the principles upon which we support any given part of our constitution; or even the whole of it together. I could easily, if I had not already tired you, give you very striking and convincing instances of it. This is nothing but what is natural and proper. All government, indeed every human benefit and enjoyment, every virtue, and every prudent act, is founded on compromise and barter. We balance inconveniencies; we give and take; we remit some rights, that we may enjoy others; and, we chuse rather to be happy citizens, than subtle disputants. As we must give away some natural liberty, to enjoy civil advantages; so we must sacrifice some civil liberties, for the advantages to be derived from the communion and fellowship of a great empire. But in all fair dealings the thing bought, must bear some proportion to the purchase paid. None will barter away the immediate jewel of his soul. Though a great house is apt to make slaves haughty, yet it is purchasing a part of the artificial importance of a great empire too dear, to pay for it all essential rights,

rights, and all the intrinsic dignity of human nature. None of us who would not risque his life, rather than fall under a government purely arbitrary. But, although there are some amongst us who think our constitution wants many improvements, to make it a complete system of liberty, perhaps none who are of that opinion, would think it right to aim at such improvement, by disturbing his country, and risquing every thing that is dear to him. In every arduous enterprize, we consider what we are to lose, as well as what we are to gain; and the more and better stake of liberty every people possess, the less they will hazard in a vain attempt to make it more. These are *the cords of man.* Man acts from adequate motives relative to his interest; and not on metaphysical speculations. Aristotle, the great master of reasoning, cautions us, and with great weight and propriety, against this species of delusive geometrical accuracy in moral arguments, as the most fallacious of all sophistry.

The Americans will have no interest contrary to the grandeur and glory of England, when they are not oppressed by the weight of it; and they will rather be inclined to respect the acts of a superintending legislature; when they see them the acts of that power, which is itself the security, not the rival, of their secondary importance. In this assurance, my mind most
perfectly

perfectly acquiesces; and I confess, I feel not the least alarm, from the discontents which are to arise, from putting people at their ease; nor do I apprehend the destruction of this empire, from giving, by an act of free grace and indulgence, to two millions of my fellow citizens, some share of those rights, upon which I have always been taught to value myself.

It is said indeed, that this power of granting vested in American assemblies, would dissolve the unity of the empire; which was preserved, entire, although Wales, and Chester, and Durham, were added to it. Truly, Mr. Speaker, I do not know what this unity means; nor has it ever been heard of, that I know, in the constitutional policy of this country. The very idea of subordination of parts, excludes this notion of simple and undivided unity. England is the head; but she is not the head and the members too. Ireland has ever had from the beginning a separate, but not an independent, legislature; which, far from distracting, promoted the union of the whole. Every thing was sweetly and harmoniously disposed through both Islands for the conservation of English dominion, and the communication of English liberties. I do not see that the same principles might not be carried into twenty Islands, and with the same good effect. This is my model with regard to America, as far as the internal circumstances of the two countries are the fame. I know no other unity of this empire, than I can draw from its example during thefe periods, when it feemed to my poor underftanding more united than it is now, or than it is likely to be by the prefent methods.

But fince I fpeak of thefe methods, I recollect, Mr. Speaker, almoft too late, that I promifed, before I finifhed, to fay fomething of the propofition of the * Noble Lord on the floor, which has been fo lately received, and ftands on your Journals. I muft be deeply concerned, whenever it is my misfortune to continue a difference with the majority of this Houfe. But as the reafons for that difference are my apology for thus troubling you, fuffer me to ftate them in a very few words. I fhall comprefs them into as fmall a body as I poffibly can, having already debated that matter at large, when the queftion was before the Committee.

Firft, then, I cannot admit that propofition of a ranfom by auction;—becaufe it is a meer project. It is a thing new; unheard of; fupported by no experience; juftified by no analogy; without example of our anceftors, or root in the conftitution. It is neither regular parliamentary taxation, nor Colony grant. *Experimentum in corpore vili*, is a good rule, which will ever make me adverfe to any trial of experiments

* Lord North.

on what is certainly the most valuable of all subjects; the peace of this Empire.

Secondly, it is an experiment which must be fatal in the end to our constitution. For what is it but a scheme for taxing the Colonies in the antichamber of the Noble Lord and his successors? To settle the quotas and proportions in this House, is clearly impossible. You, Sir, may flatter yourself, you shall sit a state auctioneer with your hammer in your hand, and knock down to each Colony as it bids. But to settle (on the plan laid down by the Noble Lord) the true proportional payment for four or five and twenty governments, according to the absolute and the relative wealth of each, and according to the British proportion of wealth and burthen, is a wild and chimerical notion. This new taxation must therefore come in by the back-door of the constitution. Each quota must be brought to this House ready formed; you can neither add nor alter. You must register it. You can do nothing further. For on what grounds can you deliberate either before or after the proposition? You cannot hear the counsel for all these Provinces, quarrelling each on its own quantity of payment, and its proportion to others. If you should attempt it, the Committee of Provincial Ways and Means, or by whatever other name it will delight to be called, must swallow up all the time of Parliament.

Thirdly,

Thirdly, it does not give satisfaction to the complaint of the Colonies. They complain, that they are taxed without their consent; you answer, that you will fix the sum at which they shall be taxed. That is, you give them the very grievance for the remedy. You tell them indeed, that you will leave the mode to themselves. I really beg pardon: it gives me pain to mention it; but you must be sensible that you will not perform this part of the compact. For, suppose the Colonies were to lay the duties which furnished their Contingent, upon the importation of your manufactures; you know you would never suffer such a tax to be laid. You know too, that you would not suffer many other modes of taxation. So that, when you come to explain yourself, it will be found, that you will neither leave to themselves the quantum nor the mode; nor indeed any thing. The whole is delusion from one end to the other.

Fourthly, this method of ransom by auction, unless it be *universally* accepted, will plunge you into great and inextricable difficulties. In what year of our Lord are the proportions of payments to be settled? To say nothing of the impossibility that Colony agents should have general powers of taxing the Colonies at their discretion; consider, I implore you, that the communication by special messages, and orders between these agents

and

and their conſtituents on each variation of the caſe, when the parties come to contend together, and to diſpute on their relative proportions, will be a matter of delay, perplexity, and confuſion, that never can have an end.

If all the Colonies do not appear at the outcry, what is the condition of thoſe aſſemblies, who offer, by themſelves or their agents, to tax themſelves up to your ideas of their proportion? The refractory Colonies, who refuſe all compoſition, will remain taxed only to your old impoſitions; which, however grievous in principle, are trifling as to production. The obedient Colonies in this ſcheme are heavily taxed; the refractory remain unburthened. What will you do? Will you lay new and heavier taxes by Parliament on the diſobedient? Pray conſider in what way you can do it? You are perfectly convinced that in the way of taxing, you can do nothing but at the ports. Now ſuppoſe it is Virginia that refuſes to appear at your auction, while Maryland and North Carolina bid handſomely for their ranſom, and are taxed to your quota? How will you put theſe Colonies on a par? Will you tax the tobacco of Virginia? If you do, you give its deathwound to your Engliſh revenue at home, and to one of the very greateſt articles of your own foreign trade. If you tax the import of that rebellious Colony, what do you tax but your own manufactures, or the goods of ſome other

obedient,

obedient, and already well-taxed Colony? Who has said one word on this labyrinth of detail, which bewilders you more and more as you enter into it? Who has presented, who can present you, with a clue, to lead you out of it? I think, Sir, it is impossible, that you should not recollect that the Colony bounds are so implicated in one another (you know it by your other experiments in the Bill for prohibiting the New-England fishery) that you can lay no possible restraints on almost any of them which may not be presently eluded, if you do not confound the innocent with the guilty, and burthen those whom upon every principle, you ought to exonerate. He must be grosly ignorant of America, who thinks, that, without falling into this confusion of all rules of equity and policy, you can restrain any single Colony, especially Virginia and Maryland, the central, and most important of them all.

Let it also be considered, that, either in the present confusion you settle a permanent contingent, which will and must be trifling; and then you have no effectual revenue: or you change the quota at every exigency; and then on every new repartition you will have a new quarrel.

Reflect besides, that when you have fixed a quota for every Colony, you have not provided for prompt and punctual payment. Suppose one, two,

two, five, ten years arrears. You cannot iſſue a treaſury extent againſt the failing Colony. You muſt make new Boſton port bills, new reſtraining laws, new Acts for dragging men to England for trial. You muſt ſend out new fleets, new armies. All is to begin again. From this day forward the Empire is never to know an hour's tranquillity. An inteſtine fire will be kept alive in the bowels of the Colonies, which one time or other muſt conſume this whole empire. I allow indeed that the empire of Germany raiſes her revenue and her troops by quotas and contingents; but the revenue of the empire, and the army of the empire, is the worſt revenue, and the worſt army, in the world.

Inſtead of a ſtanding revenue, you will therefore have a perpetual quarrel. Indeed the noble Lord, who propoſed this project of a ranſom by auction, ſeemed himſelf to be of that opinion. His project was rather deſigned for breaking the union of the Colonies, than for eſtabliſhing a Revenue. He confeſſed, he apprehended that his propoſal would not be to *their taſte*. I ſay, this ſcheme of diſunion ſeems to be at the bottom of the project; for I will not ſuſpect that the noble Lord meant nothing but merely to delude the nation by an airy phantom which he never intended to realize. But whatever his views may be; as I propoſe the peace and union of the Colonies as the very foundation of my plan, it cannot accord

accord with one whose foundation is perpetual discord.

Compare the two. This I offer to give you is plain and simple. The other full of perplexed and intricate mazes. This is mild; that harsh. This is found by experience effectual for its purposes; the other is a new project. This is universal; the other calculated for certain Colonies only. This is immediate in its conciliatory operation; the other remote, contingent, full of hazard. Mine is what becomes the dignity of a ruling people; gratuitous, unconditional, and not held out as matter of bargain and sale. I have done my duty in proposing it to you. I have indeed tired you by a long discourse; but this is the misfortune of those to whose influence nothing will be conceded, and who must win every inch of their ground by argument. You have heard me with goodness. May you decide with wisdom! For my part, I feel my mind greatly disburthened, by what I have done to-day. I have been the less fearful of trying your patience, because on this subject I mean to spare it altogether in future. I have this comfort, that in every stage of the American affairs, I have steadily opposed the measures that have produced the confusion, and may bring on the destruction, of this empire. I now go so far as to risque a proposal of my own. If I cannot give peace to my country; I give it to my conscience.

But

But what (fays the Financier) is peace to us without money? Your plan gives us no Revenue. No! But it does—For it fecures to the fubject the power of REFUSAL; the firſt of all Revenues. Experience is a cheat, and fact a liar, if this power in the fubject of proportioning his grant, or of not granting at all, has not been found the richeſt mine of Revenue ever difcovered by the ſkill or by the fortune of man. It does not indeed vote you £152,750 : 11 : 2¼ths. nor any other paltry limited fum.—But it gives the ſtrong box itfelf, the fund, the bank, from whence only revenues can arife amongſt a people fenfible of freedom: *Pofita luditur arca.* Cannot you in England; cannot you at this time of day; cannot you, an Houfe of Commons, truſt to the principle which has raifed fo mighty a revenue, and accumulated a debt of near 140 millions in this country? Is this principle to be true in England, and falfe every where elfe? Is it not true in Ireland? Has it not hitherto been true in the Colonies? Why fhould you prefume that, in any country, a body duly conftituted for any function, will neglect to perform its duty, and abdicate its truſt? Such a prefumption would go againſt all government in all modes. But, in truth, this dread of penury of fupply, from a free affembly, has no foundation in nature. For firſt obferve, that, befides the defire which all men have naturally of fupporting the honour of their

own

own government; that sense of dignity, and that security to property, which ever attends freedom, has a tendency to increase the stock of the free community. Most may be taken where most is accumulated. And what is the soil or climate where experience has not uniformly proved, that the voluntary flow of heaped-up plenty, bursting from the weight of its own rich luxuriance, has ever run with a more copious stream of revenue, than could be squeezed from the dry husks of oppressed indigence, by the straining of all the politic machinery in the world.

Next we know, that parties must ever exist in a free country. We know too, that the emulations of such parties, their contradictions, their reciprocal necessities, their hopes, and their fears, must send them all in their turns to him that holds the balance of the state. The parties are the Gamesters; but Government keeps the table, and is sure to be the winner in the end. When this game is played, I really think it is more to be feared, that the people will be exhausted, than that Government will not be supplied. Whereas, whatever is got by acts of absolute power ill obeyed, because odious, or by contracts ill kept, because constrained; will be narrow, feeble, uncertain, and precarious. "*Ease would retract vows made in pain, as violent and void.*"

I, for one, protest against compounding our demands: I declare against compounding, for a poor limited sum, the immense, evergrowing, eternal Debt, which is due to generous Government from protected Freedom. And so may I speed in the great object I propose to you, as I think it would not only be an act of injustice, but would be the worst œconomy in the world, to compel the Colonies to a sum certain, either in the way of ransom, or in the way of compulsory compact.

But to clear up my ideas on this subject—a revenue from America transmitted hither—do not delude yourselves—you never can receive it—No, not a shilling. We have experience that from remote countries it is not to be expected. If, when you attempted to extract revenue from Bengal, you were obliged to return in loan what you had taken in imposition; what can you expect from North America? for certainly, if ever there was a country qualified to produce wealth, it is India; or an institution fit for the transmission, it is the East-India company. America has none of these aptitudes. If America gives you taxable objects, on which you lay your duties here, and gives you, at the same time, a surplus by a foreign sale of her commodities to pay the duties on these objects which you tax at home, she has performed her part to the British revenue.

But with regard to her own internal eſtabliſhments; ſhe may, I doubt not ſhe will, contribute in moderation. I ſay in moderation; for ſhe ought not to be permitted to exhauſt herſelf. She ought to be reſerved to a war; the weight of which, with the enemies that we are moſt likely to have, muſt be conſiderable in her quarter of the globe. There ſhe may ſerve you, and ſerve you eſſentially.

For that ſervice, for all ſervice, whether of revenue, trade, or empire, my truſt is in her intereſt in the Britiſh conſtitution. My hold of the Colonies is in the cloſe affection which grows from common names, from kindred blood, from ſimilar privileges, and equal protection. Theſe are ties, which, though light as air, are as ſtrong as links of iron. Let the Colonies always keep the idea of their civil rights aſſociated with your Government;—they will cling and grapple to you; and no force under heaven will be of power to tear them from their allegiance. But let it be once underſtood, that your Government may be one thing, and their Privileges another; that theſe two things may exiſt without any mutual relation; the cement is gone; the coheſion is looſened; and every thing haſtens to decay and diſſolution. As long as you have the wiſdom to keep the ſovereign authority of this country as the ſanctuary of liberty, the ſacred temple conſecrated to our common faith, wherever the choſen

race

race and sons of England worship freedom, they will turn their faces towards you. The more they multiply, the more friends you will have; the more ardently they love liberty, the more perfect will be their obedience. Slavery they can have any where. It is a weed that grows in every soil. They may have it from Spain, they may have it from Prussia. But until you become lost to all feeling of your true interest and your natural dignity, freedom they can have from none but you. This is the commodity of price, of which you have the monopoly. This is the true act of navigation, which binds to you the commerce of the Colonies, and through them secures to you the wealth of the world. Deny them this participation of freedom, and you break that sole bond, which originally made, and must still preserve, the unity of the empire. Do not entertain so weak an imagination, as that your registers and your bonds, your affidavits and your sufferances, your cockets and your clearances, are what form the great securities of your commerce. Do not dream that your letters of office, and your instructions, and your suspending clauses, are the things that hold together the great contexture of this mysterious whole. These things do not make your government. Dead instruments, passive tools as they are, it is the spirit of English communion that gives all their life and efficacy to them. It is the spirit of the English constitution, which, infused through the mighty mass, pervades;

pervades, feeds, unites, invigorates, vivifies, every part of the empire, even down to the minutest member.

Is it not the same virtue which does every thing for us here in England? Do you imagine then, that it is the land tax act which raises your revenue? that it is the annual vote in the committee of supply, which gives you your army? or that it is the Mutiny Bill which inspires it with bravery and discipline? No! surely no! It is the love of the people; it is their attachment to their government from the sense of the deep stake they have in such a glorious institution, which gives you your army and your navy, and infuses into both that liberal obedience, without which your army would be a base rabble, and your navy nothing but rotten timber.

All this, I know well enough, will sound wild and chimerical to the profane herd of those vulgar and mechanical politicians, who have no place among us; a sort of people who think that nothing exists but what is gross and material; and who therefore, far from being qualified to be directors of the great movement of empire, are not fit to turn a wheel in the machine. But to men truly initiated and rightly taught, these ruling and master principles, which, in the opinion of such men as I have mentioned, have no substantial existence, are in truth every thing,

and

and all in all. Magnanimity in politicks is not seldom the trueſt wiſdom; and a great empire and little minds go ill together. If we are conſcious of our ſituation, and glow with zeal to fill our place as becomes our ſtation and ourſelves, we ought to auſpicate all our public proceedings on America, with the old warning of the church, *Surſum corda!* We ought to elevate our minds to the greatneſs of that truſt to which the order of Providence has called us. By adverting to the dignity of this high calling, our anceſtors have turned a ſavage wilderneſs into a glorious empire; and have made the moſt extenſive, and the only honourable conqueſts; not by deſtroying, but by promoting, the wealth, the number, the happineſs, of the human race. Let us get an American revenue as we have got an American empire. Engliſh privileges have made it all that it is; Engliſh privileges alone will make it all it can be.

In full confidence of this unalterable truth, I now *(quod felix fauſtumque ſit)* — lay the firſt ſtone of the Temple of Peace; and I move you,

"*That the Colonies and Plantations of Great*
"*Britain in North America, conſiſting of Fourteen*
"*ſeparate governments, and containing Two Mil-*
"*lions and upwards of free inhabitants, have not*
"*had the liberty and privilege of electing and ſending*
"*any*

" any Knights and Burgesses, or others, to repre-
" sent them in the high Court of Parliament."

Upon this Resolution, the previous question was put, and carried;—for the previous question 270,—against it 78.

As the Propositions were opened separately in the body of the Speech, the Reader perhaps may wish to see the whole of them together, in the form in which they were moved for.

MOVED,

" That the Colonies and Plantations of Great Britain in North America, consisting of Fourteen separate Governments, and containing two Millions and upwards of Free Inhabitants, have not had the liberty and privilege of electing and sending any Knights and Burgesses, or others, to represent them in the High Court of Parliament."

" That the said Colonies and Plantations have been made liable to, and bounden by, several subsidies, payments, rates, and taxes, given and granted by Parliament; though the said Colonies and Plantations have not their Knights and Burgesses, in the said High Court of Parliament, of their own election, to represent the condition of their country; *by lack whereof, they have been oftentimes touched and grieved by subsidies given, granted, and assented to, in the said Court, in a manner prejudicial to the common wealth, quietness, rest, and peace, of the subjects inhabiting within the same.*"

" That,

"That, from the diſtance of the ſaid Colonies, and from other circumſtances, no method hath hitherto been deviſed for procuring a Repreſentation in Parliament for the ſaid Colonies."

"That each of the ſaid Colonies hath within itſelf a Body, choſen, in part or in the whole, by the Freemen, Freeholders, or other Free Inhabitants thereof, commonly called the General Aſſembly, or General Court; with powers, legally to raiſe, levy, and aſſeſs, according to the ſeveral uſage of ſuch Colonies, duties and taxes towards defraying all ſorts of public ſervices *."

"That the ſaid General Aſſemblies, General Courts, or other bodies, legally qualified as aforeſaid, have at ſundry times freely granted ſeveral large ſubſidies and public aids for his Majeſty's ſervice, according to their abilities, when required thereto by letter from one of his Majeſty's Principal Secretaries of State; and that their right to grant the ſame, and their chearfulneſs and ſufficiency in the ſaid grants, have been at ſundry times acknowledged by Parliament."

* The firſt Four Motions and the laſt had the previous queſtion put on them. The others were negatived.

The words in Italicks were, by an amendment that was carried, left out of the motion; which will appear in the Journals; though it is not the practice to inſert ſuch amendments in the Votes.

"That

"That it hath been found by experience, that
the manner of granting the said supplies and
aids, by the said General Assemblies, hath been
more agreeable to the inhabitants of the said
Colonies, and more beneficial and conducive to
the public service, than the mode of giving
and granting aids and subsidies in Parliament to
be raised and paid in the said Colonies."

"That it may be proper to repeal an act made
in the 7th year of the reign of his present Majesty, intituled, An Act for granting certain
duties in the British Colonies and Plantations in
America; for allowing a draw-back of the duties of Customs, upon the exportation from this
kingdom, of coffee and cocoa-nuts, of the produce of the said Colonies or Plantations; for
discontinuing the draw-backs payable on china
earthen ware exported to America; and for
more effectually preventing the clandestine running of goods in the said Colonies and Plantations."

"That it may be proper to repeal an Act, made
in the 14th year of the reign of his present
Majesty, intituled, An Act to discontinue, in
such manner, and for such time, as are therein
mentioned, the landing and discharging, lading
or shipping of goods, wares, and merchandize,
at the Town, and within the Harbour, of Boston,

" in the province of Maſſachuſet's Bay, in North
" America."

" That it may be proper to repeal an Act made
" in the 14th year of the reign of his preſent
" Majeſty, intituled, An Act for the impartial
" adminiſtration of juſtice, in caſes of perſons
" queſtioned for any acts done by them in the
" execution of the law, or for the ſuppreſſion
" of riots and tumults, in the province of Maſſa-
" chuſet's Bay, in New England."

" That it is proper to repeal an Act, made in
" the 14th year of the reign of his preſent Ma-
" jeſty, intituled, An Act for the better regu-
" lating the government of the province of the
" Maſſachuſet's Bay in New England."

" That it is proper to explain and amend an Act
" made in the 35th year of the reign of King
" Henry VIII, intituled, An Act for the trial
" of treaſons committed out of the King's do-
" minions."

" That, from the time when the General Aſ-
" ſembly, or General Court, of any Colony or
" Plantation, in North America, ſhall have ap-
" pointed, by act of Aſſembly duly confirmed,
" a ſettled ſalary to the offices of the Chief Juſtice
" and Judges of the ſuperior courts, it may be
" proper that the ſaid Chief Juſtice and other
" Judges

"Judges of the superior Courts of such Colony shall hold his and their office and offices during their good behaviour; and shall not be removed therefrom, but when the said removal shall be adjudged by his Majesty in Council, upon a hearing on complaint from the General Assembly, or on a complaint from the Governor, or Council, or the House of Representatives, severllay, of the Colony in which the said Chief Justice and other Judges have exercised the said office."

"That it may be proper to regulate the Courts of Admiralty, or Vice-admiralty, authorized by the 15th chapter of the 4th of George III, in such a manner, as to make the same more commodious to those who sue, or are sued, in the said courts; *and to provide for the more decent maintenance of the Judges of the same.*"

FINIS.

MR. *BURKE's*
SPEECH,

ON

MR. FOX's *East India* Bill.

[Price 2 *s.*]

MR. *BURKE'S* SPEECH,

On the 1st DECEMBER 1783,

UPON

THE QUESTION FOR THE SPEAKER'S LEAVING THE CHAIR,

IN ORDER FOR THE HOUSE TO RESOLVE ITSELF INTO A COMMITTEE

ON

MR. FOX's *East India* Bill.

LONDON:

Printed for J. DODSLEY, in PALL-MALL.

M.DCC.LXXXIV.

BURKE'S
SPEECH

SPEECH, &c.

Mr. Speaker,

I THANK you for pointing to me. I really wished much to engage your attention in an early stage of the debate. I have been long very deeply, though perhaps ineffectually, engaged in the preliminary enquiries, which have continued without intermission for some years. Though I have felt, with some degree of sensibility, the natural and inevitable impressions of the several matters of fact, as they have been successively disclosed, I have not at any time attempted to trouble you on the merits of the subject; and very little on any of the points which incidentally arose in the course of our proceedings. But I should be sorry to be found totally silent upon this day. Our enquiries are now come to their final issue:—It is now to be determined whether the three years of laborious parliamentary research, whether the twenty years of patient Indian suffering, are to produce a substantial reform in our Eastern administration; or whether our knowledge of the grievances has abated our zeal for the correction of them, and whether our very enquiry into the evil was only a pretext to elude the remedy which is demanded from us by humanity, by justice, and by every principle of true policy. Depend upon it, this business cannot be indifferent to our fame. It will turn out a matter of great disgrace or great glory to the whole British nation. We are on a conspicuous stage, and the world marks our demeanour.

I am therefore a little concerned to perceive the spirit and temper in which the debate has been all along pursued, upon one side of the House. The declamation of the Gentlemen who oppose the bill has been abundant and vehement, but they have been reserved and even silent about the fitness or unfitness of the plan to attain the direct object it has in view. By some gentlemen it is taken up (by way of exercise I presume) as a point of law on a question of private property, and corporate franchise; by others it is regarded as the petty intrigue of a faction at court, and argued merely as it tends to set this man a little higher, or that a little lower in situation and power. All the void has been filled up with invectives against coalition; with allusions to the loss of America; with the activity and inactivity of ministers. The total silence of these gentlemen concerning the interest and well-being of the people of India, and concerning the interest which this nation has in the commerce and revenues of that country, is a strong indication of the value which they set upon these objects.

It

It has been a little painful to me to obſerve the intruſion into this important debate of ſuch company as *Quo Warranto*, and *Mandamus*, and *Certiorari*; as if we were on a trial about mayors and aldermen, and capital burgeſſes; or engaged in a ſuit concerning the borough of Penryn, or Saltaſh, or St. Ives, or St. Mawes. Gentlemen have argued with as much heat and paſſion, as if the firſt things in the world were at ſtake; and their topics are ſuch, as belong only to matter of the loweſt and meaneſt litigation. It is not right, it is not worthy of us, in this manner to depreciate the value, to degrade the majeſty of this grave deliberation of policy and empire.

For my part, I have thought myſelf bound, when a matter of this extraordinary weight came before me, not to conſider (as ſome Gentlemen are ſo fond of doing) whether the bill originated from a Secretary of State for the home department, or from a Secretary for the foreign; from a miniſter of influence or a miniſter of the people; from Jacob or from Eſau[*]. I aſked myſelf, and I aſked myſelf nothing elſe, what part it was fit for a member of parliament, who has ſupplied a mediocrity of talents by the extreme of diligence, and who has thought himſelf obliged, by the reſearch of years, to wind himſelf into the inmoſt receſſes and labyrinths of the Indian detail, what part, I ſay, it became ſuch a member of parliament to take, when a miniſter of ſtate, in conformity to a recommendation from the throne, has brought before us a ſyſtem for the better government of the territory and commerce of the Eaſt. In this light, and in this only, I will trouble you with my ſentiments.

[*] An alluſion made by Mr. Powis.

It is not only agreed but demanded, by the Right Honourable gentleman [*], and by those who act with him, that a *whole* system ought to be produced; that it ought not to be an *half measure*; that it ought to be no *palliative*; but a legislative provision, vigorous, substantial, and effective.—I believe that no man who understands the subject can doubt for a moment, that those must be the conditions of any thing deserving the name of a reform in the Indian government; that any thing short of them would not only be delusive, but, in this matter which admits no medium, noxious in the extreme.

To all the conditions proposed by his adversaries the mover of the bill perfectly agrees; and on his performance of them he rests his cause. On the other hand, not the least objection has been taken, with regard to the efficiency, the vigour, or the completeness of the scheme. I am therefore warranted to assume, as a thing admitted, that the bills accomplish what both sides of the House demand as essential. The end is completely answered, so far as the direct and immediate object is concerned.

But though there are no direct, yet there are various collateral objections made; objections from the effects, which this plan of reform for Indian administration may have on the privileges of great public bodies in England; from its probable influence on the constitutional rights, or on the freedom and integrity of the several branches of the legislature.

[*] Mr. Pitt.

Before I answer these objections I must beg leave to observe, that if we are not able to contrive some method of governing India *well*, which will not of necessity become the means of governing Great Britain *ill*, a ground is laid for their eternal separation; but none for sacrificing the people of that country to our constitution. I am however far from being persuaded that any such incompatibility of interest does at all exist. On the contrary I am certain that every means, effectual to preserve India from oppression, is a guard to preserve the British constitution from its worst corruption. To shew this, I will consider the objections, which I think are four.

1st. That the bill is an attack on the chartered rights of men.

2dly. That it increases the influence of the crown.

3dly. That it does *not* increase, but diminishes, the influence of the crown, in order to promote the interests of certain ministers and their party.

4thly. That it deeply affects the national credit.

As to the first of these objections; I must observe that the phrase of "the chartered rights *of men*," is full of affectation; and very unusual in the discussion of privileges conferred by charters of the present description. But it is not difficult to discover what end that ambiguous mode of expression, so often reiterated, is meant to answer.

The rights of *men*, that is to say, the natural rights of mankind, are indeed sacred things; and if any public measure is proved mischievously to affect them, the objection ought to be fatal to that measure,

measure, even if no charter at all could be set up against it. If these natural rights are further affirmed and declared by express covenants, if they are clearly defined and secured against chicane, against power, and authority, by written instruments and positive engagements, they are in a still better condition: they partake not only of the sanctity of the object so secured, but of that solemn public faith itself, which secures an object of such importance. Indeed this formal recognition, by the sovereign power, of an original right in the subject, can never be subverted, but by rooting up the holding radical principles of government, and even of society itself. The charters, which we call by distinction *great*, are public instruments of this nature; I mean the charters of King John and King Henry the Third. The things secured by these instruments may, without any deceitful ambiguity, be very fitly called the *chartered rights of men*.

These charters have made the very name of a charter dear to the heart of every Englishman—But, Sir, there may be, and there are charters, not only different in nature, but formed on principles the *very reverse* of those of the great charter. Of this kind is the charter of the East India Company. *Magna charta* is a charter to restrain power, and to destroy monopoly. The East India charter is a charter to establish monopoly, and to create power. Political power and commercial monopoly are *not* the rights of men; and the rights to them derived from charters, it is fallacious and sophistical to call " the chartered rights of men." These chartered rights, (to speak of such charters and of their effects in terms of the greatest possible

possible moderation) do at least suspend the natural rights of mankind at large; and in their very frame and constitution are liable to fall into a direct violation of them.

It is a charter of this latter description (that is to say a charter of power and monopoly) which is affected by the bill before you. The bill, Sir, does, without question, affect it; it does affect it essentially and substantially. But, having stated to you of what description the chartered rights are which this bill touches, I feel no difficulty at all in acknowledging the existence of those chartered rights, in their fullest extent. They belong to the Company in the surest manner; and they are secured to that body by every sort of public sanction. They are stamped by the faith of the King; they are stamped by the faith of Parliament; they have been bought for money, for money honestly and fairly paid; they have been bought for valuable consideration, over and over again.

I therefore freely admit to the East India Company their claim to exclude their fellow-subjects from the commerce of half the globe. I admit their claim to administer an annual territorial revenue of seven millions sterling; to command an army of sixty thousand men; and to dispose, (under the control of a sovereign imperial discretion, and with the due observance of the natural and local law) of the lives and fortunes of thirty millions of their fellow-creatures. All this they possess by charter and by acts of parliament, (in my opinion) without a shadow of controversy.

Those who carry the rights and claims of the Company the furthest do not contend for more than this; and all this I freely grant. But granting all this, they must grant to me in my turn, that all political power which is set over men, and that all privilege claimed or exercised in exclusion of them, being wholly artificial, and for so much, a derogation from the natural equality of mankind at large, ought to be some way or other exercised ultimately for their benefit.

If this is true with regard to every species of political dominion, and every description of commercial privilege, none of which can be original self-derived rights, or grants for the mere private benefit of the holders, then such rights, or privileges, or whatever else you choose to call them, are all in the strictest sense a *trust*; and it is of the very essence of every trust to be rendered *accountable*; and even totally to *cease*, when it substantially varies from the purposes for which alone it could have a lawful existence.

This I conceive, Sir, to be true of trusts of power vested in the highest hands, and of such as seem to hold of no human creature. But about the application of this principle to subordinate *derivative* trusts, I do not see how a controversy can be maintained. To whom then would I make the East India Company accountable? Why, to Parliament to be sure; to Parliament, from whom their trust was derived; to Parliament, which alone is capable of comprehending the magnitude of its object, and its abuse; and alone capable of an effectual legislative remedy. The very charter, which is held out to exclude Parliament from correcting malversation with regard to the high trust vested in the Company, is the very thing which at once gives a title and imposes a duty on us to interfere with effect, wherever power and authority originating from ourselves are perverted from their purposes, and become instruments of wrong and violence.

If Parliament, Sir, had nothing to do with this charter, we might have some sort of Epicurean excuse to stand aloof, indifferent spectators of what passes in the Company's name in India and in London. But if we are the very cause of the evil, we are in a special manner engaged to the redress; and for us passively to bear with oppressions committed under the sanction of our own authority, is in truth and reason for this House to be an active accomplice in the abuse.

That the power notoriously, grossly, abused has been bought from us is very certain. But this circumstance, which is urged against the bill, becomes an additional motive for our interference; lest we should be thought to have sold the blood of millions of men, for the base consideration of money. We sold, I admit, all that we had to sell; that is our authority, not our controul. We had not a right to make a market of our duties.

I ground myself therefore on this principle—that if the abuse is proved, the contract is broken; and we re-enter into all our rights; that is, into the exercise of all our duties. Our own authority is indeed as much a trust originally, as the Company's authority is a trust derivatively; and it is the use we make of the resumed power that must justify or condemn us in the resumption of it. When we have perfected the plan laid before us by the Right Honourable mover, the world will then see what it is we destroy, and what it is we create. By that test we stand or fall; and by that test I trust that it will be found in the issue, that we are going to supersede a charter abused to the full extent of all the powers which it could abuse, and exercised in the plenitude of despotism, tyranny, and corruption;

and

and that, in one and the same plan, we provide a real chartered security for the *rights of men* cruelly violated under that charter.

This bill, and those connected with it, are intended to form the *Magna Charta* of Hindostan. Whatever the treaty of Westphalia is to the liberty of the princes and free cities of the empire, and to the three religions there professed—Whatever the great charter, the statute of tallage, the petition of right, and the declaration of right, are to Great Britain, these bills are to the people of India. Of this benefit, I am certain, their condition is capable; and when I know that they are capable of more, my vote shall most assuredly be for our giving to the full extent of their capacity of receiving; and no charter of dominion shall stand as a bar in my way to their charter of safety and protection.

The strong admission I have made of the Company's rights (I am conscious of it) binds me to do a great deal. I do not presume to condemn those who argue *a priori*, against the propriety of leaving such extensive political powers in the hands of a company of merchants. I know much is, and much more may be said against such a system. But, with my particular ideas and sentiments, I cannot go that way to work. I feel an insuperable reluctance in giving my hand to destroy any established institution of government, upon a theory, however plausible it may be. My experience in life teaches me nothing clear upon the subject. I have known merchants with the sentiments and the abilities of great statesmen; and I have seen persons in the rank of statesmen, with the conceptions and character of pedlars. Indeed, my observation has furnished me with

nothing

nothing that is to be found in any habits of life or education, which tends wholly to difqualify men for the functions of government, but that, by which the power of exercifing thofe functions is very frequently obtained, I mean, a fpirit and habits of low cabal and intrigue; which I have never, in one inftance, feen united with a capacity for found and manly policy.

To juftify us in taking the adminiftration of their affairs out of the hands of the Eaft India Company, on my principles, I muft fee feveral conditions. 1ft. The object affected by the abufe fhould be great and important. 2d. The abufe affecting this great object ought to be a great abufe. 3d. It ought to be habitual, and not accidental. 4th. It ought to be utterly incurable in the body as it now ftands conftituted. All this ought to be made as vifible to me as the light of the fun, before I fhould ftrike off an atom of their charter. A Right Honourable gentleman * has faid, and faid I think but once, and that very flightly (whatever his original demand for a plan might feem to require) that " there are abufes in the " Company's government." If that were all, the fcheme of the mover of this bill, the fcheme of his learned friend, and his own fcheme of reformation (if he has any) are all equally needlefs. There are, and muft be, abufes in all governments. It amounts to no more than a nugatory propofition. But before I confider of what nature thefe abufes are, of which the gentleman fpeaks fo very lightly, permit me to recall to your recollection the map of the country which this abufed chartered right affects. This I fhall do, that you

* Mr. Pitt.

may judge whether in that map I can difcover any thing like the firſt of my conditions; that is, Whether the object affected by the abufe of the Eaſt India Company's power be of importance fufficient to juſtify the meaſure and means of reform applied to it in this bill.

With very few, and thoſe inconſiderable intervals, the Britiſh dominion, either in the Company's name, or in the names of princes abſolutely dependent upon the Company, extends from the mountains that ſeparate India from Tartary, to Cape Comorin, that is, one-and-twenty degrees of latitude!

In the northern parts it is a ſolid maſs of land, about eight hundred miles in length, and four or five hundred broad. As you go ſouthward, it becomes narrower for a ſpace. It afterwards dilates; but narrower or broader, you poſſeſs the whole eaſtern and north-eaſtern coaſt of that vaſt country, quite from the borders of Pegu. — Bengal, Bahar, and Oriſſa, with Benares (now unfortunately in our immediate poſſeſſion) meaſure 161,978 ſquare Engliſh miles; a territory conſiderably larger than the whole kingdom of France. Oude, with its dependent provinces, is 53,286 ſquare miles, not a great deal leſs than England. The Carnatic, with Tanjour and the Circars, is 65,948 ſquare miles, very conſiderably larger than England; and the whole of the Company's dominion comprehending Bombay and Salſette, amounts to 281,412 ſquare miles; which forms a territory larger than any European dominion, Ruſſia and Turkey excepted. Through all that vaſt extent of country there is not a man who eats a mouthful of rice but by permiſſion of the Eaſt India Company.

So

So far with regard to the extent. The population of this great empire is not eafy to be calculated. When the countries, of which it is compofed, came into our poffeffion, they were all eminently peopled, and eminently productive; though at that time confiderably declined from their antient profperity. But fince they are come into our hands!————! However if we take the period of our eftimate immediately before the utter defolation of the Carnatic, and if we allow for the havoc which our government had even then made in thefe regions, we cannot, in my opinion, rate the population at much lefs than thirty millions of fouls; more than four times the number of perfons in the ifland of Great Britain.

My next enquiry to that of the number, is the quality and defcription of the inhabitants. This multitude of men does not confift of an abject and barbarous populace; much lefs of gangs of favages, like the Guaranies and Chiquitos, who wander on the wafte borders of the river of Amazons, or the Plate; but a people for ages civilized and cultivated; cultivated by all the arts of polifhed life, whilft we were yet in the woods. There, have been (and ftill the fkeletons remain) princes once of great dignity, authority, and opulence. There, are to be found the chiefs of tribes and nations. There is to be found an antient and venerable priefthood, the depofitory of their laws, learning, and hiftory, the guides of the people whilft living, and their confolation in death; a nobility of great antiquity and renown; a multitude of cities, not exceeded in population and trade by thofe of the firft clafs in Europe; merchants and bankers, individual

houfes

houses of whom have once vied in capital with the Bank of England; whose credit had often supported a tottering state, and preserved their governments in the midst of war and desolation; millions of ingenious manufacturers and mechanicks; millions of the most diligent, and not the least intelligent, tillers of the earth. Here are to be found almost all the religions professed by men, the Bramincal, the Mussulmen, the Eastern and the Western Christians.

If I were to take the whole aggregate of our possessions there, I should compare it, as the nearest parallel I can find, with the empire of Germany. Our immediate possessions I should compare with the Austrian dominions, and they would not suffer in the comparison. The Nabob of Oude might stand for the King of Prussia; the Nabob of Arcot I would compare, as superior in territory, and equal in revenue, to the Elector of Saxony. Cheyt Sing, the Rajah of Benares, might well rank with the Prince of Hesse at least; and the Rajah of Tanjore (though hardly equal in extent of dominion, superior in revenue) to the Elector of Bavaria. The Polygars and the northern Zemindars, and other great chiefs, might well class with the rest of the Princes, Dukes, Counts, Marquisses, and Bishops in the empire; all of whom I mention to honour, and surely without disparagement to any or all of those most respectable princes and grandees.

All this vast mass, composed of so many orders and classes of men, is again infinitely diversified by manners, by religion, by hereditary employment, through all their possible combinations. This renders the handling of India a matter in an
high

high degree critical and delicate. But oh! it has been handled rudely indeed. Even some of the reformers seem to have forgot that they had any thing to do but to regulate the tenants of a manor, or the shopkeepers of the next county town.

It is an empire of this extent, of this complicated nature, of this dignity and importance, that I have compared to Germany, and the German government; not for an exact resemblance, but as a sort of a middle term, by which India might be approximated to our understandings, and if possible to our feelings; in order to awaken something of sympathy for the unfortunate natives, of which I am afraid we are not perfectly susceptible, whilst we look at this very remote object through a false and cloudy medium.

My second condition, necessary to justify me in touching the charter, is, Whether the Company's abuse of their trust, with regard to this great object, be an abuse of great atrocity. I shall beg your permission to consider their conduct in two lights; first the political, and then the commercial. Their political conduct (for distinctness) I divide again into two heads; the external, in which I mean to comprehend their conduct in their federal capacity, as it relates to powers and states independent, or that not long since were such; the other internal, namely their conduct to the countries either immediately subject to the Company, or to those who, under the apparent government of native sovereigns, are in a state much lower, and much more miserable, than common subjection.

The attention, Sir, which I wish to preserve to method will not be considered as unnecessary or affected.

affected. Nothing else can help me to selection out of the infinite mass of materials which have passed under my eye; or can keep my mind steady to the great leading points I have in view.

With regard therefore to the abuse of the external federal trust, I engage myself to you to make good these three positions:—First, I say, that from Mount Imaus, (or whatever else you call that large range of mountains that walls the northern frontier of India) where it touches us in the latitude of twenty-nine, to Cape Comorin, in the latitude of eight, that there is not a *single* prince, state, or potentate, great or small, in India, with whom they have come into contact, whom they have not sold. I say *sold*, though sometimes they have not been able to deliver according to their bargain.—Secondly, I say, that there is not a *single treaty* they have ever made, which they have not broken.—Thirdly, I say, that there is not a single prince or state, who ever put any trust in the Company, who is not utterly ruined; and that none are in any degree secure or flourishing, but in the exact proportion to their settled distrust and irreconcileable enmity to this nation.

These assertions are universal. I say in the full sense *universal*. They regard the external and political trust only; but I shall produce others fully equivalent, in the internal. For the present, I shall content myself with explaining my meaning; and if I am called on for proof whilst these bills are depending (which I believe I shall not) I will put my finger on the Appendixes to the Reports, or on papers of record in the House, or the Committees, which I have distinctly present to my memory, and which I think I can lay before you at half an hour's warning.

The first potentate sold by the Company for money was the Great Mogul—the descendant of Tamerlane. This high personage, as high as human veneration can look at, is by every account amiable in his manners, respectable for his piety according to his mode, and accomplished in all the Oriental literature. All this, and the title derived under his *charter*, to all that we hold in India, could not save him from the general *sale*. Money is coined in his name; In his name justice is administered; He is prayed for in every temple through the countries we possess—But he was sold.

It is impossible, Mr. Speaker, not to pause here for a moment, to reflect on the inconstancy of human greatness, and the stupendous revolutions that have happened in our age of wonders. Could it be believed, when I entered into existence, or when you, a younger man, were born, that on this day, in this House, we should be employed in discussing the conduct of those British subjects who had disposed of the power and person of the Grand Mogul? This is no idle speculation. Awful lessons are taught by it, and by other events, of which it is not yet too late to profit.

This is hardly a digression; but I return to the sale of the Mogul. Two districts, Corah and Allahabad, out of his immense grants, were reserved as a royal demesne to the donor of a kingdom, and the rightful sovereign of so many nations. — After withholding the tribute of £.260,000 a year, which the Company was, by the *charter* they had received from this prince, under the most solemn obligation to pay, these districts were sold to his chief minister Sujah ul Dowlah; and, what may appear to some the worst part of the tranfaction, thefe two diftricts were fold for scarcely two years purchafe. The defcendant of Tamerlane now ftands in need almoft of the common neceffaries of life; and in this fituation we do not even allow him, as bounty, the fmalleft portion of what we owe him in juftice.

The next fale was that of the whole nation of the Rohillas, which the grand falefman, without a pretence of quarrel, and contrary to his own declared fenfe of duty and rectitude, fold to the fame Sujah ul Dowlah. He fold the people to utter *extirpation*, for the fum of four hundred thoufand pounds. Faithfully was the bargain performed upon our fide. Hafiz Rhamet, the moft eminent of their chiefs, one of the braveft men of his time, and as famous throughout the Eaft for the elegance of his literature, and the fpirit of his poetical compofitions (by which he fupported the name of Hafiz), as for his courage, was invaded with an army of an hundred thoufand men, and an Englifh brigade. This man, at the head of inferior forces, was flain valiantly fighting for his country. His head was cut off, and delivered for money to a barbarian. His wife and children, perfons of that rank, were feen begging an handful of rice through the Englifh camp. The whole nation, with inconfiderable exceptions, was flaughtered or banifhed. The country was laid wafte with fire and fword; and that land diftinguifhed above moft others, by the chearful face of paternal government and protected labour, the chofen feat of cultivation and plenty, is now almoft throughout a dreary defart, covered with rufhes and briars, and jungles full of wild beafts.

The Britifh officer who commanded in the delivery of the people thus fold, felt fome compunction

compunction at his employment. He reprefented thefe enormous exceffes to the prefident of Bengal, for which he received a fevere reprimand from the civil governor; and I much doubt whether the breach caufed by the conflict, between the compaffion of the military and the firmnefs of the civil governor, be clofed at this hour.

In Bengal, Seraja Dowla was fold to Mir Jaffier; Mir Jaffier was fold to Mir Coffim; and Mir Coffim was fold to Mir Jaffier again. The fucceffion to Mir Jaffier was fold to his eldeft fon;—another fon of Mir Jaffier, Mobarech ul Dowla, was fold to his ftep-mother—The Maratta empire was fold to Ragoba; and Ragoba was fold and delivered to the Peifhwa of the Marattas. Both Ragoba and the Peifhwa of the Marattas were offered to fale to the Rajah of Berar. Scindia, the chief of Malva, was offered to fale to the fame Rajah; and the Subah of the Decan was fold to the great trader Mahomet Ali, Nabob of Arcot. To the fame Nabob of Arcot they fold Hyder Ali and the kingdom of Myfore. To Mahomet Ali they twice fold the kingdom of Tanjore. To the fame Mahomet Ali they fold at leaft twelve fovereign princes, called the Polygars. But to keep things even, the territory of Tinnivelly, belonging to their Nabob, they would have fold to the Dutch; and to conclude the account of fales, their great cuftomer, the Nabob of Arcot himfelf, and his lawful fucceffion, has been fold to his fecond fon, Amir ul Omrah, whofe character, views, and conduct, are in the accounts upon your table. It remains with you whether they fhall finally perfect this laft bargain.

All thefe bargains and fales were regularly attended with the wafte and havoc of the country, always by the buyer, and fometimes by the object of the sale. This was explained to you by the Honourable mover, when he stated the mode of paying debts due from the country powers to the Company. An Honourable gentleman, who is not now in his place, objected to his jumping near two thousand miles for an example. But the southern example is perfectly applicable to the northern claim, as the northern is to the southern;—for, throughout the whole space of these two thousand miles, take your stand where you will, the proceeding is perfectly uniform, and what is done in one part will apply exactly to the other.

My second assertion is, that the Company never has made a treaty which they have not broken. This position is so connected with that of the sales of provinces and kingdoms, with the negotiation of universal distraction in every part of India, that a very minute detail may well be spared on this point. It has not yet been contended, by any enemy to the reform, that they have observed any public agreement. When I hear that they have done so in any one instance (which hitherto, I confess, I never heard alledged) I shall speak to the particular treaty. The governor general has even amused himself and the Court of Directors in a very singular letter to that board, in which he admits he has not been very delicate with regard to public faith; and he goes so far as to state a regular estimate of the sums which the Company would have lost, or never acquired, if the rigid ideas of public faith entertained by his colleagues had been observed. * The learned gentleman over against me has indeed saved me much trouble. On a former occasion he obtained no small credit, for the clear and forcible manner in which he

* Mr. Dundas, Lord Advocate of Scotland.

stated

stated what we have not forgot, and I hope he has not forgot, that universal systematic breach of treaties which had made the British faith proverbial in the East.

It only remains, Sir, for me just to recapitulate some heads.—The treaty with the Mogul, by which we stipulated to pay him £.260,000 annually, was broken. This treaty they have broken, and not paid him a shilling. They broke their treaty with him, in which they stipulated to pay £.400,000 a year to the Soubah of Bengal. They agreed with the Mogul, for services admitted to have been performed, to pay Nudjif Cawn a pension. They broke this article with the rest, and stopped also this small pension. They broke their treaties with the Nizam, and with Hyder Ali. As to the Marattas, they had so many cross treaties with the States General of that nation, and with each of the chiefs, that it was notorious, that no one of these agreements could be kept without grossly violating the rest. It was observed, that if the terms of these several treaties had been kept, two British armies would at one and the same time have met in the field to cut each other's throats. The wars which desolate India, originated from a most atrocious violation of public faith on our part. In the midst of profound peace, the Company's troops invaded the Maratta territories, and surprised the island and fortress of Salsette. The Marattas nevertheless yielded to a treaty of peace, by which solid advantages were procured to the Company. But this treaty, like every other treaty, was soon violated by the Company. Again the Company invaded the Maratta dominions. The disaster that ensued gave occasion to a new treaty.

treaty. The whole army of the Company was obliged, in effect, to surrender to this injured, betrayed, and insulted people. Justly irritated however, as they were, the terms which they prescribed were reasonable and moderate; and their treatment of their captive invaders, of the most distinguished humanity. But the humanity of the Marattas was of no power whatsoever to prevail on the Company to attend to the observance of the terms dictated by their moderation. The war was renewed with greater vigour than ever; and such was their insatiable lust of plunder, that they never would have given ear to any terms of peace, if Hyder Ali had not broke through the Gauts, and rushing like a torrent into the Carnatic, swept away every thing in his career. This was in consequence of that confederacy, which by a sort of miracle united the most discordant powers for our destruction, as a nation in which no other could put any trust, and who were the declared enemies of the human species.

It is very remarkable, that the late controversy between the several presidencies, and between them and the Court of Directors, with relation to these wars and treaties, has not been, which of the parties might be defended for his share in them; but on which of the parties the guilt of all this load of perfidy should be fixed. But I am content to admit all these proceedings to be perfectly regular, to be full of honour and good faith; and wish to fix your attention solely to that single transaction which the advocates of this system select for so transcendant a merit as to cancel the guilt of all the rest of their proceedings; I mean the late treaties with the Marattas.

I make no observation on the total cession of territory,

territory, by which they surrendered all they had obtained by their unhappy successes in war, and almost all that they had obtained under the treaty of Poorunder. The restitution was proper, if it had been voluntary and seasonable. I attach on the spirit of the treaty, the dispositions it shewed, the provisions it made for a general peace, and the faith kept with allies and confederates; in order that the House may form a judgment, from this chosen piece, of the use which has been made (and is likely to be made, if things continue in the same hands) of the trust of the federal powers of this country.

It was the wish of almost every Englishman, that the Maratta peace might lead to a general one; because the Maratta war was only a part of a general confederacy formed against us on account of the universal abhorrence of our conduct which prevailed in every state and almost in every house in India. Mr. Hastings was obliged to pretend some sort of acquiescence in this general and rational desire. He therefore consented, in order to satisfy the point of honour of the Marattas, that an article should be inserted to admit Hyder Ali to accede to the pacification. But observe, Sir, the spirit of this man (which if it were not made manifest by a thousand things, and particularly by his proceedings with regard to Lord Macartney) would be sufficiently manifest by this—What sort of article think you does he require this essential head of a solemn treaty of general pacification to be? In his instruction to Mr. Anderson, he desires him to admit " a *vague* " article" in favour of Hyder. Evasion and fraud were the declared basis of the treaty. These *vague* articles, intended for a more vague performance,

formance, are the things which have damned our reputation in India.

Hardly was this vague article inserted, than, without waiting for any act on the part of Hyder, Mr. Haftings enters into a negociation with the Maratta Chief, Scindia, for a partition of the territories of the prince who was one of the objects to be secured by the treaty. He was to be parcelled out in three parts—one to Scindia; one to the Peifhwa of the Marattas; and the third to the Eaft India Company, or to (the old dealer and chapman) Mahomet Ali.

During the formation of this project, Hyder dies; and before his fon could take any one ftep, either to conform to the tenour of the article, or to contravene it, the treaty of partition is renewed on the old footing, and an inftruction is fent to Mr. Anderfon to conclude it in form.

A circumftance intervened, during the pendency of this negociation, to fet off the good faith of the Company with an additional brilliancy, and to make it fparkle and glow with a variety of fplendid faces. General Matthews had reduced that moft valuable part of Hyder's dominions called the Country of Biddenore. When the news reached Mr. Haftings he inftructed Mr. Anderfon to contend for an alteration in the treaty of partition, and to take the Biddenore country out of the common ftock which was to be divided, and to keep it for the Company.

The firft ground for this variation was its being a feparate conqueft made before the treaty had actually taken place. Here was a new proof given of the fairnefs, equity, and moderation, of the Company. But the fecond of Mr. Haftings's reafons for retaining the Biddenore as a feparate portion,

portion, and his conduct on that second ground, is still more remarkable. He asserted that that country could not be put into the partition stock, because General Matthews had received it on the terms of some convention, which might be incompatible with the partition proposed. This was a reason in itself both honourable and solid; and it shewed a regard to faith somewhere, and with some persons. But in order to demonstrate his utter contempt of the plighted faith which was alledged on one part as a reason for departing from it on another, and to prove his impetuous desire for sowing a new war, even in the prepared soil of a general pacification, he directs Mr. Anderson, if he should find strong difficulties impeding the partition, on the score of the subtraction of Biddenore, wholly to abandon that claim, and to conclude the treaty on the original terms. General Matthews's convention was just brought forward sufficiently to demonstrate to the Marattas the slippery hold which they had on their new confederate; on the other hand that convention being instantly abandoned, the people of India were taught, that no terms on which they can surrender to the Company are to be regarded, when farther conquests are in view.

Next, Sir, let me bring before you the pious care that was taken of our allies under that treaty which is the subject of the Company's applauses. These allies were Ragonaut Row, for whom we had engaged to find a throne; the Guickwar, (one of the Guzerat princes) who was to be emancipated from the Maratta authority, and to grow great by several accessions of dominion; and lastly, the Rana of Gohud, with whom we had entered into a treaty of partition for eleven sixteenths of our joint conquests. Some of these inestimable
securities,

(26)

securities, called *vague* articles, were inserted in favour of them all.

As to the first, the unhappy abdicated Peshwa, and pretender to the Maratta throne, Ragonaut Row, was delivered up to his people, with an article for safety, and some provision. This man, knowing how little vague the hatred of his countrymen was towards him, and well apprised of what black crimes he stood accused (among which our invasion of his country would not appear the least) took a mortal alarm at the security we had provided for him. He was thunderstruck at the article in his favour, by which he was surrendered to his enemies. He never had the least notice of the treaty; and it was apprehended that he would fly to the protection of Hyder Ali, or some other, disposed or able to protect him. He was therefore not left without comfort; for Mr. Anderson did him the favour to send a special messenger, desiring him to be of good cheer and to fear nothing. And his old enemy, Scindia, at our request, sent him a message equally well calculated to quiet his apprehensions.

By the same treaty the Guickwar was to come again, with no better security, under the dominion of the Maratta state. As to the Rana of Gohud, a long negotiation depended for giving him up. At first this was refused by Mr. Hastings with great indignation; at another stage it was admitted as proper, because he had shewn himself a most perfidious person. But at length a method of reconciling these extremes was found out, by contriving one of the usual articles in his favour. What I believe will appear beyond all belief, Mr. Anderson exchanged the final ratifications of that treaty by which the Rana was nominally secured in his possessions, in the camp of the Maratta

chief,

chief, Scindia, whilst he was (really, and not nominally) battering the castle of Gualior, which we had given, agreeably to treaty, to this deluded ally. Scindia had already reduced the town; and was at the very time, by various detachments, reducing, one after another, the fortresses of our protected ally, as well as in the act of chastising all the Rajahs who had assisted Colonel Camaq in his invasion. I have seen in a letter from Calcutta, that the Rana of Gohud's agent would have represented these hostilities (which went hand in hand with the protecting treaty) to Mr. Hastings; but he was not admitted to his presence.

In this manner the Company has acted with their allies in the Maratta war. But they did not rest here: the Marattas were fearful lest the persons delivered to them by that treaty should attempt to escape into the British territories, and thus might elude the punishment intended for them, and by reclaiming the treaty, might stir up new disturbances. To prevent this, they desired an article to be inserted in the supplemental treaty, to which they had the ready consent of Mr. Hastings and the rest of the Company's representatives in Bengal. It was this, " That " the English and Maratta governments mutual- " ly agree not to afford refuge to any *chiefs,* " *merchants, or other persons,* flying for protec- " tion to the territories of the other." This was readily assented to, and assented to without any exception whatever, in favour of our surrendered allies. On their part a reciprocity was stipulated which was not unnatural for a government like the Company's to ask; a government, conscious that many subjects had been, and would in future, be driven to fly from its jurisdiction.

To complete the system of pacific intention

and

and public faith, which predominate in thefe treaties, Mr. Haftings fairly refolved to put all peace, except on the terms of abfolute conqueft, wholly out of his own power. For, by an article in this fecond treaty with Scindia, he binds the Company not to make any peace with Tippoo Saheb, without the confent of the Peifhwa of the Marattas; and binds Scindia to him by a reciprocal engagement. The treaty between France and England obliges us mutually to withdraw our forces, if our allies in India do not accede to the peace within four months; Mr. Haftings's treaty obliges us to continue the war as long as the Peifhwa thinks fit. We are now in that happy fituation, that the breach of the treaty with France, or the violation of that with the Marattas, is inevitable; and we have only to take our choice.

My third affertion, relative to the abufe made of the right of war and peace is, that there are none who have ever confided in us who have not been utterly ruined. The examples I have given of Ragonaut Row, of Guickwar, of the Ranah of Gohud, are recent. There is proof more than enough in the condition of the Mogul; in the flavery and indigence of the Nabob of Oude; the exile of the Rajah of Benares; the beggary of the Nabob of Bengal; the undone and captive condition of the Rajah and kingdom of Tanjour; the deftruction of the Polygars; and laftly, in the deftruction of the Nabob of Arcot himfelf, who when his dominions were invaded was found entirely deftitute of troops, provifions, ftores, and (as he afferts) of money, being a million in debt to the Company, and four millions to others: the many millions which he had extorted from fo many extirpated princes and their defolated countries

tries having (as he has frequently hinted) been expended for the ground-rent of his manfion-houfe in an alley in the fuburbs of Madras. Compare the condition of all thefe princes with the power and authority of all the Maratta ftates; with the independence and dignity of the Soubah of the Decan; and the mighty ftrength, the refources, and the manly ftruggle of Hyder Ali; and then the Houfe will difcover the effects, on every power in India, of an eafy confidence, or of a rooted diftruft in the faith of the Company.

Thefe are fome of my reafons, grounded on the abufe of the external political truft of that body, for thinking myfelf not only juftified but bound to declare againft thofe chartered rights which produce fo many wrongs. I fhould deem myfelf the wickedeft of men, if any vote of mine could contribute to the continuance of fo great an evil.

Now, Sir, according to the plan I propofed, I fhall take notice of the Company's internal government, as it is exercifed firft on the dependent provinces, and then as it affects thofe under the direct and immediate authority of that body. And here, Sir, before I enter into the fpirit of their interior government, permit me to obferve to you, upon a few of the many lines of difference which are to be found between the vices of the Company's government, and thofe of the conquerors who preceded us in India; that we may be enabled a little the better to fee our way in an attempt to the neceffary reformation.

The feveral irruptions of Arabs, Tartars, and Perfians, into India were, for the greater part, ferocious, bloody, and wafteful in the extreme: our entrance into the dominion of that country was, as generally, with fmall comparative effufion of blood; being introduced by various frauds

and

and delusions; and by taking advantage of the incurable, blind, and senseless animosity, which the several country powers bear towards each other, rather than by open force. But the difference in favour of the first conquerors is this; the Asiatic conquerors very soon abated of their ferocity, because they made the conquered country their own. They rose or fell with the rise or fall of the territory they lived in. Fathers there deposited the hopes of their posterity; and children there beheld the monuments of their fathers. Here their lot was finally cast; and it is the natural wish of all, that their lot should not be cast in a bad land. Poverty, sterility, and desolation, are not a recreating prospect to the eye of man; and there are very few who can bear to grow old among the curses of a whole people. If their passion or their avarice drove the Tartar lords to acts of rapacity or tyranny, there was time enough, even in the short life of man, to bring round the ill effects of an abuse of power upon the power itself. If hoards were made by violence and tyranny, they were still domestic hoards; and domestic profusion, or the rapine of a more powerful and prodigal hand, restored them to the people. With many disorders, and with few political checks upon power, Nature had still fair play; the sources of acquisition were not dried up; and therefore the trade, the manufactures, and the commerce of the country flourished. Even avarice and usury itself operated, both for the preservation and the employment of national wealth. The husbandman and manufacturer paid heavy interest, but then they augmented the fund from whence they were again to borrow. Their resources were dearly bought, but they were sure; and the general stock of the community grew by the general effort.

But

But under the English government all this order is reversed. The Tartar invasion was mischievous; but it is our protection that destroys India. It was their enmity, but it is our friendship. Our conquest there, after twenty years, is as crude as it was the first day. The natives scarcely know what it is to see the grey head of an Englishman. Young men (boys almost) govern there, without society, and without sympathy with the natives. They have no more social habits with the people, than if they still resided in England; nor indeed any species of intercourse but that which is necessary to making a sudden fortune, with a view to a remote settlement. Animated with all the avarice of age, and all the impetuosity of youth, they roll in one after another; wave after wave; and there is nothing before the eyes of the natives but an endless, hopeless prospect of new flights of birds of prey and passage, with appetites continually renewing for a food that is continually wasting. Every rupee of profit made by an Englishman is lost for ever to India. With us are no retributory superstitions, by which a foundation of charity compensates, through ages, to the poor, for the rapine and injustice of a day. With us no pride erects stately monuments which repair the mischiefs which pride had produced, and which adorn a country out of its own spoils. England has erected no churches, no hospitals*, no palaces, no schools; England has built no bridges, made no high roads, cut no navigations, dug out no reservoirs. Every other conqueror of every other description has left some monument, either of state

---

* The paltry foundation at Calcutta is scarcely worth naming as an exception.

or beneficence, behind him. Were we to be driven out of India this day, nothing would remain, to tell that it had been poſſeſſed, during the inglorious period of our dominion, by any thing better than the ouran-outang or the tiger.

There is nothing in the boys we ſend to India worſe than the boys whom we are whipping at ſchool, or that we ſee trailing a pike, or bending over a deſk at home. But as Engliſh youth in India drink the intoxicating draught of authority and dominion before their heads are able to bear it, and as they are full grown in fortune long before they are ripe in principle, neither nature nor reaſon have any opportunity to exert themſelves for remedy of the exceſſes of their premature power. The conſequences of their conduct, which in good minds, (and many of theirs are probably ſuch) might produce penitence or amendment, are unable to purſue the rapidity of their flight. Their prey is lodged in England; and the cries of India are given to ſeas and winds, to be blown about, in every breaking up of the monſoon, over a remote and unhearing ocean. In India all the vices operate by which ſudden fortune is acquired; in England are often diſplayed, by the ſame perſons, the virtues which diſpenſe hereditary wealth. Arrived in England, the deſtroyers of the nobility and gentry of a whole kingdom will find the beſt company in this nation, at a board of elegance and hoſpitality. Here the manufacturer and huſbandman will bleſs the juſt and punctual hand, that in India has torn the cloth from the loom, or wreſted the ſcanty portion of rice and ſalt from the peaſant of Bengal, or wrung from him the very opium in which he forgot his oppreſſions and his oppreſſor. They marry into your families;

they

they enter into your senate; they ease your estates by loans; they raise their value by demand; they cherish and protect your relations which lie heavy on your patronage; and there is scarcely an house in the kingdom that does not feel some concern and interest that makes all reform of our eastern government appear officious and disgusting; and, on the whole, a most discouraging attempt. In such an attempt you hurt those who are able to return kindness or to resent injury. If you succeed, you save those who cannot so much as give you thanks. All these things shew the difficulty of the work we have on hand: but they shew its necessity too. Our Indian government is in its best state a grievance. It is necessary that the correctives should be uncommonly vigorous; and the work of men sanguine, warm, and even impassioned in the cause. But it is an arduous thing to plead against abuses of a power which originates from your own country, and affects those whom we are used to consider as strangers.

I shall certainly endeavour to modulate myself to this temper; though I am sensible that a cold style of describing actions which appear to me in a very affecting light, is equally contrary to the justice due to the people, and to all genuine human feelings about them. I ask pardon of truth and nature for this compliance. But I shall be very sparing of epithets either to persons or things. It has been said (and, with regard to one of them, with truth) that Tacitus and Machiavel, by their cold way of relating enormous crimes, have in some sort appeared not to disapprove them; that they seem a sort of professors of the art of tyranny, and that they corrupt the minds of their readers by not expressing the detestation and horror that naturally belong to horrible and

D   detestable

detestable proceedings. But we are in general, Sir, so little acquainted with Indian details; the instruments of oppression under which the people suffer are so hard to be understood; and even the very names of the sufferers are so uncouth and strange to our ears, that it is very difficult for our sympathy to fix upon these objects. I am sure that some of us have come down stairs from the committee-room, with impressions on our minds, which to us were the inevitable results of our discoveries, yet if we should venture to express ourselves in the proper language of our sentiments, to other gentlemen not at all prepared to enter into the cause of them, nothing could appear more harsh and dissonant, more violent and unaccountable, than our language and behaviour. All these circumstances are not, I confess, very favourable to the idea of our attempting to govern India at all. But there we are; there we are placed by the Sovereign Disposer: and we must do the best we can in our situation. The situation of man is the preceptor of his duty.

Upon the plan which I laid down, and to which I beg leave to return, I was considering the conduct of the Company to those nations which are indirectly subject to their authority. The most considerable of the dependent princes is the Nabob of Oude. * My Right Honourable friend, to whom we owe the remedial bills on your table, has already pointed out to you, in one of the Reports, the condition of that prince, and as it stood in the time he alluded to. I shall only add a few circumstances that may tend to awaken some sense of the manner in which the condition of the people is affected by that of the prince, and

* Mr. Fox.

involved

involved in it; and to shew you, that when we talk of the sufferings of princes, we do not lament the oppression of individuals; and that in these cases the high and the low suffer together.

In the year 1779 the Nabob of Oude represented, through the British resident at his court, that the number of Company's troops stationed in his dominions was a main cause of his distress; and that all those which he was not bound by treaty to maintain should be withdrawn, as they had greatly diminished his revenue, and impoverished his country. I will read you, if you please, a few extracts from these representations.

He states " that the country and cultivation
" are abandoned; and this year in particular, from
" the excessive drought of the season, deductions
" of many lacks having been allowed to the far-
" mers, who are still left unsatisfied;" and then he proceeds with a long detail of his own distress, and that of his family, and all his dependants; and adds, " that the new-raised brigade is not only
" quite useless to my government, but is more-
" over the cause of much loss, both in revenues and
" customs. The detached body of troops under
" European officers bring nothing *but confusion to*
" *the affairs of my government, and are entirely*
" *their own masters.*" Mr. Middleton, Mr. Hastings's confidential Resident, vouches for the truth of this representation in its fullest extent. " I
" am concerned to confess, that there is too good
" ground for this plea. *The misfortune has been*
" *general throughout the whole of the Vizier's* [the
" Nabob of Oude] *dominions*, obvious to every
" body; and so *fatal* have been its consequences,
" that no person, of either credit or character,
" would enter into engagements with government

" for

" for farming the country." He then proceeds to give ſtrong inſtances of the general calamity, and its effects.

It was now to be ſeen what ſteps the governor general and council took for the relief of this diſtreſſed country, long labouring under the vexations of men, and now ſtricken by the hand of God. The caſe of a general famine is known to relax the ſeverity even of the moſt rigorous government.—Mr. Haſtings does not deny, or ſhew the leaſt doubt of the fact. The repreſentation is humble, and almoſt abject. On this repreſentation from a great prince, of the diſtreſs of his ſubjects, Mr. Haſtings falls into a violent paſſion; ſuch as (it ſeems) would be unjuſtifiable in any one who ſpeaks of any part of *his* conduct. He declares " that the *demands*, the *tone* in which they were af-
" ſerted, and the *ſeaſon* in which they were made, are
" all equally alarming, and appear to him to require
" an adequate degree of firmneſs in this board, in
" *oppoſition* to them." He proceeds to deal out very unreſerved language, on the perſon and character of the Nabob and his miniſters. He declares, that in a diviſion between him and the Nabob, " *the ſtrongeſt muſt decide*." With regard to the urgent and inſtant neceſſity, from the failure of the crops, he ſays, " that *perhaps* ex-
" pedients *may be found* for affording a *gradual*
" relief from the burthen of which he ſo heavily
" complains, and it ſhall be my endeavour to
" ſeek them out:" and, leſt he ſhould be ſuſpected of too much haſte to alleviate ſufferings, and to remove violence, he ſays, " that theſe
" muſt be *gradually* applied, and their complete
" *effect* may be *diſtant*; and this I conceive *is all*
" he can claim of right."

This

This complete effect of his lenity is distant indeed. Rejecting this demand (as he calls the Nabob's abject supplication) he attributes it, as he usually does all things of the kind, to the division in their government; and says, " this is a " powerful motive with *me* (however inclined I " might be, *upon any other occasion*, to yield to some " *part* of his demand) to give them an *absolute* " *and unconditional refusal* upon the present; and " even *to bring to punishment, if my influence can* " *produce that effect, those incendiaries who have* " *endeavoured to make themselves the instruments* " *of division between us*."

Here, Sir, is much heat and passion; but no more consideration of the distress of the country, from a failure of the means of subsistence, and (if possible) the worse evil of an useless and licentious soldiery, than if they were the most contemptible of all trifles. A letter is written in consequence, in such a style of lofty despotism, as I believe has hitherto been unexampled and unheard of in the records of the East. The troops were continued. The *gradual* relief, whose effect was to be so *distant*, has *never* been substantially and beneficially applied—and the country is ruined.

Mr. Hastings, two years after, when it was too late, saw the absolute necessity of a removal of the intolerable grievance of this licentious soldiery, which, under a pretence of defending it, held the country under military execution. A new treaty and arrangement, according to the pleasure of Mr. Hastings, took place; and this new treaty was broken in the old manner, in every essential article. The soldiery were again sent, and again set loose. The effect of all his manœuvres, from which it seems he was sanguine enough

enough to entertain hopes, upon the state of the country, he himself informs us, " the event has proved the *reverse* of these hopes, and *accumulation of distress, debasement, and dissatisfaction* to the Nabob, and *disappointment and disgrace to me*.—Every measure [which he had himself proposed] has been *so conducted* as to give him cause of displeasure; there are no officers established by which his affairs could be regularly conducted; mean, incapable, and indigent men have been appointed. A number of the districts without authority, and without the means of personal protection; some of them have been murdered by the Zemindars, and those Zemindars, instead of punishment, have been permitted to retain their Zemindaries, with independent authority; *all* the other Zemindars suffered to rise up in rebellion, and to insult the authority of the Sircar, without any attempt made to suppress them; and the Company's debt, instead of being discharged by the assignments and extraordinary sources of money provided for that *purpose, is likely to exceed even the amount at which it stood at the time in which the arrangement with his Excellency was concluded.*" The House will smile at the resource on which the Directors take credit as such a certainty in their curious account.

This is Mr. Hastings's own narrative of the effects of his own settlement. This is the state of the country which we have been told is in perfect peace and order; and, what is curious, he informs us, that *every part of this was foretold to him in the order and manner in which it happened,* at the very time he made his arrangement of men and measures.

The invariable course of the Company's policy is this: Either they set up some prince too odious to maintain himself without the necessity of their assistance; or they soon render him odious, by making him the instrument of their government. In that case troops are bountifully sent to him to maintain his authority. That he should have no want of assistance, a civil gentleman, called a Resident, is kept at his court, who, under pretence of providing duly for the pay of these troops, gets assignments on the revenue into his hands. Under his provident management, debts soon accumulate; new assignments are made for these debts; until, step by step, the whole revenue, and with it the whole power of the country, is delivered into his hands. The military do not behold without a virtuous emulation the moderate gains of the civil department. They feel that, in a country driven to habitual rebellion by the civil government, the military is necessary; and they will not permit their services to go unrewarded. Tracts of country are delivered over to their discretion. Then it is found proper to convert their commanding officers into farmers of revenue. Thus, between the well paid civil, and well rewarded military establishment, the situation of the natives may be easily conjectured. The authority of the regular and lawful government is every where and in every point extinguished. Disorders and violences arise; they are repressed by other disorders and other violences. Wherever the collectors of the revenue, and the farming colonels and majors move, ruin is about them, rebellion before and behind them. The people in crowds fly out of the country; and the frontier is guarded by lines of troops, not to exclude an enemy, but to prevent the escape of the inhabitants.

By these means, in the course of not more than four or five years, this once opulent and flourishing country, which, by the accounts given in the Bengal consultations, yielded more than three crore of Sicca rupees, that is, above three millions sterling, annually, is reduced, as far as I can discover, in a matter purposely involved in the utmost perplexity, to less than one million three hundred thousand pounds, and that exacted by every mode of rigour that can be devised. To complete the business, most of the wretched remnants of this revenue are mortgaged, and delivered into the hands of the usurers at Benares (for there alone are to be found some lingering remains of the ancient wealth of these regions) at an interest of near *thirty per cent. per annum.*

The revenues in this manner failing, they seized upon the estates of every person of eminence in the country, and, under the name of *resumption,* confiscated their property. I wish, Sir, to be understood universally and literally, when I assert, that there is not left one man of property and substance for his rank, in the whole of these provinces, in provinces which are nearly the extent of England and Wales taken together. Not one landholder, not one banker, not one merchant, not one even of those who usually perish last, the *ultimum moriens* in a ruined state, no one farmer of revenue.

One country for a while remained, which stood as an island in the midst of the grand waste of the Company's dominion. My Right Honourable friend, in his admirable speech on moving the bill, just touched the situation, the offences, and the punishment, of a native prince, called

Fizulla

Fizulla Khân. This man, by policy and force, had protected himself from the general extirpation of the Rohilla chiefs. He was secured (if that were any security) by a treaty. It was stated to you, as it was stated by the enemies of that unfortunate man—" that the whole of his country " *is* what the whole country of the Rohillas *was*, " cultivated like a garden, without one neglected " spot in it."—Another accuser says, " Fyzoolah " Khan though a bad soldier [that is the true " source of his misfortune] has approved himself a " good aumil; having, it is supposed, in the course " of a few years, at least *doubled* the population, " and revenue of his country."—In another part of the correspondence he is charged with making his country an asylum for the oppressed peasants, who fly from the territories of Oude. The improvement of his revenue, arising from this single crime, (which Mr. Hastings considers as tantamount to treason) is stated at an hundred and fifty thousand pounds a year.

Dr. Swift somewhere says, that he who could make two blades of grass grow where but one grew before, was a greater benefactor to the human race than all the politicians that ever existed. This prince, who would have been deified by antiquity, who would have been ranked with Osiris, and Bacchus, and Ceres, and the divinities most propitious to men, was, for those very merits, by name attacked by the Company's government, as a cheat, a robber, a traitor. In the same breath in which he was accused as a rebel, he was ordered at once to furnish 5,000 horse. On delay, or (according to the technical phrase, when any remonstrance is made to them) " *on evasion*," he was declared a violator of treaties, and every thing he had was to be taken from him.

him.—Not one word, however, of horse in this treaty.

The territory of this Fizulla Khân, Mr. Speaker, is less than the county of Norfolk. It is an inland country, full seven hundred miles from any sea port, and not distinguished for any one considerable branch of manufacture whatsoever. From this territory a punctual payment was made to the British Resident of £. 150,000 sterling a year. The demand of cavalry, without a shadow or decent pretext of right, amounted to three hundred thousand a year more, at the lowest computation; and it is stated, by the last person sent to negotiate, as a demand of little use, if it could be complied with; but that the compliance was impossible, as it amounted to more than his territories could supply, if there had been no other demand upon him——four hundred and fifty thousand pounds a year from an inland country not so large as Norfolk!

The thing most extraordinary was to hear the culprit defend himself from the imputation of his virtues, as if they had been the blackest offences. He extenuated the superior cultivation of his country. He denied its population. He endeavoured to prove that he had often sent back the poor peasant that sought shelter with him.—I can make no observation on this.

After a variety of extortions and vexations, too fatiguing to you, too disgusting to me, to go through with, they found " that they ought to be " in a better state to warrant forcible means;" they therefore contented themselves with a gross sum of 150,000 pounds, for their present demand. They offered him indeed an indemnity from their
exactions

exactions in future, for three hundred thousand pounds more. But he refused to buy their securities; pleading (probably with truth) his poverty: but if the plea were not founded, in my opinion very wisely; not choosing to deal any more in that dangerous commodity of the Company's faith; and thinking it better to oppose distress and unarmed obstinacy to uncoloured exaction, than to subject himself to be considered as a cheat, if he should make a treaty in the least beneficial to himself. Thus they executed an exemplary punishment on Fizulla Khân for the culture of his country. But, conscious that the prevention of evils is the great object of all good regulation, they deprived him of the means of encreasing that criminal cultivation in future, by exhausting his coffers; and, that the population of his country should no more be a standing reproach and libel on the Company's government, they bound him, by a positive engagement, not to afford any shelter whatsoever to the farmers and labourers who should seek refuge in his territories, from the exactions of the British Residents in Oude. When they had done all this effectually, they gave him a full and complete acquittance from all charges of rebellion, or of any intention to rebel, or of his having originally had any interest in, or any means of rebellion.

These intended rebellions are one of the Company's standing resources. When money has been thought to be heaped up any where, its owners are universally accused of rebellion, until they are acquitted of their money and their treasons at once. The money once taken, all accusation, trial, and punishment ends. It is so settled a resource, that I rather wonder how it comes to be omitted in the Directors account;
but

but I take it for granted this omiſſion will be ſupplied in their next edition. The Company ſtretched this reſource to the full extent, when they accuſed two old women, in the remoteſt corner of India (who could have no poſſible view or motive to raiſe diſturbances) of being engaged in rebellion, with an intent to drive out the Engliſh nation in whoſe protection, purchaſed by money and ſecured by treaty, reſted the ſole hope of their exiſtence. But the Company wanted money, and the old women *muſt* be guilty of a plot. They were accuſed of rebellion, and they were convicted of wealth. Twice had great ſums been extorted from them, and as often had the Britiſh faith guaranteed the remainder. A body of Britiſh troops, with one of the military farmers general at their head, was ſent to ſeize upon the caſtle in which theſe helpleſs women reſided. Their chief eunuchs, who were their agents, their guardians, protectors, perſons of high rank according to the Eaſtern manners and of great truſt, were thrown into dungeons, to make them diſcover their hidden treaſures; and there they lie at preſent. The lands aſſigned for the maintenance of the women were ſeized and confiſcated. Their jewels and effects were taken, and ſet up to a pretended auction in an obſcure place, and bought at ſuch a price as the gentlemen thought proper to give. No account has ever been tranſmitted of the articles or produce of this ſale. What money was obtained is unknown, or what terms were ſtipulated for the maintenance of theſe deſpoiled and forlorn creatures; for by ſome particulars it appears as if an engagement of the kind was made.

Let me here remark, once for all, that though
tho

the act of 1773 requires that an account of all proceedings should be diligently transmitted, that this, like all the other injunctions of the law, is totally despised; and that half at least of the most important papers are intentionally withheld.

I wish you, Sir, to advert particularly, in this transaction, to the quality and the numbers of the persons spoiled, and the instrument by whom that spoil was made. These ancient matrons called the Begums or Princesses, were of the first birth and quality in India, the one mother, the other wife, of the late Nabob of Oude, Sujah Dowlah, a prince possessed of extensive and flourishing dominions, and the second man in the Mogul empire. This prince (suspicious, and not unjustly suspicious, of his son and successor) at his death committed his treasures and his family to the British faith. That family and houshold, consisted of *two thousand women*; to which were added two other seraglios of near kindred, and said to be extremely numerous, and (as I am well informed) of about fourscore of the Nabob's children, with all the eunuchs, the ancient servants, and a multitude of the dependants of his splendid court. These were all to be provided, for present maintenance and future establishment, from the lands assigned as dower, and from the treasures which he left to these matrons, in trust for the whole family.

So far as to the objects of the spoil. The *instrument* chosen by Mr. Hastings to despoil the relict of Sujah Dowlah was *her own son*, the reigning Nabob of Oude. It was the pious hand of a son that was selected to tear from his mother and grandmother the provision of their age, the maintenance of his brethren, and of
all

all the ancient houshold of his father. [Here a laugh from some young members]—The laugh is *seasonable*, and the occasion decent and proper.

By the last advices something of the sum extorted remained unpaid. The women in despair refuse to deliver more, unless their lands are restored and their ministers released from prison: but Mr. Hastings and his council, steady to their point, and consistent to the last in their conduct, write to the Resident to stimulate the son to accomplish the filial acts he had brought so near to their perfection.—" We " desire," say they in their letter to the Resident (written so late as March last) " that you will " inform us if any, and what means, have been " taken for recovering the balance due from " the Begum [Princess] at Fizabad; and that, " if necessary, you *recommend* it to the Vizier to " enforce *the most effectual means* for that pur-" pose."

What their effectual means of enforcing demands on women of high rank and condition are, I shall shew you, Sir, in a few minutes; when I represent to you another of these plots and rebellions, which *always*, in India, though so *rarely* any where else, are the offspring of an easy condition, and hoarded riches.

Benares is the capital city of the Indian religion. It is regarded as holy by a particular and distinguished sanctity; and the Gentûs in general think themselves as much obliged to visit it once in their lives as the Mahometans to perform their pilgrimage to Mecca. By this means that city grew great in commerce and opulence; and so effectually was it secured by the pious veneration

of

of that people, that in all wars and in all violences of power, there was so sure an asylum, both for poverty and wealth, (as it were under a divine protection) that the wisest laws and best assured free constitution could not better provide for the relief of the one, or the safety of the other; and this tranquillity influenced to the greatest degree the prosperity of all the country, and the territory of which it was the capital. The interest of money there was not more than half the usual rate in which it stood in all other places. The reports have fully informed you of the means and of the terms in which this city and the territory called Gazipour, of which it was the head, came under the sovereignty of the East India Company.

If ever there was a subordinate dominion pleasantly circumstanced to the superior power, it was this; a large rent or tribute, to the amount of two hundred and sixty thousand pounds a year, was paid in monthly instalments with the punctuality of a dividend at the Bank. If ever there was a prince who could not have an interest in disturbances, it was its sovereign, the Rajah Cheit Sing. He was in possession of the capital of his religion, and a willing revenue was paid by the devout people who resorted to him from all parts. His sovereignty and his independence, except his tribute, was secured by every tie. His territory was not much less than half of Ireland, and displayed in all parts a degree of cultivation, ease, and plenty, under his frugal and paternal management, which left him nothing to desire, either for honour or satisfaction.

This was the light in which this country appeared to almost every eye. But Mr. Hastings beheld it askance. Mr. Hastings tells us that it

was

was *reported* of this Cheit Sing, that his father left him a million sterling, and that he made annual accessions to the hoard. Nothing could be so obnoxious to indigent power. So much wealth could not be innocent. The House is fully acquainted with the unfounded and unjust requisitions which were made upon this prince. The question has been most ably and conclusively cleared up in one of the Reports of the Select Committee, and in an answer of the Court of Directors to an extraordinary publication against them by their servant, Mr. Hastings. But I mean to pass by these exactions, as if they were perfectly just and regular; and, having admitted them, I take what I shall now trouble you with, only as it serves to shew the spirit of the Company's government, the mode in which it is carried on, and the maxims on which it proceeds.

Mr. Hastings, from whom I take the doctrine, endeavours to prove that Cheit Sing was no sovereign prince; but a mere Zemindar or common subject, holding land by rent. If this be granted to him, it is next to be seen under what terms he is of opinion such a land-holder, that is a British subject, holds his life and property under the Company's government. It is proper to understand well the doctrines of the person whose administration has lately received such distinguished approbation from the Company. His doctrine is —" that the Company, or the *person delegated by it*,
" holds *an absolute* authority over such Zemindars ;
" —that he [such a subject] owes *an implicit* and
" *unreserved* obedience to its authority, at the
" *forfeiture* even of his *life* and *property*, at the
" DISCRETION of those who held *or fully represented*
" the sovereign authority ;—and that *these* rights
" are *fully* delegated *to him* Mr. Hastings."

Such

Such is a British governor's idea of the condition of a great Zemindar holding under a British authority; and this kind of authority he supposes fully delegated to *him*; though no such delegation appears in any commission, instruction, or act of parliament. At his *discretion* he may demand, of the substance of any Zemindar over and above his rent or tribute, even what he pleases, with a sovereign authority; and if he does not yield an *implicit unreserved* obedience to all his commands, he forfeits his lands, his life, and his property, at Mr. Hastings's *discretion*. But, extravagant and even frantic as these positions appear, they are less so than what I shall now read to you; for he asserts, that if any one should urge an exemption from more than a stated payment, or should consider the deeds, which passed between him and the board, " as bearing *the quality and force* of a treaty between equal states," he says, " that such an opinion is itself criminal to the state of which he is a subject; and that he was himself amenable to its justice, if he gave *countenance* to such a *belief*." Here is a new species of crime invented, that of countenancing a belief—but a belief of what? A belief of that which the Court of Directors, Hastings's masters, and a Committee of this House, have decided as this prince's indisputable right.

But supposing the Rajah of Benares to be a mere subject, and that subject a criminal of the highest form; let us see what course was taken by an upright English magistrate. Did he cite this culprit before his tribunal? Did he make a charge? Did he produce witnesses? These are not forms; they are parts of substantial and eternal justice. No, not a word of all this. Mr. Hastings concludes him, *in his own mind*, to be guilty;

guilty; he makes this conclusion on reports, on hear-says, on appearances, on rumours, on conjectures, on presumptions; and even these never once hinted to the party, nor publicly to any human being, till the whole business was done.

But the governor tells you his motive for this extraordinary proceeding, so contrary to every mode of justice towards either a prince or a subject, fairly and without disguise; and he puts into your hands the key of his whole conduct:—" I will
" suppose, for a moment, that I have acted with
" unwarrantable rigour towards Cheit Sing, and
" even with injustice.—Let my MOTIVE be con-
" sulted. I left Calcutta, impressed with a belief
" that *extraordinary means* were necessary, and
" those exerted with a *steady hand*, to preserve the
" Company's *interests from sinking under the ac-*
" *cumulated weight which oppressed them*. I saw a
" *political necessity* for curbing the *overgrown*
" power of a great member of their dominion,
" and for *making it contribute to the relief of their*
" *pressing exigencies*." This is plain speaking; after this, it is no wonder that the Rajah's wealth and his offence, the necessities of the judge, and the opulence of the delinquent, are never separated, through the whole of Mr. Hastings's apology. " The justice and *policy* of exacting *a large*
" *pecuniary mulct*." The resolution " *to draw from*
" *his guilt* the means *of relief to the Company's*
" *distresses.*" His determination " to make him *pay*
" *largely* for his pardon, or to execute a severe
" vengeance for past delinquency." That " as his
" *wealth was great*, and the *Company's exigencies*
" pressing, he thought it a measure of justice and
" policy to exact from him a large pecuniary mulct
" for *their relief.*"—" The sum (says Mr. Wheler, bearing evidence, at his desire, to his intentions)
" to

" to which the governor declared his resolution
" to extend his fine; was forty or fifty lacks, *that is
" four or five hundred thousand pounds*; and that if
" he refused, he was to be removed from his ze-
" mindary entirely; or by taking possession of his
" forts, to obtain, *out of the treasure deposited in
" them*, the above sum for the Company."

Crimes so convenient, crimes so politic, crimes so necessary, crimes so alleviating of distress, can never be wanting to those who use no process, and who produce no proofs.

But there is another serious part (what is not so?) in this affair. Let us suppose that the power, for which Mr. Hastings contends, a power which no sovereign ever did, or ever can vest in any of his subjects, namely, his own sovereign authority, to be conveyed by the act of parliament to any man or body of men whatsoever; it certainly was never given to Mr. Hastings. The powers given by the act of 1773 were formal and official; they were given, not to the governor general, but to the major vote of the board, as a board, on discussion amongst themselves, in their public character and capacity; and their acts in that character and capacity were to be ascertained by records and minutes of council. The despotic acts exercised by Mr. Hastings were done merely in his *private* character; and, if they had been moderate and just, would still be the acts of an usurped authority, and without any one of the legal modes of proceeding which could give him competence for the most trivial exertion of power. There was no proposition or deliberation whatsoever in council, no minute on record, by circulation or otherwise, to authorize his proceedings. No delegation of power to impose a fine, or to take any step to deprive the Rajah of Benares of his government, his property, or his liberty. The minutes of confultation affign to his journey a totally different object, duty, and deftination. Mr. Wheler, at his defire, tells us long after, that he had a confidential converfation with him on various fubjects, of which this was the principal, in which Mr. Haftings notified to him his fecret intentions; " and that he *befpoke* his fupport of the meafures " which he intended to purfue towards him (the " Rajah.)" This confidential difcourfe, and *befpeaking* of fupport, could give him no power, in oppofition to an exprefs act of parliament, and the whole tenor of the orders of the Court of Directors.

In what manner the powers thus ufurped were employed, is known to the whole world. All the Houfe knows, that the defign on the Rajah proved as unfruitful as it was violent. The unhappy prince was expelled, and his more unhappy country was enflaved and ruined; but not a rupee was acquired. Inftead of treafure to recruit the Company's finances, wafted by their wanton wars and corrupt jobbs, they were plunged into a new war, which fhook their power in India to its foundation; and, to ufe the governor's own happy fimile, might have diffolved it like a magic ftructure, if the talifman had been broken.

But the fuccefs is no part of my confideration, who fhould think juft the fame of this bufinefs, if the fpoil of one Rajah had been fully acquired, and faithfully applied to the deftruction of twenty other Rajahs. Not only the arreft of the Rajah in his palace was unneceffary and unwarrantable, and calculated to ftir up any manly blood which remained in his fubjects; but the defpotic ftyle,

and

and the extreme infolence of language and demeanour, ufed to a perfon of great condition among the politeft people in the world, was intolerable. Nothing aggravates tyranny fo much as contumely. *Quicquid fuperbia in contumeliis* was charged by a great man of antiquity, as a principal head of offence againft the governor general of that day. The unhappy people were ftill more infulted. A relation, but an *enemy* to the family, a notorious robber and villain, called Uffaun Sing, kept as a hawk in a mew, to fly upon this nation, was fet up to govern there, inftead of a prince honoured and beloved. But when the bufinefs of infult was accomplifhed, the revenue was too ferious a concern to be entrufted to fuch hands. Another was fet up in his place, as guardian to an infant.

But here, Sir, mark the effect of all thefe *extraordinary* means, of all this policy and juftice. The revenues which had been hitherto paid with fuch aftonifhing punctuality, fell into arrear. The new prince guardian was depofed without ceremony; and with as little, caft into prifon. The government of that once happy country has been in the utmoft confufion ever fince fuch good order was taken about it. But, to complete the contumely offered to this undone people, and to make them feel their fervitude in all its degradation, and all its bitternefs, the government of their facred city, the government of that Benares which had been fo refpected by Perfian and Tartar conquerors, though of the Muffulman perfuafion, that, even in the plenitude of their pride, power, and bigotry, no magiftrate of that fect entered the place, was now delivered over by English hands to a Mahometan; and an Ali Ibrahim Khân was introduced, under the Company's authority, with power of life and death, into the sanctuary of the Gentû religion.

After this, the taking off a flight payment, chearfully made by pilgrims to a chief of their own rites, was represented as a mighty benefit. It remains only to shew, through the conduct in this business, the spirit of the Company's government, and the respect they pay towards other prejudices not less regarded in the East than those of religion; I mean the reverence paid to the female sex in general, and particularly to women of high rank and condition. During the general confusion of the country of Gazypore, Panna, the mother of Cheit Sing, was lodged with her train in a castle called Bidgé Gur, in which were likewise deposited a large portion of the treasures of her son, or more probably her own. To whomsoever they belonged was indifferent; for, though no charge of rebellion was made on this woman (which was rather singular, as it would have cost nothing) they were resolved to secure her with her fortune. The castle was besieged by Major Popham.

There was no great reason to apprehend that soldiers ill paid, that soldiers who thought they had been defrauded of their plunder on former services of the same kind, would not have been sufficiently attentive to the spoil they were expressly come for; but the gallantry and generosity of the profession was justly suspected, as being likely to set bounds to military rapaciousness. The Company's first civil magistrate discovered the greatest uneasiness lest the women should have any thing preserved to them. Terms, tending

tending to put some restraint on military violence, were granted. He writes a letter to Mr. Popham, referring to some letter written before to the same effect, which I do not remember to have seen; but it shews his anxiety on this subject. Hear himself:—" I think *every* demand she
" has made on you, except that of safety and
" respect to her person, is unreasonable. If the
" reports brought to me are true, your rejecting
" her offers, or *any negotiation*, would soon ob-
" tain you the fort upon your own terms. I
" apprehend she will attempt to *defraud the*
" *captors of a considerable part of their booty,*
" *by being suffered to retire without examination.*
" But this is your concern, not mine. I should
" *be very sorry* that your officers and soldiers lost
" *any* part of the reward to which they are so well
" entitled; but you must be the best judge of
" the *promised* indulgence to the Ranny: what
" you have engaged for I will certainly ratify; but
" as to suffering the Ranny to hold the purgunna of
" Hurlich, or any other zemindary, without be-
" ing subject to the authority of the Zemindar, *or*
" *any lands whatsoever,* or indeed making *any*
" condition with her for a *provision,* I will *never*
" *consent.*"

Here your governor stimulates a rapacious and licentious soldiery to the personal search of women, lest these unhappy creatures should avail themselves of the protection of their sex to secure any supply for their necessities; and he positively orders that no stipulation should be made for any provision for them. The widow and mother of a prince, well informed of her miserable situation, and the cause of it, a woman of this rank became

a suppliant

a suppliant to the domestic servant of Mr. Hastings (they are his own words that I read); "imploring his intercession, that she may be relieved *from the hardships and dangers of her present situation*; and offering to surrender the fort, and the *treasure and valuable effects contained* in it, provided she can be assured *of safety and protection to her person and honour*, and to that of her family and attendants." He is so good as to consent to this, "provided she surrenders every thing of value, with the reserve *only* of such articles as *you* shall think *necessary* to her condition, or as you *yourself* shall be disposed to indulge her with.—But should she refuse to execute the promise she has made, or delay it beyond the term of twenty-four hours, it is *my positive* injunction, that you immediately put a stop to any further intercourse or negociation with her, and on no pretext renew it. If she disappoints or *trifles* with me, after I have subjected *my Duan* to the disgrace of returning ineffectually, and of course myself to discredit, I shall consider it as a *wanton* affront and indignity *which I can never forgive*; nor will I grant her *any* conditions whatever, but leave her exposed *to those* dangers which she has chosen to risque, rather than trust to the clemency and generosity of our government. I think she cannot be ignorant of these consequences, and will not venture to incur them; and it is for this reason I place a dependance on her offers, and have consented to send my Duan to her." The dreadful secret hinted at by the merciful governor in the latter part of the letter, is well understood in India; where those who
suffer

suffer corporeal indignities, generally expiate the offences of others with their own blood. However, in spite of all these, the temper of the military did, some way or other, operate. They came to terms which have never been transmitted. It appears that a fifteenth *per cent.* of the plunder was reserved to the captives, of which the unhappy mother of the prince of Benares was to have a share. This antient matron, born to better things [a laugh from certain young gentlemen]—I see no cause for this mirth. A good author of antiquity reckons among the calamities of his time, *Nobilissimarum fœminarum exilia et fugas.* I say, Sir, this antient lady was compelled to quit her house with three hundred helpless women, and a multitude of children in her train; but the lower sort in the camp it seems could not be restrained. They did not forget the good lessons of the governor general. They were unwilling " to be defrauded of a con-
" siderable part of their booty, by suffering them
" to pass without examination."—They examined them, Sir, with a vengeance, and the sacred protection of that awful character, Mr. Hastings's maitre d'hotel, could not secure them from insult and plunder. Here is Popham's narrative of the affair:—" The Ranny came out of the fort,
" with her family and dependants, the 10th at
" night, owing to which such attention was not
" paid to her as I wished; and I am exceedingly
" sorry to inform you, that the *licentiousness of*
" *our followers was beyond the bounds of con-*
" *troul; for, notwithstanding all I could do, her*
" *people were plundered on the road of most of*
" *the things which they brought out of the fort,*
" *by which means one of the articles of surrender*
" has

" *has been much infringed.* The diſtreſs I have
" felt upon this occaſion cannot be expreſſed, and
" can only be allayed by a firm performance of
" the other articles of the treaty, which I ſhall
" make it my buſineſs to enforce.

" The ſuſpicions which the officers had of trea-
" chery, and the delay made to our getting poſ-
" ſeſſion, had enraged them, as well as the troops,
" ſo much, that the treaty was at firſt regarded
" as void, but this determination was ſoon ſuc-
" ceeded by pity and compaſſion for the unfor-
" tunate beſieged."—After this comes, in his due
order, Mr. Haſtings; who is full of ſorrow and
indignation, &c. &c. &c. according to the beſt
and moſt authentic precedents eſtabliſhed upon
ſuch occaſions.

The women being thus diſpoſed of, that is, completely deſpoiled, and pathetically lamented, Mr. Haſtings at length recollected the great object of his enterprize, which, during his zeal left the officers and ſoldiers ſhould loſe any part of their reward, he ſeems to have forgot; that is to ſay, " to draw from the Rajah's guilt the means
" of relief to the Company's diſtreſſes." This was to be the ſtrong hold of his defence. This compaſſion to the Company, he knew by experience would ſanctify a great deal of rigour towards the natives. But the military had diſtreſſes of their own, which they conſidered firſt. Neither Mr. Haſtings's authority, nor his ſupplications, could prevail on them to aſſign a ſhilling to the claim he made on the part of the Company. They divided the booty amongſt themſelves. Driven from his claim he was reduced to petition for the ſpoil as a loan. But the ſoldiers were too

wife to venture as a loan, what the borrower claimed as a right. In defiance of all authority, they shared amongst themselves about two hundred thousand pounds sterling, besides what had been taken from the women.

In all this there is nothing wonderful. We may rest assured, that when the maxims of any government establish among its resources extraordinary means, and those exerted with a strong hand, that strong hand will provide those extraordinary means for *itself*. Whether the soldiers had reason or not (perhaps much might be said for them) certain it is, the military discipline of India was ruined from that moment; and the same rage for plunder, the same contempt of subordination, which blasted all the hopes of extraordinary means from your strong hand at Benares, have very lately lost you an army in Mysore. This is visible enough from the accounts in the last Gazette.

There is no doubt but that the country and city of Benares, now brought into the same order, will very soon exhibit, if it does not already display the same appearance with those countries and cities which are under better subjection. A great master, Mr. Hastings, has himself been at the pains of drawing a picture of one of these countries, I mean the province and city of Farruckabad. There is no reason to question his knowledge of the facts; and his authority (on this point at least) is above all exception, as well for the state of the country, as for the cause. In his minute of consultation, Mr. Hastings describes forcibly the consequences which arise from the degradation into which we have sunk the native government. " The total want (says he) of all
" order,

"order, regularity, or authority, in his (the Nabob
"of Farruckabad's) government, and to which,
"among other obvious causes, it may no doubt
"be owing that the country of Farruckabad is
"become *almost an entire waste, without culti-
"vation or inhabitants*; that the capital, which,
"but a very short time ago, was distinguished as
"one of the most populous and opulent com-
"mercial cities in Hindostan, at present exhibits
"nothing but *scenes of the most wretched poverty,
"desolation, and misery*; and that the *Nabob
"himself*, tho' in the possession of a tract of country
"which, with only common care, is notoriously
"capable of yielding an annual revenue of be-
"tween thirty and forty lacks, (three or four
"hundred thousand pounds) with *no military
"establishment* to maintain, scarcely commands
"*the means of a bare subsistance.*"

This is a true and unexaggerated picture, not only of Farruckabad, but of at least three-fourths of the country which we possess, or rather lay waste, in India. Now, Sir, the House will be desirous to know, for what purpose this picture was drawn. It was for a purpose, I will not say laudable, but necessary, that of taking the unfortunate Prince and his country out of the hands of a sequestrator sent thither by the Nabob of Oude, the mortal enemy of the Prince thus ruined, and to protect him by means of a British Resident, who might carry his complaints to the superior Resident at Oude, or transmit them to Calcutta. But mark, how the reformer persisted in his reformation. The effect of the measure was better than was probably expected. The Prince began to be at ease; the country began to recover; and the revenue began to be
collected

collected. These were alarming circumstances. Mr. Hastings not only recalled the Resident, but he entered into a formal stipulation with the Nabob of Oude, never to send an English subject again to Farruckabad; and thus the country, described as you have heard by Mr. Hastings, is given up for ever to the very persons to whom he had attributed its ruin, that is to the Sezawals or sequestrators of the Nabob of Oude.

Such was the issue of the first attempt to relieve the distresses of the dependent provinces. I shall close what I have to say on the condition of the northern dependencies, with the effect of the last of these attempts. You will recollect, Sir, the account I have not long ago stated to you as given by Mr. Hastings, of the ruined condition of the destroyer of others, the Nabob of Oude, and of the recal, in consequence, of Hannay, Middleton, and Johnson. When the first little sudden gust of passion against these gentlemen was spent, the sentiments of old friendship began to revive. Some healing conferences were held between them and the superior government. Mr. Hannay was permitted to return to Oude; but death prevented the further advantages intended for him, and the future benefits proposed for the country by the provident care of the council general.

These three gentlemen were accused of the grossest peculations. The Court of Directors were informed, by the governor general and council, that a severe enquiry would be instituted against the two survivors; and they requested that court to suspend its judgment, and to wait the event of their proceedings. But no enquiry has been instituted, nor any steps taken towards it. By means of the bland and conciliatory dispositions of the charter governors,

governors, and proper private explanations, the public enquiry has died away, the fuppofed peculators and deftroyers of Oude repofe in all fecurity in the bofoms of their accufers; whilft others fucceed to them to be inftructed by their example.

It is only to complete the view I propofed of the conduct of the Company, with regard to the dependent provinces, that I fhall fay *any* thing at all of the Carnatic, which is the fcene, if poffible, of greater diforder than the northern provinces. Perhaps it were better to fay of this center and metropolis of abufe, whence all the reft in India and in England diverge; from whence they are fed and methodized, what was faid of Carthage—*de Carthagine fatius eft filere quam parum dicere.* This country, in all its denominations, is about 46,000 fquare miles. It may be affirmed univerfally, that not one perfon of fubftance or property, landed, commercial, or monied, excepting two or three bankers, who are neceffary depofits and diftributors of the general fpoil, is left in all that region. In that country the moifture, the bounty of Heaven, is given but at a certain feafon. Before the æra of our influence, the induftry of man carefully hufbanded that gift of God. The Gentûs preferved, with a provident and religious care, the precious depofit of the periodical rain in refervoirs, many of them works of royal grandeur; and from thefe, as occafion demanded, they fructified the whole country. To maintain thefe refervoirs, and to keep up an annual advance to the cultivators, for feed and cattle, formed a principal object of the piety and policy of the priefts and rulers of the Gentû religion.

This object required a command of money; and there was no Pollam, or castle, which in the happy days of the Carnatic was without some hoard of treasure, by which the governors were enabled to combat with the irregularity of the seasons, and to resist or to buy off the invasion of an enemy. In all the cities were multitudes of merchants and bankers, for all occasions of monied assistance; and on the other hand, the native princes were in condition to obtain credit from them. The manufacturer was paid by the return of commodities, or by imported money, and not, as at present, in the taxes that had been originally exacted from his industry. In aid of casual distress, the country was full of choultries, which were inns and hospitals, where the traveller and the poor were relieved. All ranks of people had their place in the public concern, and their share in the common stock and common prosperity; but *the chartered rights of men*, and the right which it was thought proper to set up in the Nabob of Arcot, introduced a new system. It was their policy to consider hoards of money as crimes; to regard moderate rents as frauds on the sovereign; and to view, in the lesser princes, any claim of exemption from more than settled tribute, as an act of rebellion. Accordingly all the castles were, one after the other, plundered and destroyed. The native princes were expelled; the hospitals fell to ruin; the reservoirs of water went to decay; the merchants, bankers, and manufacturers disappeared; and sterility, indigence, and depopulation, overspread the face of these once flourishing provinces.

The Company was very early sensible of these mischiefs, and of their true cause. They gave precise orders,

orders, " that the native princes, called Polygars, " fhould *not be extirpated.*—That the rebellion [fo " they choofe to call it] of the Polygars, may (they " fear) *with too much juftice*, be attributed to the " mal-adminiftration of the Nabob's collectors." That " they obferve with concern, that their " troops have been put to *difagreeable fervices*." They might have ufed a ftronger expreffion without impropriety. But they make amends in another place. Speaking of the Polygars, the Directors fay, that " it was repugnant to humanity " to *force* them to fuch dreadful extremities *as* " *they underwent.*" That fome examples of feverity *might* be neceffary, " when they fell into " the Nabob's hands," *and not by the deftruction of the country.* " That *they fear* his government " is *none of the mildeft*; and that there is *great* " *oppreffion* in collecting his revenues." They ftate, that the wars in which he has involved the Carnatic, had been a caufe of its diftreffes. " That thefe diftreffes have been certainly great; " but thofe by *the Nabob's oppreffions* we believe " *to be greater than all.*" Pray, Sir, attend to the reafon for their opinion that the government of this their inftrument is more calamitous to the country than the ravages of war. —Becaufe, fay they, his oppreffions are " *without intermiffion.*—The others are temporary; " by all which *oppreffions* we believe the Nabob " has great wealth in ftore." From this ftore neither he nor they could derive any advantage whatfoever, upon the invafion of Hyder Ali in the hour of their greateft calamity and difmay.

It is now proper to compare thefe declarations with the Company's conduct. The principal reafon which they affigned againft the *extirpation*
of

of the Polygars was, that the *weavers* were protected in their fortresses. They might have added, that the Company itself, which stung them to death, had been warmed in the bosom of these unfortunate princes: for, on the taking of Madras by the French, it was in their hospitable Pollams, that most of the inhabitants found refuge and protection. But, notwithstanding all these orders, reasons, and declarations, they at length gave an indirect sanction, and permitted the use of a very direct and irresistible force, to measures which they had, over and over again, declared to be false policy, cruel, inhuman, and oppressive. Having, however, forgot all attention to the princes and the people, they remembered that they had some sort of interest in the trade of the country; and it is matter of curiosity to observe the protection which they afforded to this their natural object.

Full of anxious cares on this head, they direct, "that in reducing the Polygars they (their ser-"vants) were to be *cautious*, not to deprive the "*weavers and manufacturers* of the protection "they often met with in the strong holds of the "Polygar countries;"—and they write to their instrument, the Nabob of Arcot, concerning these poor people in a most pathetic strain. "We en-"*treat* your Excellency (say they) in particular, "to make the manufacturers the object of your "*tenderest care*; particularly when you *root out* "the Polygars, you do not deprive the *weavers* "*of the protection they enjoyed under them*." When they root out the protectors in favour of the oppressor, they shew themselves religiously cautious of the rights of the protected. When they extirpate the shepherd and the shepherd's dogs, they piously recommend the helpless flock to the mercy,

mercy, and even to the *tenderest care*, of the wolf. This is the uniform strain of their policy, strictly forbidding, and at the same time strenuously encouraging and enforcing, every measure that can ruin and desolate the country committed to their charge. After giving the Company's idea of the government of this their instrument, it may appear singular, but it is perfectly consistent with their system, that, besides wasting for him, at two different times, the most exquisite spot upon the earth, Tanjour, and all the adjacent countries, they have even voluntarily put their own territory, that is, a large and fine country adjacent to Madras, called their Jaghire, wholly out of their protection; and have continued to farm their subjects, and their duties towards these subjects, to that very Nabob, whom they themselves constantly represent as an habitual oppressor, and a relentless tyrant. This they have done without any pretence of ignorance of the objects of oppression for which this prince has thought fit to become their renter; for he has again and again told them, that it is for the sole purpose of exercising authority he holds the Jaghire lands; and he affirms (and I believe with truth) that he pays more for that territory than the revenues yield. This deficiency he must make up from his other territories; and thus, in order to furnish the means of oppressing one part of the Carnatic, he is led to oppress all the rest.

 The House perceives that the livery of the Company's government is uniform. I have described the condition of the countries indirectly, but most substantially, under the Company's authority. And now I ask, whether, with this map of misgovernment before me, I can suppose myself bound by my vote

vote to continue, upon any principles of pretended public faith, the management of thefe countries in thofe hands. If I kept fuch a faith (which in reality is no better than a *fides latronum*) with what is called the Company, I muft break the faith, the covenant, the folemn, original, indifpenfable oath, in which I am bound, by the eternal frame and conftitution of things, to the whole human race.

As I have dwelt fo long on thefe who are indirectly under the Company's adminiftration, I will endeavour to be a little fhorter upon the countries immediately under this charter government.—Thefe are the Bengal provinces. The condition of thefe provinces is pretty fully detailed in the Sixth and Ninth Reports, and in their Appendixes. I will felect only fuch principles and inftances as are broad and general. To your own thoughts I fhall leave it, to furnifh the detail of oppreffions involved in them. I fhall ftate to you, as fhortly as I am able, the conduct of the Company;—1ft, towards the landed interefts;— next, the commercial interefts;—3dly, the native government;—and laftly, to their own government.

Bengal, and the provinces that are united to it, are larger than the kingdom of France; and once contained, as France does contain, a great and independent landed intereft, compofed of princes, of great lords, of a numerous nobility and gentry, of freeholders, of lower tenants, of religious communities, and public foundations. So early as 1769, the Company's fervants perceived the decay into which thefe provinces had fallen under Englifh adminiftration, and they made a ftrong reprefentation upon this decay, and what they apprehended

apprehended to be the causes of it. Soon after Mr. Hastings became president of Bengal. Instead of administering a remedy, upon the heels of a dreadful famine, in the year 1772, the succour which the new president and the council lent to this afflicted nation was—shall I be believed in relating it?—the landed interest of a whole kingdom, of a kingdom to be compared to France, was set up to public auction! They set up (Mr. Hastings set up) the whole nobility, gentry, and freeholders, to the highest bidder. No preference was given to the ancient proprietors. They must bid against every usurer, every temporary adventurer, every jobber and schemer, every servant of every European, or they were obliged to content themselves, in lieu of their extensive domains, with their house, and such a pension as the state auctioneers thought fit to assign. In this general calamity, several of the first nobility thought (and in all appearance justly) that they had better submit to the necessity of this pension, than continue, under the name of Zemindars, the objects and instruments of a system, by which they ruined their tenants, and were ruined themselves. Another reform has since come upon the back of the first; and a pension having been assigned to these unhappy persons, in lieu of their hereditary lands, a new scheme of œconomy has taken place, and deprived them of that pension.

 The menial servants of Englishmen, persons (to use the emphatical phrase of a ruined and patient Eastern chief) " *whose fathers they would not have* " *set with the dogs of their flock,*" entered into their patrimonial lands. Mr. Hastings's banian was, after this auction, found possessed of territories yielding a rent of one hundred and forty thousand pounds a year.

Such an univerſal proſcription, upon any pretence, has few examples. Such a proſcription, without even a pretence of delinquency, has none. It ſtands by itſelf. It ſtands as a monument to aſtoniſh the imagination, to confound the reaſon of mankind. I confeſs to you, when I firſt came to know this buſineſs in its true nature and extent, my ſurpriſe did a little ſuſpend my indignation. I was in a manner ſtupified by the deſperate boldneſs of a few obſcure young men, who having obtained, by ways which they could not comprehend, a power of which they ſaw neither the purpoſes nor the limits, toſſed about, ſubverted, and tore to pieces, as if it were in the gambols of a boyiſh unluckineſs and malice, the moſt eſtabliſhed rights, and the moſt ancient and moſt revered inſtitutions, of ages and nations. Sir, I will not now trouble you with any detail with regard to what they have ſince done with theſe ſame lands and land-holders; only to inform you, that nothing has been ſuffered to ſettle for two ſeaſons together upon any baſis; and that the levity and inconſtancy of theſe mock legiſlators were not the leaſt afflicting parts of the oppreſſions ſuffered under their uſurpation; nor will any thing give ſtability to the property of the natives, but an adminiſtration in England at once protecting and ſtable. The country ſuſtains, almoſt every year, the miſeries of a revolution. At preſent, all is uncertainty, miſery, and confuſion. There is to be found through theſe vaſt regions no longer one landed man, who is a reſource for voluntary aid, or an object for particular rapine. Some of them were, not long ſince, great princes; they poſſeſſed treaſures, they levied armies. There was a Zemindar in Bengal (I forget his name) that, on the threat of an invaſion, ſupplied the Soubah of theſe provinces with the loan of a

million

million sterling. The family this day wants credit for a breakfast at the bazar.

I shall now say a word or two on the Company's care of the commercial interest of those kingdoms. As it appears in the Reports, that persons in the highest stations in Bengal have adopted, as a fixed plan of policy, the destruction of all intermediate dealers between the Company and the manufacturer, native merchants have disappeared of course. The spoil of the revenues is the sole capital which purchases the produce and manufactures; and through three or four foreign companies transmits the official gains of individuals to Europe. No other commerce has an existence in Bengal. The transport of its plunder is the only traffic of the country. I wish to refer you to the Appendix to the Ninth Report for a full account of the manner in which the Company have protected the commercial interests of their dominions in the East.

As to the native government and the administration of justice, it subsisted in a poor tottering manner for some years. In the year 1781, a total revolution took place in that establishment. In one of the usual freaks of legislation of the council of Bengal, the whole criminal jurisdiction of these courts, called the Phoujdary Judicature, exercised till then by the principal Mussulmen, was in one day, without notice, without consultation with the magistrates or the people there, and without communication with the directors or ministers here, totally subverted. A new institution took place, by which this jurisdiction was divided between certain English servants of the Company and the Gentû Zemindars of the country, the latter of whom never petitioned for it, nor, for ought that appears, ever desired this boon. But its natural use was

made

made of it; it was made a pretence for new extortions of money.

The natives had however one confolation in the ruin of their judicature; they foon faw that it fared no better with the Englifh government itfelf. That too, after deftroying every other, came to its period. This revolution may well be rated for a moft daring act, even among the extraordinary things that have been doing in Bengal fince our unhappy acquifition of the means of fo much mifchief.

An eftablifhment of Englifh government for civil juftice, and for the collection of revenue, was planned and executed by the prefident and council of Bengal, fubject to the pleafure of the Directors, in the year 1772. According to this plan, the country was divided into fix great diftricts, or provinces. In each of thefe was eftablifhed a provincial council, which adminiftered the revenue; and of that council one member, by monthly rotation, prefided in the courts of civil refort; with an appeal to the council of the province, and thence to Calcutta. In this fyftem (whether, in other refpects, good or evil) there were fome capital advantages. There was in the very number of perfons in each provincial council, authority, communication, mutual check, and controul. They were obliged, on their minutes of confultation, to enter their reafons and diffents; fo that a man of diligence, of refearch, and tolerable fagacity, fitting in London, might, from thefe materials, be enabled to form fome judgment of the fpirit of what was going on on the furtheft banks of the Ganges and Burrampûter.

The Court of Directors fo far ratified this eftablifhment, (which was confonant enough to their general plan of government) that they gave

precife

precise orders, that no alteration should be made in it, without their consent. So far from being apprised of any design against this constitution, they had reason to conceive that on trial it had been more and more approved by their council general, at least by the governor general, who had planned it. At the time of the revolution, the council general was nominally in two persons, virtually in one. At that time measures of an arduous and critical nature ought to have been forborne, even if, to the fullest council, this specific measure had not been prohibited by the superior authority. It was in this very situation, that one man had the hardiness to conceive, and the temerity to execute, a total revolution in the form and the persons composing the government of a great kingdom. Without any previous step, at one stroke, the whole constitution of Bengal, civil and criminal, was swept away. The counsellors were recalled from their provinces. Upwards of fifty of the principal officers of government were turned out of employ, and rendered dependent on Mr. Hastings for their immediate subsistence, and for all hope of future provision. The chief of each council, and one European collector of revenue, was left in each province.

But here, Sir, you may imagine a new government, of some permanent description, was established in the place of that which had been thus suddenly overturned. No such thing. Lest these chiefs without councils should be conceived to form the ground plan of some future government, it was publicly declared, that their continuance was only temporary and permissive. The whole subordinate British administration of revenue was then vested in a committee in Calcutta, all
creatures

creatures of the governor general; and the provincial management, under the permiffive chief, was delivered over to native officers.

But, that the revolution, and the purpofes of the revolution, might be complete, to this committee were delegated, not only the functions of all the inferior, but, what will furprize the Houfe, thofe of the fupreme adminiftration of revenue alfo. Hitherto the governor general and council had, in their revenue department, adminiftered the finances of thofe kingdoms. By the new fcheme they are delegated to this committee, who are only to report their proceedings for approbation.

The key to the whole tranfaction is given in one of the inftructions to the committee, "that it is not neceffary that they fhould enter diffents." By this means the ancient plan of the Company's adminiftration was deftroyed; but the plan of concealment was perfected. To that moment the accounts of the revenues were tolerably clear; or at leaft means were furnifhed for enquiries, by which they might be rendered fatisfactory. In the obfcure and filent gulph of this committee every thing is now buried. The thickeft fhades of night furround all their tranfactions. No effectual means of detecting fraud, mifmanagement, or mifreprefentation, exift. The Directors, who have dared to talk with fuch confidence on their revenues, know nothing about them. What ufed to fill volumes is now comprifed under a few dry heads on a fheet of paper. The natives, a people habitually made to concealment, are the chief managers of the revenue thoughout the provinces. I mean by natives, fuch wretches as your rulers felect out of them as moft fitted for their purpofes. As a

proper

proper key-ſtone to bind the arch, a native, one Gunga Govind Sing, a man turned out of his employment by Sir John Clavering, for malverſation in office, is made the correſponding ſecretary; and indeed the great moving principle of their new board.

As the whole revenue and civil adminiſtration was thus ſubverted, and a clandeſtine government ſubſtituted in the place of it, the judicial inſtitution underwent a like revolution. In 1772 there had been ſix courts formed out of the ſix provincial councils. Eighteen new ones are appointed in their place, with each a judge, taken from the *junior* ſervants of the Company. To maintain theſe eighteen courts, a tax is levied on the ſums in litigation, of $2\frac{1}{2}$ *per cent.* on the great, and of 5 *per cent.* on the leſs. This money is all drawn from the provinces to Calcutta. The chief juſtice (the ſame who ſtays in defiance of a vote of this Houſe, and of His Majeſty's recal) is appointed at once the treaſurer and diſpoſer of theſe taxes, levied, without any ſort of authority, from the Company, from the Crown, or from Parliament.

In effect, Sir, every legal regular authority in matters of revenue, of political adminiſtration, of criminal law, of civil law, in many of the moſt eſſential parts of military diſcipline, is laid level with the ground; and an oppreſſive, irregular, capricious, unſteady, rapacious, and peculating deſpotiſm, with a direct diſavowal of obedience to any authority at home, and without any fixed maxim, principle, or rule of proceeding, to guide them in India, is at preſent the ſtate of your charter-government over great kingdoms.

As the Company has made this uſe of their truſt, I ſhould ill diſcharge mine, if I refuſed to

give

give my moſt chearful vote for the redreſs of theſe abuſes, by putting the affairs of ſo large and valuable a part of the intereſts of this nation and of mankind, into ſome ſteady hands, poſſeſſing the confidence, and aſſured of the ſupport of this Houſe, until they can be reſtored to regularity, order, and confiſtency.

I have touched the heads of ſome of the grievances of the people, and the abuſes of government. But I hope and truſt, you will give me credit, when I faithfully aſſure you, that I have not mentioned one fourth part of what has come to my knowledge in your committee; and further, I have full reaſon to believe, that not one fourth part of the abuſes are come to my knowledge, by that or by any other means. Pray conſider what I have ſaid only as an index to direct you in your enquiries.

If this then, Sir, has been the uſe made of the truſt of political powers internal and external, given by you in the charter, the next thing to be ſeen is the conduct of the Company with regard to the commercial truſt. And here I will make a fair offer:—If it can be proved that they have acted wiſely, prudently, and frugally, as merchants, I ſhall paſs by the whole maſs of their enormities as ſtateſmen. That they have not done this their preſent condition is proof ſufficient. Their diſtreſſes are ſaid to be owing to their wars. This is not wholly true. But if it were, is not that readineſs to engage in wars which diſtinguiſhes them, and for which the Committee of Secrecy has ſo branded their politics, founded on the falſeſt principles of mercantile ſpeculation?

The principle of buying cheap and ſelling dear is the firſt, the great foundation of mercantile
dealing.

dealing. Have they ever attended to this principle? Nay, for years have they not actually authorized in their servants a total indifference as to the prices they were to pay?

A great deal of strictness in driving bargains for whatever we contract, is another of the principles of mercantile policy. Try the Company by that test! Look at the contracts that are made for them. Is the Company so much as a good commissary to their own armies? I engage to select for you, out of the innumerable mass of their dealings, all conducted very nearly alike, one contract only, the excessive profits on which during a short term would pay the whole of their year's dividend. I shall undertake to shew, that upon two others, that the inordinate profits given, with the losses incurred in order to secure those profits, would pay a year's dividend more.

It is a third property of trading men, to see that their clerks do not divert the dealings of the master to their own benefit. It was the other day only, when their governor and council taxed the Company's investment with a sum of fifty thousand pounds, as an inducement to persuade only seven members of their board of trade to give their *honour* that they would abstain from such profits upon that investment as they must have violated their *oaths* if they had made at all.

It is a fourth quality of a merchant to be exact in his accounts. What will be thought, when you have fully before you the mode of accounting made use of in the treasury of Bengal?—I hope you will have it soon. With regard to one of their agencies, when it came to the material part, the prime cost of the goods

goods on which a commiſſion of fifteen *per cent.* was allowed, to the aſtoniſhment of the factory to whom the commodities were ſent, the accountant general reports that he did not think himſelf authorized to call for *vouchers* relative to this and other particulars,—becauſe the agent was upon his *honour* with regard to them. A new principle of account upon honour ſeems to be regularly eſtabliſhed in their dealings and their treaſury, which in reality amounts to an entire annihilation of the principle of all accounts.

It is a fifth property of a merchant, who does not meditate a fraudulent bankruptcy, to calculate his probable profits upon the money he takes up to veſt in buſineſs. Did the Company, when they bought goods on bonds bearing 8 *per cent.* intereſt, at ten and even twenty *per cent.* diſcount, even aſk themſelves a queſtion concerning the poſſibility of advantage from dealing on theſe terms?

The laſt quality of a merchant I ſhall advert to, is the taking care to be properly prepared, in caſh or goods, in the ordinary courſe of ſale, for the bills which are drawn on them. Now I aſk, whether they have ever calculated the clear produce of any given ſales, to make them tally with the four million of bills which are come and coming upon them, ſo as at the proper periods to enable the one to liquidate the other? No, they have not. They are now obliged to borrow money of their own ſervants to purchaſe their inveſtment. The ſervants ſtipulate five *per cent.* on the capital they advance, if their bills ſhould not be paid at the time when they become due; and the value of the rupee on which they charge this intereſt is taken at two ſhillings and a penny. Has the Company ever troubled themſelves to enquire whether their ſales can bear the

payment

payment of that interest, and at that rate of exchange? Have they once considered the dilemma in which they are placed—the ruin of their credit in the East Indies, if they refuse the bills—the ruin of their credit and existence in England, if they accept them? Indeed no trace of equitable government is found in their politics; not one trace of commercial principle in their mercantile dealing; and hence is the deepest and maturest wisdom of Parliament demanded, and the best resources of this kingdom must be strained, to restore them; that is, to restore the countries destroyed by the misconduct of the Company, and to restore the Company itself, ruined by the consequences of their plans for destroying what they were bound to preserve.

I required, if you remember, at my outset a proof that these abuses were habitual. But surely this it is not necessary for me to consider as a separate head; because I trust I have made it evident beyond a doubt, in considering the abuses themselves, that they are regular, permanent, and systematical.

I am now come to my last condition, without which, for one, I will never readily lend my hand to the destruction of any established government; which is, That in its present state, the government of the East India Company is absolutely incorrigible.

Of this great truth I think there can be little doubt, after all that has appeared in this House. It is so very clear, that I must consider the leaving any power in their hands, and the determined resolution to continue and countenance every mode and every degree of peculation, oppression, and tyranny, to be one and the same thing. I look upon that body incorrigible, from the fullest consideration both of their uniform conduct,

conduct, and their prefent real and virtual conftitution.

If they had not conftantly been apprized of
all the enormities committed in India under their
authority; if this ftate of things had been as
much a difcovery to them as it was to many
of us; we might flatter ourfelves that the detection of the abufes would lead to their reformation. I will go further: If the Court of Directors had not uniformly condemned every act
which this Houfe or any of its Committees had
condemned; if the language in which they ex-
preffed their difapprobation againft enormities and
their authors had not been much more vehement
and indignant than any ever ufed in this Houfe,
I fhould entertain fome hopes. If they had not,
on the other hand, as uniformly commended all
their fervants who had done their duty and obeyed
their orders, as they had heavily cenfured thofe
who rebelled; I might fay, Thefe people have been
in an error, and when they are fenfible of it they
will mend. But when I reflect on the uniformity
of their fupport to the objects of their uniform
cenfure; and the ftate of infignificance and difgrace to which all of thofe have been reduced
whom they approved; and that even utter ruin
and premature death have been among the fruits
of their favour; I muft be convinced, that in this
cafe, as in all others, hypocrify is the only vice
that never can be cured.

Attend, I pray you, to the fituation and profperity of Benfield, Haftings, and others of that
fort. The laft of thefe has been treated by the
company with an afperity of reprehenfion that has
no parallel. They lament, "that the power of dif-
"pofing of their property for perpetuity, fhould
"fall into fuch hands." Yet for fourteen years,
with

with little interruption, he has governed all their affairs, of every description, with an absolute sway. He has had himself the means of heaping up immense wealth; and, during that whole period, the fortunes of hundreds have depended on his smiles and frowns. He himself tells you he is incumbered with two hundred and fifty young gentlemen, some of them of the best families in England, all of whom aim at returning with vast fortunes to Europe in the prime of life. He has then two hundred and fifty of your children as his hostages for your good behaviour; and loaded for years, as he has been, with the execrations of the natives, with the censures of the Court of Directors, and struck and blasted with resolutions of this House, he still maintains the most despotic power ever known in India. He domineers with an overbearing sway in the assemblies of his pretended masters; and it is thought in a degree rash to venture to name his offences in this House, even as grounds of a legislative remedy.

On the other hand, consider the fate of those who have met with the applauses of the Directors. Colonel Monson, one of the best of men, had his days shortened by the applauses, destitute of the support, of the Company. General Clavering, whose panegyric was made in every dispatch from England, whose hearse was bedewed with the tears, and hung round with eulogies of the Court of Directors, burst an honest and indignant heart at the treachery of those who ruined him by their praises. Uncommon patience and temper, supported Mr. Francis a while longer under the baneful influence of the commendation of the Court of Directors. His health however gave way at length; and, in utter despair

he

he returned to Europe. At his return the doors of the India House were shut to this man, who had been the object of their constant admiration. He has indeed escaped with life, but he has forfeited all expectation of credit, consequence, party, and following. He may well say, *Me nemo ministro fur erit, atque ideo nulli comes exeo.* This man, whose deep reach of thought, whose large legislative conceptions, and whose grand plans of policy, make the most shining part of our Reports, from whence we have all learned our lessons, if we have learned any good ones; this man, from whose materials those gentlemen who have least acknowledged it have yet spoken as from a brief; this man, driven from his employment, discountenanced by the Directors, has had no other reward, and no other distinction, but that inward "sun-"shine of the soul" which a good conscience can always bestow upon itself. He has not yet had so much as a good word, but from a person too insignificant to make any other return for the means with which he has been furnished for performing his share of a duty which is equally urgent on us all.

Add to this, that from the highest in place to the lowest, every British subject, who, in obedience to the Company's orders, has been active in the discovery of peculations, has been ruined. They have been driven from India. When they made their appeal at home they were not heard; when they attempted to return they were stopped. No artifice of fraud, no violence of power, has been omitted, to destroy them in character as well as in fortune.

Worse, far worse, has been the fate of the poor creatures, the natives of India, whom the hypocrisy of the Company has betrayed into complaint of oppreſſion, and diſcovery of peculation. The firſt woman in Bengal, the Ranni of Rajeſhahi, the Ranni of Burdwan, the Ranni of Amboa, by their weak and thoughtleſs truſt in the Company's honour and protection, are utterly ruined: the firſt of theſe women, a perſon of princely rank, and once of correſpondent fortune, who paid above two hundred thouſand a year quit-rent to the ſtate, is, according to very credible information, ſo completely beggared as to ſtand in need of the relief of alms. Mahomed Reza Khân, the ſecond Muſſulman in Bengal, for having been diſtinguiſhed by the ill-omened honour of the countenance and protection of the Court of Directors, was, without the pretence of any enquiry whatſoever into his conduct, ſtripped of all his employments, and reduced to the loweſt condition. His ancient rival for power, the Rajah Nundcomar, was, by an inſult on every thing which India holds reſpectable and ſacred, hanged in the face of all his nation, by the judges you ſent to protect that people; hanged for a pretended crime, upon an *ex poſt facto* Britiſh act of parliament, in the midſt of his evidence againſt Mr. Haſtings. The accuſer they ſaw hanged. The culprit, without acquittal or enquiry, triumphs on the ground of that murder: a murder not of Nundcomar only, but of all living teſtimony, and even of evidence yet unborn. From that time not a complaint has been heard from the natives againſt their governors. All the grievances of India have found a complete remedy.

Men will not look to acts of parliament, to regulations, to declarations, to votes, and reſolutions. No, they are not ſuch fools. They will aſk, what is the road to power, credit, wealth, and honours? They will aſk, what conduct ends in neglect,

neglect, difgrace, poverty, exile, prifon, and gibbet? Thefe will teach them the courfe which they are to follow. It is your diftribution of thefe that will give the character and tone to your government. All the reft is miferable grimace.

When I accufe the Court of Directors of this habitual treachery, in the ufe of reward and punifhment, I do not mean to include all the individuals in that Court. There have been, Sir, very frequently, men of the greateft integrity and virtue amongft them; and the contrariety in the declarations and conduct of that Court has arifen, I take it, from this:—That the honeft Directors have, by the force of matter of fact on the records, carried the reprobation of the evil meafures of the fervants in India. This could not be prevented, whilft thefe records ftared them in the face; nor were the delinquents, either here or there, very folicitous about their reputation, as long as they were able to fecure their power. The agreement of their partizans to cenfure them, blunted for a while the edge of a fevere proceeding. It obtained for them a character of impartiality, which enabled them to recommend, with fome fort of grace, what will always carry a plaufible appearance, thofe treacherous expedients, called moderate meafures. Whilft thefe were under difcuffion, new matter of complaint came over, which feemed to antiquate the firft. The fame circle was here trod round once more; and thus through years they proceeded in a compromife of cenfure for punifhment; until, by fhame and defpair, one after another, almoft every man, who preferred his duty to the Company to the interefts of their fervants, has been driven from that Court.

This, Sir, has been their conduct; and it has been the refult of the alteration which was infenfibly made in their constitution. The change was made insensibly; but it is now strong and adult, and as public and declared, as it is fixed beyond all power of reformation. So that there is none who hears me, that is not as certain as I am, that the Company, in the sense in which it was formerly understood, has no existence. The question is not, what injury you may do to the proprietors of India stock; for there are no such men to be injured. If the active ruling part of the Company who form the general court, who fill the offices, and direct the measures (the rest tell for nothing) were persons who held their stock as a means of their subsistence, who in the part they took were only concerned in the government of India, for the rise or fall of their dividend, it would be indeed a defective plan of policy. The interest of the people who are governed by them would not be their primary object; perhaps a very small part of their consideration at all. But then they might well be depended on, and perhaps more than persons in other respects preferable, for preventing the peculations of their servants to their own prejudice. Such a body would not easily have left their trade as a spoil to the avarice of those who received their wages. But now things are totally reversed. The stock is of no value, whether it be the qualification of a director or proprietor; and it is impossible that it should. A director's qualification may be worth about two thousand five hundred pounds—and the interest, at eight *per cent.* is about one hundred and sixty pounds a year. Of what value is that, whether it rise to ten, or fall to six, or to nothing, to him whose son, before he is in Bengal two months, and before he descends the steps of the council chamber, sells the grant of a single contract for forty thousand pounds?

pounds? Accordingly the stock is bought up in qualifications. The vote is not to protect the stock, but the stock is bought to acquire the vote; and the end of the vote is to cover and support, against justice, some man of power who has made an obnoxious fortune in India; or to maintain in power those who are actually employing it in the acquisition of such a fortune; and to avail themselves in return of his patronage, that he may shower the spoils of the East, " barbaric pearl and gold," on them, their families, and dependents. So that all the relations of the Company are not only changed, but inverted. The servants in India are not appointed by the Directors, but the Directors are chosen by them. The trade is carried on with their capitals. To them the revenues of the country are mortgaged. The seat of the supreme power is in Calcutta. The house in Leadenhall Street is nothing more than a change for their agents, factors, and deputies to meet in, to take care of their affairs, and support their interests; and this so avowedly, that we see the known agents of the delinquent servants marshalling and disciplining their forces, and the prime spokesmen in all their assemblies.

Every thing has followed in this order, and according to the natural train of events. I will close what I have to say on the incorrigible condition of the Company, by stating to you a few facts, that will leave no doubt of the obstinacy of that corporation, and of their strength too, in resisting the reformation of their servants. By these facts you will be enabled to discover the sole grounds upon which they are tenacious of their charter. It is now more than two years that, upon account of the gross abuses and ruinous situation of the Company's affairs, (which occasioned the cry of the whole world long before it was taken up here) that we instituted

instituted two Committees to enquire into the mismanagements by which the Company's affairs had been brought to the brink of ruin. These enquiries had been pursued with unremitting diligence; and a great body of facts was collected and printed for general information. In the result of those enquiries, although the Committees consisted of very different descriptions, they were unanimous. They joined in censuring the conduct of the Indian administration, and enforcing the responsibility upon two men, whom this House, in consequence of these reports, declared it to be the duty of the Directors to remove from their stations, and recal to Great Britain, "*because they had acted in a manner repugnant to the honour and policy of this nation, and thereby brought great calamities on India, and enormous expences on the East India Company.*"

Here was no attempt on the charter. Here was no question of their privileges. To vindicate their own honour, to support their own interests, to enforce obedience to their own orders; these were the sole object of the monitory resolution of this House. But as soon as the general court could assemble, they assembled to demonstrate who they really were. Regardless of the proceedings of this House, they ordered the Directors not to carry into effect any resolution they might come to for the removal of Mr. Hastings and Mr. Hornby. The Directors, still retaining some shadow of respect to this House, instituted an enquiry themselves, which continued from June to October; and after an attentive perusal and full consideration of papers, resolved to take steps for removing the persons who had been the objects of our resolution; but not without a violent struggle against evidence. Seven Directors went so far as to enter a protest against the vote of their court.

Upon

Upon this the general court takes the alarm; it re-assembles; it orders the Directors to rescind their resolution, that is, not to recal Mr. Hastings and Mr. Hornby, and to despise the resolution of the House of Commons. Without so much as the pretence of looking into a single paper, without the formality of instituting any committee of enquiry, they superseded all the labours of their own Directors, and of this House.

It will naturally occur to ask, how it was possible that they should not attempt some sort of examination into facts, as a colour for their resistance to a public authority, proceeding so very deliberately; and exerted, apparently at least, in favour of their own? The answer, and the only answer which can be given, is, that they were afraid that their true relation should be mistaken. They were afraid that their patrons and masters in India should attribute their support of them, to an opinion of their cause, and not to an attachment to their power. They were afraid it should be suspected, that they did not mean blindly to support them in the use they made of that power. They determined to shew that they at least were set against reformation; that they were firmly resolved to bring the territories, the trade, and the stock of the Company, to ruin, rather than be wanting in fidelity to their nominal servants and real masters, in the ways they took to their private fortunes.

Even since the beginning of this session, the same act of audacity was repeated, with the same circumstances of contempt of all the decorum of enquiry, on their part, and of all the proceedings of this House. They again made it a request to their favourite, and your culprit, to keep his post; and thanked and applauded him, without calling for a paper which could afford light into the merit or demerit of the tranfaction, and without giving themfelves a moment's time to confider, or even to underftand, the articles of the Maratta peace. The fact is, that for a long time there was a ftruggle, a faint one indeed, between the Company and their fervants. But it is a ftruggle no longer. For fome time the fuperiority has been decided. The interefts abroad are become the fettled preponderating weight both in the Court of Proprietors, and the Court of Directors. Even the attempt you have made to enquire into their practices and to reform abufes, has raifed and piqued them to a far more regular and fteady fupport. The Company has made a common caufe, and identified themfelves, with the deftroyers of India. They have taken on themfelves all that mafs of enormity; they are fupporting what you have reprobated; thofe you condemn they applaud; thofe you order home to anfwer for their conduct, they requeft to ftay, and thereby encourage to proceed in their practices. Thus the fervants of the Eaft India Company triumph, and the reprefentatives of the people of Great Britain are defeated.

I therefore conclude, what you all conclude, that this body, being totally perverted from the purpofes of its inftitution, is utterly incorrigible; and becaufe they are incorrigible, both in conduct and conftitution, power ought to be taken out of their hands; juft on the fame principles on which have been made all the juft changes and revolutions of government that have taken place fince the beginning of the world.

I will now fay a few words to the general principle of the plan which is fet up againft that of my Right Honourable friend. It is to re-commit the government of India to the Court of Directors. Thofe who would commit the reformation of India to the destroyers of it, are the enemies to that reformation. They would make a distinction between Directors and Proprietors, which, in the present state of things, does not, cannot exist. But a Right Honourable gentleman says, he would keep the present government of India in the Court of Directors; and would, to curb them, provide salutary regulations;—wonderful! That is, he would appoint the old offenders to correct the old offences; and he would render the vicious and the foolish wife and virtuous, by salutary regulations. He would appoint the wolf as guardian of the sheep; but he has invented a curious muzzle, by which this protecting wolf shall not be able to open his jaws above an inch or two at the utmost. Thus his work is finished. But I tell the Right Honourable gentleman, that controuled depravity is not innocence; and that it is not the labour of delinquency in chains, that will correct abuses. Will these gentlemen of the direction animadvert on the partners of their own guilt? Never did a serious plan of amending of any old tyrannical establishment propose the authors and abettors of the abuses as the reformers of them. If the undone people of India see their old oppressors in confirmed power, even by the reformation, they will expect nothing but what they will certainly feel, a continuance, or rather an aggravation, of all their former sufferings. They look to the seat of power, and to the persons who fill it; and they despise those gentlemen's regulations as much as the gentlemen do who talk of them.

But there is a cure for every thing. Take away, say they, the Court of Proprietors, and the Court of Directors will do their duty. Yes; as they have done it hitherto. That the evils in India have solely arisen from the Court of Proprietors,

is

is grossly false. In many of them, the Directors were heartily concurring; in most of them they were encouraging, and sometimes commanding; in all they were conniving.

But who are to choose this well-regulated and reforming Court of Directors?—Why, the very proprietors who are excluded from all management, for the abuse of their power. They will choose undoubtedly, out of themselves, men like themselves; and those who are most forward in resisting your authority, those who are most engaged in faction or interest with the delinquents abroad, will be the objects of their selection. But Gentlemen say, that when this choice is made, the proprietors are not to interfere in the measures of the Directors, whilst those Directors are busy in the control of their common patrons and masters in India. No, indeed, I believe they will not desire to interfere. They will choose those whom they know may be trusted, safely trusted, to act in strict conformity to their common principles, manners, measures, interests, and connections. They will want neither monitor nor control. It is not easy to choose men to act in conformity to a public interest against their private: but a sure dependance may be had on those who are chosen to forward their private interest, at the expence of the public. But if the Directors should slip, and deviate into rectitude, the punishment is in the hands of the general court, and it will surely be remembered to them at their next election.

If the government of India wants no reformation; but gentlemen are amusing themselves with a theory, conceiving a more democratic or aristocratic mode of government for their dependances, or if they are in a dispute only about patronage; the dispute is with me of so little concern, that I should not take the pains to utter an

affirmative

affirmative or negative to any propofition in it. If it be only for a theoretical amufement that they are to propofe a bill; the thing is at beft frivolous and unneceffary. But if the Company's government is not only full of abufe, but is one of the moft corrupt and deftructive tyrannies, that probably ever exifted in the world (as I am fure it is) what a cruel mockery would it be in me, and in thofe who think like me, to propofe this kind of remedy for this kind of evil!

I now come to the third objection, That this bill will increafe the influence of the Crown. An Honourable gentleman has demanded of me, whether I was in earneft when I propofed to this Houfe a plan for the reduction of that influence. Indeed, Sir, I was much, very much, in earneft. My heart was deeply concerned in it; and I hope the public has not loft the effect of it. How far my judgment was right, for what concerned perfonal favour and confequence to myfelf, I fhall not prefume to determine; nor is its effect upon *me* of any moment. But as to this bill, whether it encreafes the influence of the Crown, or not, is a queftion I fhould be afhamed to afk. If I am not able to correct a fyftem of oppreffion and tyranny, that goes to the utter ruin of thirty millions of my fellow-creatures and fellow-fubjects, but by fome increafe to the influence of the Crown, I am ready here to declare, that I, who have been active to reduce it, fhall be at leaft as active and ftrenuous to reftore it again. I am no lover of names; I contend for the fubftance of good and protecting government, let it come from what quarter it will.

But I am not obliged to have recourfe to this expedient. Much, very much the contrary. I am fure that the influence of the Crown will by no means aid a reformation of this kind; which

can

can neither be originated nor supported, but by the uncorrupt public virtue of the representatives of the people of England. Let it once get into the ordinary course of administration, and to me all hopes of reformation are gone. I am far from knowing or believing, that this bill will encrease the influence of the Crown. We all know, that the Crown has ever had some influence in the Court of Directors; and that it has been extremely increased by the acts of 1773 and 1780. The gentlemen who, as part of their reformation, propose " a more active controul on the part of the " Crown," which is to put the Directors under a Secretary of State, specially named for that purpose, must know, that their project will increase it further. But that old influence has had, and the new will have, incurable inconveniences, which cannot happen under the parliamentary establishment proposed in this bill. * An Honourable gentleman not now in his place, but who is well acquainted with the India Company, and by no means a friend to this bill, has told you that a ministerial influence has always been predominant in that body; and that to make the Directors pliant to their purposes, Ministers generally caused persons meanly qualified to be chosen Directors. According to his idea, to secure subserviency, they submitted the Company's affairs to the direction of incapacity. This was to ruin the Company, in order to govern it. This was certainly influence in the very worst form in which it could appear. At best it was clandestine and irresponsible. Whether this was done so much upon system as that gentleman supposes, I greatly doubt. But such in effect the operation of Government on that court unquestionably was; and such under a similar constitution, it will be for ever.

* Governor Johnstone.

Ministers

Ministers must be wholly removed from the management of the affairs of India, or they will have an influence in its patronage. The thing is inevitable. Their scheme of a new Secretary of State, " with a more vigorous " control," is not much better than a repetition of the measure which we know by experience will not do. Since the year 1773 and the year 1780, the Company has been under the control of the Secretary of State's office, and we had then three Secretaries of State. If more than this is done, then they annihilate the direction which they pretend to support; and they augment the influence of the Crown, of whose growth they affect so great an horror. But in truth this scheme of reconciling a direction really and truly deliberative, with an office really and substantially controlling, is a sort of machinery that can be kept in order but a very short time. Either the Directors will dwindle into clerks, or the Secretary of State, as hitherto has been the course, will leave every thing to them, often through design, often through neglect. If both should affect activity, collision, procrastination, delay, and in the end, utter confusion must ensue.

But, Sir, there is one kind of influence far greater than that of the nomination to office. This gentlemen in opposition have totally overlooked, although it now exists in its full vigour; and it will do so, upon their scheme, in at least as much force as it does now. That influence this bill cuts up by the roots; I mean the *influence of protection*. I shall explain myself:—The office given to a young man going to India is of trifling consequence. But he that goes out an insignificant boy, in a few years returns a great Nabob. Mr. Hastings says he has two hundred and fifty of that kind of raw materials, who expect to be

speedily

speedily manufactured into the merchantable quality I mention. One of these gentlemen, suppose, returns hither, loaded with odium and with riches. When he comes to England he comes as to a prison or as to a sanctuary; and either are ready for him, according to his demeanor. What is the influence in the grant of any place in India, to that which is acquired by the protection or compromise with such guilt, and with the command of such riches, under the dominion of the hopes and fears which power is able to hold out to every man in that condition? That man's whole fortune, half a million perhaps, becomes an instrument of influence, without a shilling of charge to the Civil List; and the influx of fortunes which stand in need of this protection is continual. It works both ways; it influences the delinquent, and it may corrupt the minister. Compare the influence acquired by appointing for instance even a governor general, and that obtained by protecting him. I shall push this no further. But I wish gentlemen to roll it a little in their own minds.

The bill before you cuts off this source of influence. Its design and main scope is to regulate the administration of India upon the principles of a Court of Judicature; and to exclude, as far as human prudence can exclude, all possibility of a corrupt partiality, in appointing to office or supporting in office, or covering from enquiry and punishment, any person who has abused or shall abuse his authority. At the board, as appointed and regulated by this bill, reward and punishment cannot be shifted and reversed by a whisper. That commission becomes fatal to cabal, to intrigue, and to secret representation, those instruments of the ruin of India.

He that cuts off the means of premature fortune, and the power of protecting it when acquired, strikes a deadly blow at the great fund, the Bank, the capital stock of Indian influence, which cannot be vested any where, or in any hands, without most dangerous consequences to the public.

The third and contradictory objection, is, That this bill does not increase the influence of the Crown. On the contrary, That the just power of the Crown will be lessened, and transferred to the use of a party, by giving the patronage of India to a commission nominated by parliament, and independent of the Crown. The contradiction is glaring, and it has been too well exposed to make it necessary for me to insist upon it. But passing the contradiction, and taking it without any relation, of all objections that is the most extraordinary. Do not gentlemen know, that the Crown has not at present the grant of a single office under the Company, civil or military, at home or abroad? So far as the Crown is concerned, it is certainly rather a gainer; for the vacant offices in the new commission are to be filled up by the King.

It is argued as a part of the bill, derogatory to the prerogatives of the Crown, that the commissioners named in the bill are to continue for a short term of years (too short in my opinion) and because, during that time, they are not at the mercy of every predominant faction of the court. Does not this objection lie against the present Directors; none of whom are named by the Crown, and a proportion of whom hold for this very term of four years? Did it not lie against the governor general and council named in the act of 1773—who were invested by name, as the present commissioners are to be appointed

pointed in the body of the act of parliament, who were to hold their places for a term of years, and were not removable at the difcretion of the Crown? Did it not lie againft the re-appointment, in the year 1780, upon the very fame terms? Yet at none of thefe times, whatever other objections the fcheme might be liable to, was it fuppofed to be a derogation to the juft prerogative of the Crown, that a commiffion created by act of parliament fhould have its members named by the authority which called it into exiftence? This is not the difpofal by parliament of any office derived from the authority of the Crown, or now difpofable by that authority. It is fo far from being any thing new, violent, or alarming, that I do not recollect, in any parliamentary commiffion, down to the commiffioners of the land tax, that it has ever been otherwife.

The objection of the tenure for four years is an objection to all places that are not held during pleafure; but in that objection I pronounce the gentlemen, from my knowledge of their complexion and of their principles, to be perfectly in earneft. The party (fay thefe gentlemen) of the minifter who propofes this fcheme will be rendered powerful by it; for he will name his party friends to the commiffion. This objection againft party is a party objection; and in this too thefe gentlemen are perfectly ferious. They fee that if, by any intrigue, they fhould fucceed to office, they will lofe the *clandeftine* patronage, the true inftrument of clandeftine influence, enjoyed in the name of fubfervient Directors, and of wealthy trembling Indian delinquents. But as often as they are beaten off this ground, they return to it again. The minifter will name his friends, and perfons of his own party. —Who fhould he name? Should he name his adverfaries? Should he name thofe whom he cannot truft?

Should

Should he name thofe to execute his plans, who are the declared enemies to the principles of his reform? His character is here at ftake. If he propofes for his own ends (but he never will propofe) fuch names as, from their want of rank, fortune, character, ability, or knowledge, are likely to betray or to fall fhort of their truft, he is in an independent Houfe of Commons; in an Houfe of Commons which has, by its own virtue, deftroyed the inftruments of parliamentary fubfervience. This Houfe of Commons would not endure the found of fuch names. He would perifh by the means which he is fuppofed to purfue for the fecurity of his power. The firft pledge he muft give of his fincerity in this great reform will be in the confidence which ought to be repofed in thofe names.

For my part, Sir, in this bufinefs I put all indirect confiderations wholly out of my mind. My fole queftion, on each claufe of the bill, amounts to this:—Is the meafure propofed required by the neceffities of India? I cannot confent totally to lofe fight of the real wants of the people who are the objects of it, and to hunt after every matter of party fquabble that may be ftarted on the feveral provifions. On the queftion of the duration of the commiffion I am clear and decided. Can I, can any one who has taken the fmalleft trouble to be informed concerning the affairs of India, amufe himfelf with fo ftrange an imagination, as that the habitual defpotifm and oppreffion, that the monopolies, the peculations, the univerfal deftruction of all the legal authority of this kingdom, which have been for twenty years maturing to their prefent enormity, combined with the diftance of the fcene, the boldnefs and artifice of delinquents, their combination, their exceſſive wealth, and the faction they have made in England, can be fully corrected in a ſhorter term than four years? None has hazarded ſuch an aſſertion—None, who has a regard for his reputation, will hazard it.

Sir, the gentlemen, whoever they are, who ſhall be appointed to this commiſſion, have an undertaking of magnitude on their hands, and their ſtability muſt not only be, but it muſt be thought, real;—and who is it will believe, that any thing ſhort of an eſtabliſhment made, ſupported, and fixed in its duration, with all the authority of parliament, can be thought ſecure of a reaſonable ſtability? The plan of my Honourable friend is the reverſe of that of reforming by the authors of the abuſe. The beſt we could expect from them is, that they ſhould not continue their ancient pernicious activity. To thoſe we could think of nothing but applying *control*; as we are ſure, that even a regard to their reputation (if any ſuch thing exiſts in them) would oblige them to cover, to conceal, to ſuppreſs, and conſequently to prevent, all cure of the grievances of India. For what can be diſcovered, which is not to their diſgrace? Every attempt to correct an abuſe would be a ſatire on their former adminiſtration. Every man they ſhould pretend to call to an account, would be found their inſtrument or their accomplice. They can never ſee a beneficial regulation, but with a view to defeat it. The ſhorter the tenure of ſuch perſons, the better would be the chance of ſome amendment.

But the ſyſtem of the bill is different. It calls in perſons no wiſe concerned with any act cenſured by parliament; perſons generated with, and for the reform of which, they are themſelves the moſt

most essential part. To these the chief regulations in the bill are helps, not fetters; they are authorities to support, not regulations to restrain them. From these we look for much more than innocence. From these we expect zeal, firmness, and unremitted activity. Their duty, their character, binds them to proceedings of vigour; and they ought to have a tenure in their office which precludes all fear, whilst they are acting up to the purposes of their trust; a tenure without which, none will undertake plans that require a series and system of acts. When they know that they cannot be whispered out of their duty, that their public conduct cannot be censured without a public discussion; that the schemes which they have begun will not be committed to those who will have an interest and credit in defeating and disgracing them; then we may entertain hopes. The tenure is for four years, or during their good behaviour. That good behaviour is as long as they are true to the principles of the bill; and the judgment is in either House of Parliament. This is the tenure of your judges; and the valuable principle of the bill is, to make a judicial administration for India. It is to give confidence in the execution of a duty, which requires as much perseverance and fortitude as can fall to the lot of any that is born of woman.

As to the gain by party, from the Right Honourable gentleman's bill, let it be shewn, that this supposed party advantage is pernicious to its object, and the objection is of weight; but until this is done, and this has not been attempted, I shall consider the sole objection, from its tendency to promote the interest of a party, as altogether contemptible. The kingdom is divided

divided into parties, and it ever has been so divided, and it ever will be so divided; and if no system for relieving the subjects of this kingdom from oppression, and snatching its affairs from ruin, can be adopted, until it is demonstrated that no party can derive an advantage from it, no good can ever be done in this country. If party is to derive an advantage from the reform of India, (which is more than I know, or believe) it ought to be that party which alone, in this kingdom, has its reputation, nay its very being, pledged to the protection and preservation of that part of the empire. Great fear is expressed, that the commissioners named in this bill will shew some regard to a minister out of place. To men made like the objectors, this must appear criminal. Let it however be remembered by others, that if the commissioners should be his friends, they cannot be his slaves. But dependants are not in a condition to adhere to friends, nor to principles, nor to any uniform line of conduct. They may begin censors, and be obliged to end accomplices. They may be even put under the direction of those whom they were appointed to punish.

The fourth and last objection is, That the bill will hurt public credit. I do not know whether this requires an answer. But if it does, look to your foundations. The sinking fund is the pillar of credit in this country; and let it not be forgot, that the distresses, owing to the mismanagement of the East India Company, have already taken a million from that fund by the non-payment of duties. The bills drawn upon the Company, which are about four millions, cannot be accepted without the consent of the treasury. The treasury, acting under a parliamentary trust and authority,

authority, pledges the public for thefe millions. If they pledge the public, the public muſt have a ſecurity in its hands for the management of this intereſt, or the national credit is gone. For otherwiſe it is not only the Eaſt India Company, which is a great intereſt, that is undone, but, clinging to the ſecurity of all your funds, it drags down the reſt, and the whole fabric perifhes in one ruin. If this bill does not provide a direction of integrity and of ability competent to that truſt, the objection is fatal. If it does, public credit muſt depend on the ſupport of the bill.

It has been ſaid, if you violate this charter, what ſecurity has the charter of the Bank, in which public credit is ſo deeply concerned, and even the charter of London, in which the rights of ſo many ſubjects are involved? I anſwer, In the like caſe they have no ſecurity at all—No—no ſecurity at all. If the Bank ſhould, by every ſpecies of miſmanagement, fall into a ſtate ſimilar to that of the Eaſt India Company; if it ſhould be oppreſſed with demands it could not anſwer, engagements which it could not perform, and with bills for which it could not procure payment; no charter ſhould protect the miſmanagement from correction, and ſuch public grievances from redreſs. If the city of London had the means and will of deſtroying an empire, and of cruelly oppreſſing and tyrannizing over millions of men as good as themſelves, the charter of the city of London ſhould prove no ſanction to ſuch tyranny and ſuch oppreſſion. Charters are kept, when their purpoſes are maintained: they are violated when the privilege is ſupported againſt its end and its object.

Now, Sir, I have finiſhed all I propoſed to ſay, as my reaſons for giving my vote to this Bill. If

I am

I am wrong, it is not for want of pains to know what is right. This pledge, at least, of my rectitude I have given to my country.

And now, having done my duty to the Bill, let me say a word to the author. I should leave him to his own noble sentiments, if the unworthy and illiberal language with which he has been treated, beyond all example of parliamentary liberty, did not make a few words necessary; not so much in justice to him, as to my own feelings. I must say then, that it will be a distinction honourable to the age, that the rescue of the greatest number of the human race that ever were so grievously oppressed, from the greatest tyranny that was ever exercised, has fallen to the lot of abilities and dispositions equal to the task; that it has fallen to one who has the enlargement to comprehend, the spirit to undertake, and the eloquence to support, so great a measure of hazardous benevolence. His spirit is not owing to his ignorance of the state of men and things; he well knows what snares are spread about his path, from personal animosity, from court intrigues, and possibly from popular delusion. But he has put to hazard his ease, his security, his interest, his power, even his darling popularity, for the benefit of a people whom he has never seen. This is the road that all heroes have trod before him. He is traduced and abused for his supposed motives. He will remember, that obloquy is a necessary ingredient in the composition of all true glory: he will remember, that it was not only in the Roman customs, but it is in the nature and constitution of things, that calumny and abuse are essential parts of triumph. These thoughts will support
a mind,

a mind, which only exifts for honour, under the burthen of temporary reproach. He is doing indeed a great good; fuch as rarely falls to the lot, and almoft as rarely coincides with the defires, of any man. Let him ufe his time. Let him give the whole length of the reins to his benevolence. He is now on a great eminence, where the eyes of mankind are turned to him. He may live long, he may do much. But here is the fummit. He never can exceed what he does this day.

He has faults; but they are faults that, though they may in a fmall degree tarnifh the luftre, and fometimes impede the march of his abilities, have nothing in them to extinguifh the fire of great virtues. In thofe faults, there is no mixture of deceit, of hypocrify, of pride, of ferocity, of complexional defpotifm, or want of feeling for the diftreffes of mankind. His are faults which might exift in a defcendant of Henry the Fourth of France, as they did exift in that father of his country. Henry the Fourth wifhed that he might live to fee a fowl in the pot of every peafant of his kingdom. That fentiment of homely benevolence was worth all the fplendid fayings that are recorded of kings. But he wifhed perhaps for more than could be obtained, and the goodnefs of the man exceeded the power of the King. But this gentleman, a fubject, may this day fay this at leaft, with truth, that he fecures the rice in his pot to every man in India. A poet of antiquity thought it one of the firft diftinctions to a prince whom he meant to celebrate, that through a long fucceffion of generations, he had been the progenitor of an able and virtuous citizen, who by force of the arts of peace, had corrected
governments

governments of oppression, and suppressed wars of rapine.

> Indole proh quanta juvenis, quantumque daturus
> Aufoniæ populis, ventura in fæcula civem.
> Ille super Gangem, super exauditus et Indos,
> Implebit terras voce ; et furialia bella
> Fulmine compescet linguæ.——

This was what was said of the predecessor of the only person to whose eloquence it does not wrong that of the mover of this bill to be compared. But the Ganges and the Indus are the patrimony of the fame of my Honourable friend, and not of Cicero. I confess, I anticipate with joy the reward of those, whose whole consequence, power, and authority, exist only for the benefit of mankind; and I carry my mind to all the people, and all the names and descriptions, that, relieved by this bill, will bless the labours of this Parliament, and the confidence which the best House of Commons has given to him who the best deserves it. The little cavils of party will not be heard, where freedom and happiness will be felt. There is not a tongue, a nation, or religion in India, which will not bless the presiding care and manly beneficence of this House, and of him who proposes to you this great work. Your names will never be separated before the throne of the Divine Goodness, in whatever language, or with whatever rites, pardon is asked for sin, and reward for those who imitate the Godhead in his universal bounty to his creatures. These honours you deserve, and they will surely be paid, when all the jargon, of influence, and party, and patronage, are swept into oblivion.

I have

I have spoken what I think, and what I feel, of the mover of this Bill. An Honourable friend of mine, speaking of his merits, was charged with having made a studied panegyric. I don't know what his was. Mine, I am sure, is a studied panegyric; the fruit of much meditation; the result of the observation of near twenty years. For my own part, I am happy that I have lived to see this day; I feel myself overpaid for the labours of eighteen years, when, at this late period, I am able to take my share, by one humble vote, in destroying a tyranny that exists to the disgrace of this nation, and the destruction of so large a part of the human species.

FINIS.

THE
SUBSTANCE
OF
GENERAL BURGOYNE'S
SPEECHES.

PRICE ONE SHILLING.

Speedily will be Published,

A Genuine Copy of the PROCEEDINGS of the COURT MARTIAL, held upon Colonel HENLEY of the American Troops, at *Cambridge*, in the Month of *February*, 1778; upon the Profecution of General BURGOYNE, for Ill-treatment of the *British* Troops.

Printed for *J. Almon*, oppofite Burlington-Houfe in Piccadilly.

THE SUBSTANCE

OF

GENERAL BURGOYNE'S SPEECHES,

ON

MR. VYNER'S MOTION,

On the 26th of May;

AND UPON

MR. HARTLEY'S MOTION,

On the 28th of May, 1778.

WITH AN

APPENDIX,

CONTAINING

General Wafhington's Letter

TO

General Burgoyne,

&c.

LONDON:

PRINTED FOR J. ALMON, OPPOSITE BURLINGTON-HOUSE, PICCADILLY, MDCCLXXVIII.

SPEECH

OF

GENERAL BURGOYNE.

MOTION by Mr. VYNER,

Martis 26° die Maii, 1778.

" THAT this house will now resolve it-
" self into a committee of the whole
" house to consider of the state and condition
" of the army which surrendered themselves
" on convention at Saratoga, in America;
" and also by what means Lieutenant Gene-
" ral Burgoyne, who commanded that army,
" and was included in that convention, was
" released, and is now returned to England?"

Mr. Vyner, in opening the motion, stated some questions to General Burgoyne, which he proposed to ask in the committee.

The motion was seconded by Mr. Wilkes, who also stated further questions in respect to the treaty with the Indians, their conduct during the campaign, and the burning the country.

An amendment was proposed by Mr. Fox to insert, after the word *consider*, these words " of the transactions of the northern army " under Lieutenant General Burgoyne, and " of "

The motion thus amended, would have run as follows: " That this house will now " resolve itself into a committee of the whole " house to consider of the transactions of the " northern army under Lieutenant General " Burgoyne, and of the state and condition " of the said army, &c."

In the course of the debate General Burgopne spoke nearly as follows:

Mr. Speaker, not imagining there would be any motion by the honourable gentleman who spoke first, but that merely a desire of information would be expressed upon certain subjects, I had myself prepared a motion for an address to the king, to have such papers laid before the house, as are now in possession of the secretary of state, and contain an account in detail, much too long for me to give in my place, of every circumstance expressed in the questions of the honourable gentleman. Those papers are of the utmoſt importance to the ſtate, to parliament, and to the public.

The turn the buſineſs has taken precludes me at preſent from my intended motion; but I riſe to give my warmeſt ſupport to the amendment propoſed; and as reaſons for the expediency of inſtituting a full enquiry, to which the amendment points, I ſhall endeavour, as far as I can do it without breach of order in debate, to give to *both the gentlemen ſatisfaction upon the particular ſubjects of their enquiries.

[* Mr. Vyner and Mr. Wilkes.]

I agree with the honourable gentleman who ſeconded the motion, that all the conduct reſpecting the Indian nations is a matter that ought to be thoroughly canvaſſed; and I look upon his calling upon me openly, and in my place, as ſome reparation for the very free, and not very generous comments he made upon my conduct in my abſence.

Sir, I ever eſteemed the Indian alliances, at beſt, a neceſſary evil. I ever believed their ſervices to be over-valued; ſometimes inſignificant, often barbarous, always capricious; and that the employment of them was only juſtifiable, when by being united to a regular army, they could be kept under controul, and made ſubſervient to a general ſyſtem.

Upon this principle I heartily concurred with that gallant and humane general, Sir Guy Carleton, in the year 1776, to decline the offers and folicitations of the Indians to be then employed feparately: the impoffibility of compleating the preparations for paffing the regular troops over the lakes made it impoffible to employ them conjunctively.

In that year, Sir, it was my lot, by delegation from Sir Guy Carleton, who was then at Quebec, to prefide at one of the greateft councils with the Indians that had been held at Montreal. Many gentlemen here know, that the ceremony preceding the taking up the hatchet, is, to offer to the reprefentative of the power they mean to ferve, the pipe of war. It was preffed upon me by the chiefs prefent; and it was in my power, by a fingle whif of tobacco, to have given flame and explofion to a dozen nations. I never felt greater fatisfaction than in being able to fulfil the inftructions I was charged with, for reftraining the impetuous paffions of thefe people: it was a fecondary fatisfaction, at my return to England in the winter, to juftify the conduct of Sir Guy Carleton in this refpect, though the juftification was very unpopular, among thofe—I mean not to particularize
minifters,

ministers, or ministers of ministers—but among those men, who, in their zeal against the colonists, had adopted the reasoning, that " partial severity was general mercy," provided by carrying terrors it conduced to finishing the war. How just so ever this principle may be, my mind is not of a texture for carrying it into effect; and I returned to Canada the following spring, when I succeeded to the command, determined to be the soldier, not the executioner of the state.

I found care had been already taken by General Carleton, upon the same principles of humanity which always direct his conduct, to officer the Indians with gentlemen selected from the British troops, upon a distinction of their temper and judgment, as well as upon that of their valour; and in much greater number than ever was destined to that service before. To these precautions I added that of a favourite priest, who had more controul over the passions of the Indians than all their chiefs put together; and I trust the expence put upon government to engage that gentleman's assistance through the course of the campaign, will not be esteemed an improper article in my accounts.

Sir,

Sir, with these assistances I was able to enforce obedience to the injunctions of my speech at the great council, upon assembling the army, which has been made public. Barbarity was prevented—So much so, that in one instance, two wounded provincial officers were brought off in the midst of fire upon the backs of Indians; and a captain, and his whole detachment, placed in ambuscade, were brought prisoners to my camp by Indians, without a man hurt, though it was evident they were placed for the special purpose of destroying me upon a reconnoitring party, and I was at that time very popular with the Indians.

I could produce many more instances to shew, that every possible exertion of humanity was used; and that the case of Miss Mecree excepted, which was accident, not premeditated cruelty, the stories upon which the honourable gentleman founded his accusation of me, were merely those fabricated by committees, and propagated in news-papers, for temporary purposes. The proclamation, which the honourable gentleman, in my absence treated with so harsh terms, I avow, was penned by myself. The design was to excite obedience, first by encouragement, and next by the dread, not the commission of severity;

—" to

—" to speak daggers, but use none." And so far were the Americans, in their hearts, from putting upon that proclamation the interpretation that gentleman has done, that it served to procure me respect and acknowledgment wherever I afterwards travelled through the country.

Sir, a gentleman has been in London great part of the winter, who I wish had been called to your bar.—It is for the sake of truth only I wish it; for he is certainly not my friend. His name is St. Luc le Corne, a distinguished partisan of the French in the last war, and now in the British service as a leader of the Indians.—He owes us indeed some service, having been formerly instrumental in scalping many hundred British soldiers upon the very ground where, though with a different sort of latitude, he was this year employed. He is by nature, education, and practice, artful, ambitious, and a courtier. To the grudge he owed me for controlling him in the use of the hatchet and scalping knife, it was natural to his character to recommend himself to ministerial favour, by any censure in his power to cast upon an unfashionable general. He was often closeted by a noble Lord in my eye*, and, with all these disadvantages, as he has

* Lord G. Germaine.

not

not been examined here, I wish the noble lord to inform the house, what this man has presumed to say of my conduct with the Indians. I know, in private companies, his language has been, that the Indians might have done great services, but they were discharged. Sir, if to restrain them from murder was to discharge them, I take with pride the blame---They were discharged. That circumstance apart, I should say that the Indians, and Mr. St. Luc at the head of them, deserted.

[*Sir, in regard to the call made upon me by the same honourable gentleman, for explanation respecting the burning of the country during the progress of the army under my command, I am ignorant of any such circumstance; I do not recollect more than one accident by fire; I positively assert there was no fire by order or countenance of myself, or any other officer, except at Saratoga. That district is the property of Major General Scuyler of the American troops; there were large barracks built by him, which took fire the day after the army arrived upon the

---

* This part of the speech included between crotchets, was omitted at the time of the preceding and following parts, and delivered separately upon a second call of Mr. Wilkes; but now is inserted in its proper place, as better connecting the whole matter spoke to by General Burgoyne.

ground

ground in their retreat; and I believe I need not ſtate any other proof of that matter being merely accident, than that the barracks were then made uſe of as my hoſpital, and full of ſick and wounded ſoldiers. General Scuyler had likewiſe a very good dwelling-houſe, exceeding large ſtorehouſes, great ſaw-mills, and other out-buildings, to the value altogether perhaps of ten thouſand pounds; a few days before the negotiation with General Gates, the enemy had formed a plan to attack me; a large column of troops were approaching to paſs the ſmall river, preparatory to a general action, and were entirely covered from the fire of my artillery by thoſe buildings. Sir, I avow that I gave the order to ſet them on fire; and in a very ſhort time that whole property, I have deſcribed, was conſumed. But, to ſhew that the perſon moſt deeply concerned in that calamity, did not put the conſtruction upon it, which it has pleaſed the honourable gentleman to do, I muſt inform the houſe, that one of the firſt perſons I ſaw, after the convention was ſigned, was General Scuyler. I expreſſed to him my regret at the event which had happened, and the reaſons which had occaſioned it. He deſired me to think no more of it; ſaid

said that the occasion juſtified it, according to the principles and rules of war, and he ſhould have done the ſame upon the ſame occaſion, or words to that effect. He did more---He ſent an aid-de-camp to conduct me to Albany, in order, as he expreſſed, to procure me better quarters than a ſtranger might be able to find. This gentleman conducted me to a very elegant houſe, and to my great ſurpriſe, preſented me to Mrs. Scuyler and her family; and in this general's houſe I remained during my whole ſtay at Albany, with a table of more than twenty covers for me and my friends, and every other poſſible demonſtration of hoſpitality: a ſituation, painful it is true in point of ſenſibility at the time, but which I now contemplate with ſome ſatisfaction, as carrying undeniable teſtimony how little I deſerved the charges of the honourable gentleman; and I leave it to his feelings, whether, after this explanation, ſome farther apology is not due to me.]

In regard to the firſt and moſt material queſtion aſked me by the honourable gentleman who propoſed the motion, viz. In what ſituation is the army at Cambridge? It is with ſome ſurprize I find that any part of this country is ignorant of the extraordinary circumſtances

cumstances that have attended it, as I conceive government must have received intelligence of them some time ago. In regard to the report made by myself, I acquit the king's ministers of any blame in not yet having made it public; because it was so voluminous that the papers could not be digested and copied, with the constant labour of three clerks, before last Saturday, when they were put into the hands of the noble lord secretary of state for the American department. But I trust that noble lord will now lose no time to make public, matters of such importance. Let them undergo the scrutiny of the committee as proposed by the amended motion, and let the world judge, upon their report, whether the spirit of the troops and the honour of the nation have been sustained and vindicated during those transactions. In confidence that these papers cannot possibly be withheld, I refer the honourable gentleman to them for a full delineation and explanation of the state of things at Cambridge, and will rest my present information upon a few material facts. The troops have undergone hardships and trials of patience as severe, though of a different nature, as any they experienced in the conflicts of the campaign. They have acquitted themselves

with

with equal resolution, temper, and honour. They are at present detained by a resolve of the congress, expressing that there are causes of suspicion that the convention was designed to be broke on our part, and therefore they are justifiable, without breach of public faith, to suspend the embarkation of the troops till the convention is ratified by the court of Great Britain.

In common with various pretences which involved other names in high departments to justify this measure, the congress grounded many suppositions that I knew to be unjust, upon my conduct. I thought it a duty to the state, to the army, and to myself, to refute those suppositions, and still, if possible, to give immediate effect to the convention. It will rest upon the house to judge, when they see the papers, whether I made good that refutation. And that brings me to another question asked by the honourable gentleman: "By what means and upon what condition I am in person here?" Sir, I charged my aid de camp, who carried my dispatch to the congress in answer to their vote of suspension, which the president had officially sent me, with a second letter to be delivered in case the suspension, after consideration had of my first letter, was continued:

The

The purport of this letter was to afk paffports for my perfonal return for the re-eftablifhment of my health, (which was then much affected) for the purpofe of fettling large and complicated accounts, and other reafons; and I offered to give a parole that fhould the fufpenfion of embarkation be prolonged beyond the time apprehended, I would return to America upon demand of the congrefs, and due notice given, re-deliver my perfon into their hands, and abide the fate of the reft of the army with whom I had ferved. Sir, I had many reafons, not neceffary nor proper to be alleged to the congrefs, founded upon a nearer intereft than health or any private expediency, to make me defirous to return home: to lay before government important truths, not to be communicated by other means, and to fupply, as far as in me lay, by an affiduous and honeft exertion in this houfe, the misfortune that had difenabled me from performing my duty in the field. I accompanied my letter to the congrefs by one to General Wafhington, wherein upon an opinion of his character, I afked him for his fupport to an application that could not interfere with the public duties of our refpective fituations. I fhall beg leave to read his anfwer as part of my fpeech; and I do it, Sir, not only left in

thefe

these times of doubt and aspersion, I should incur censure for holding private correspondence with an enemy, but likewise because I think this letter, though from an enemy, does honour to the human heart.

[*See the Appendix.*]

Sir, the congress readily consented to my application; and by this candid treatment of my enemies, I am here to vindicate my conduct against the false and barbarous interpretations that have arisen and have been suffered to prevail, by those who could have contradicted them, at home.

The honourable gentleman wishes to know what is the difference of numbers of the army between the time of signing the convention, and the present time; and I find the idea of great desertion very much prevails. That some men have deserted, in the worst sense of the word, is true. They are few, the scum of the regiments, and no loss of real strength. The greater part who have absconded, have had no intention to abandon the service, and if an epithet of honour could at any time be applied to a fault, theirs might be called *an honourable desertion.*[*] Some of these

---

[*] General Burgoyne took occasion in two subsequent debates to explain his meaning in this phrase, which he found had been

these men left letters or sent messages to their officers, informing them that in their present want of necessaries and comforts, and their inability to serve in arms, they had taken to trades and day labour in the country, but that they held themselves under an obligation from which they would never depart, to return to their regiments whenever the time of embarkation was ascertained: others, upon a high, though a mistaken suggestion of spirit, made efforts to effectuate a passage through the woods, to join the armies under Sir William Howe or Sir Henry Clinton, and it is believed that some of them succeeded. The whole of the absentees may amount to between five and six hundred men.

Sir, I have thus far endeavoured to give the honourable gentlemen satisfaction in the matters that seem most immediately to engage their attention, and that I could consistently

---

been misunderstood both within and without the house. He meant to apply the word *honourable* only to the common soldier's conception, who unused to consider and discriminate punctiliously the obligations of conventions with an enemy, acted only upon the principles of zeal to serve his king, and again to be actively employed in arms: that therefore their conduct was honourably intended, though misconceived. That so far from justifying that conception himself, he was persuaded that to retain such deserters when demanded, or indeed discovered, would be an infringement of the convention, and he was persuaded Sir William Howe or Sir Henry Clinton would, upon such demand or discovery, return them.

with

with order adduce in argument to support my vote for a more general enquiry.

I shall now proceed, (as yet stronger reasons for agreeing with the amendment,) to take notice of what has hitherto passed in the house, and upon very imperfect information, respecting other parts of the late campaign.

But, Sir, accustomed as I have been to be indulged by the house upon every occasion; and confident, as I ought to be, upon one where their indulgence is justice, I find cause in my own mind, in entering upon so complicated a subject, to implore anew, the fullest scope to their patience and candour, for a man, whose faculties, far too weak for such shocks, are almost unhinged by a succession of difficulties abroad, that fall to the lot of few, and whose disappointments and anxieties have been consummated, by the unexpected reception he has met at home.

And this address, Sir, is the more necessary, because I stand here unconnected and unassisted. I am ignorant who would have supported my own motion, had I made it, though confident from a prepossession of its propriety it would have found assistance somewhere. Neither courting nor fearing power, neither courting nor fearing party, I stand here upon the sole
basis

basis of truth and honour, and only ask support in proportion to the justice of my cause.

During my absence an enquiry was instituted, in which my name was very much involved. In the short space of time since my return, and in the agitated state of mind I have mentioned, it has been impossible for me to obtain from the mere conversation and recollection of friends, all that passed upon that occasion: but I have collected enough to know that I have been treated with great attention in general, and it is among my first duties to return to every quarter of the house my very sincere and grateful acknowledgments. I also know, that with all that attention and favour, much implied censure must have fallen upon me, from the nature of the proceedings, and more especially from the position, which I cannot admit to be a true one, but which I understand has been much insisted upon, " That where there is miscarriage there must be blame; and consequently, that the acquittal of one man infers the condemnation of another."

Sir, the papers which have been laid before the House are in some respects deficient and in others superfluous. The first superfluity to which I allude is a private letter from me to the

the noble Lord, acquainting him with my intention of going to Bath; of my audience with the King; of my folicitation to his Majefty for active employment the next campaign; expreffing my hopes of his Lordfhip's patronage in that purfuit, and concluding with fuch acknowledgments and profeffions as were natural to flow from a warm and unfufpicious heart impreffed with a fenfe of another's favour.

Not conceiving for what poffible public purpofe this letter was produced, I can only attend to the effects it has had to prejudice me perfonally. Sufpicions have been excited, that at the time I wrote that letter I was courting command, and by adulatory means, in preference and in prejudice to Sir Guy Carleton under whom I had had the honour to ferve, a confidential fecond, the preceding campaign. Every perfon in government might have pronounced my acquittal of fo bafe a proceeding, becaufe they knew, though the public did not, that it was decided * in the Autumn of 1776,

* This decifion was made, not only upon the expediency of the governor attending the civil duties of the province, which were thought at that time to require particular attention, but alfo upon doubts whether the general's commiffion authorifed him to act beyond the boundaries: and this whole tranfaction paffed long before the return of General Burgoyne to England, and entirely without his knowledge.

and

and notified to Sir Guy Carleton accordingly, that his military command was confined to the boundaries of the province of Quebec. It did not occur to the noble Lord to state that fact, because doubtless he did not foresee the prejudices the letter would occasion; but I cannot but lament he did not produce other letters of mine, which would have removed effectually every possible suspicion of a design so foreign to my heart as that of supplanting a gallant friend. Such letters would at the same time have rendered unnecessary the long train of correspondence laid upon your table, to shew that the preparations in Canada were duly expedited; because I should have been found to express the fullest sense of the zeal, the assiduity, and the honour with which Sir Guy Carleton acted, notwithstanding his disappointment in not being employed to conduct the campaign.

Will it be said, that the letters I allude to were withheld because they were private?— In the first place they do not properly come under that description, though it is true they were not office letters.—They could not be directed as such, because acting in subordination to Sir Guy Carleton, the official correspondence could only with decorum pass through

through him; but they were not private as applied to secresy, nor improper as they related to the distinct and separate object of the command I was entering upon. But, Sir, had any parts of these letters (or of any others necessary to my justification, of which I say there are many) been private in any sense of the word, will that excuse be alleged for detaining them, when there has appeared before you a paper of the most secret nature, I mean my thoughts upon conducting the war from the side of Canada. What officer will venture hereafter to give his opinion upon measures or men, when called upon by a minister, if his confidence, his reasonings, and his preferences are thus to be invidiously exposed; to create jealousies and differences among his fellow-officers, and at last to put an imposition upon the world, and make him responsible for the plan as well as the execution of a hazardous campaign? The plan, as originally drawn, I have no reason to be ashamed of, because it underwent the inspection, and had the sanction of some of the first and ablest officers of this country; but the plan, as it stood when my orders were framed, can with no more propriety be called mine, than any others formed by the cabinet for the distant parts of America,

or

or any other quarter of the globe where I had no participation or concern.—The noble Lord well knows, that the idea expressed in the secret paper laid before you of a latitude to act against New-England, was erased; that a power to embark the troops in case of unforeseen impediments, and make the junction with the southern army by sea, was not admitted. —Will it then be insinuated, that the plan was mine?—Why was it not produced in that changed and garbled state, by which the minister made it his own? Because it would have been one proof, if one had been wanting to unprejudiced minds, that by cutting off every proposed latitude, and confining the plan to one only object, the *forcing* a passage to Albany, the orders framed upon that plan could be no otherwise understood, than as positive, peremptory, and indispensible. But, Sir, it has been boldly insinuated, and perhaps even credited by some in this house, that the words at the latter end of the orders, which are called the saving clause, were specially dictated by me.---Sir, to suppose that, is to suppose me an ideot!---Saving clause---to whom? Surely, not to the General who was to act under it ;---for see the situation in which it puts him.----Under the words " you are to act as
" exigencies

"exigencies may require," let us suppose him to take the cautious part. He makes no attempt upon the enemy, because his *exigency* was such, that in doing so he must abandon his communications and risk his retreat. What would the government, the army, and the country have said to him? What ought every man to have said to him who read the prior part of this order? " Is this vigorous exertion? Is this
" to *force* your way to Albany. The enemy
" were panic struck before British troops;
" there numbers therefore were but as sha-
" dows. The loyalists awaited your advance
" to join by thousands—Sir H. Clinton was
" ready to move upon the lower part of Hud-
" son's river—Your interpretation of orders
" was nonsense; your inactivity was co-
" wardice—You have ignominiously lost the
" campaign."

Take the consideration the other way——The general follows the principle, the spirit, and the letter of his order—fights his ground by inches, and miscarries. " You shall be
" disgraced for your rashness," says the minister—" You had a reserve and should have
" made use of it. *Exigencies* required that
" you should have remained on the east side
" the Hudson's river." Sir, to imagine a

general

general could dictate such a dilemma for himself is preposterous. To believe that ministers could mean it, is severe credulity against them; it would be to believe them capable of the equivocation of a fiend, to insure the ruin of those who acted under their direction whatever part they should take. I charge them not so heavily. I am persuaded that saving clause was meant when it was penned, as it has been understood by me, by Sir William Howe, and by every other person who has read it, as referring solely to exigencies after the arrival of my army at Albany.

But, Sir, this ideal blame in not availing myself of the *saving clause*, has been supported by a story, that I should hardly have believed it within malevolence to invent, but which I find has been propagated with great industry, viz. that Generals Philips and Frazer remonstrated against the passage of the Hudson's River; and that finding their remonstrances of no avail, they took the parts of brave men in despair, and persevered in their duty against their reason. Upon the honor of a gentleman, without any saving or reservation soever, I pronounce that report to be a direct and abominable falsehood. Sir, those officers were the eyes and the hands by which I conducted

ducted all material operations: more able advisers, or more faithful friends, never existed that they saw. I was placed in an arduous situation, and felt for my difficulties, it is true; but that they ever dropt a syllable that implied an idea that I had an alternative, I flatly deny. The indefatigable alacrity of General Philips to bring forward the transports preparatory to the passage of the river, was uncommon even in support of a favourite object; it would have been uncommon indeed, had he acted with secret reluctancy! As to General Frazer, our communications were those of the most unreserved friendship; and it is my pride to affirm, that the consonancy of his sentiments with mine were almost invariable. Upon the passage of the Hudson's River, in particular, he thought it of uncontrovertible expediency; he thought it glorious danger; he was consulted upon all measures at the time and subsequent to it; he bore an active part in many; he approved of all; and the last sentence he uttered, was a message of affection and good wishes to me.

The other falsehoods that have been dispersed respecting the same period of time, can hardly be urged as reasons for enquiry, for they are below refutation; such as the delays
occasioned

occasioned by carrying forward *all* the artillery, and a cumberous train of baggage—" It was a merit of Eastern pomp," says a ministerial news-writer. That *all* the artillery was with the army is false, for the heavy train was sent back to Canada: the field-train which remained was that which had been destined for the expedition, when Sir Guy Carleton expected to have the conduct of it in person. That intelligent and judicious officer, General Philips, had been consulted upon the proportion; and it had been regulated upon the consideration of the nature of the war; the power of that arm in forcing posts, and against new troops; and the probability of having posts ourselves to fortify. Neither, Sir, was the artillery, in the proportion carried, cause of the least delay; because the horses that drew it were supernumerary to those which were sufficient for all the carts and waggons we had; and consequently within the time indispensibly given for the transport of the provision, the artillery was brought forward by horses that could have been no otherways employed.

The supposed quantity of baggage is equally erroneous. I cannot suffer an idea so unjust, to the spirit of the army, to remain upon the minds of the public. All baggage of bulk, to the abridgment of many material comforts, had been chearfully left behind by the officers; some of them had not beds; many lay in soldier's tents; and I know of none that had more then the common necessaries for active service.

It must be total want of knowledge of the country and the war, to suppose that, with all these precautions, the train of carriages did not still remain great. It is to be considered, there was a train of six hundred carriages; and those too few for the indispensible purpose of transporting provision, where there was no water carriage; there was another train of very cumberous carriages, equally necessary for the transport of the boats, where the rapids prevented their passage in the stream; a transport, in some places, of many miles in in length. Sir, it would be trifling with the house to dwell longer upon these censures, the offspring of malice and ignorance; the prevalence of such reports tends to one use---It will persuade the world, at least, that material faults could not abound, when detraction itself is reduced to have recourse to such accusation.

Sir, reverting therefore to the more gross injuries my reputation has sustained, I think I have

have ſtated enough to ſhew, that the character of a member has been unavoidably brought into queſtion, and upon his aſſertion that the information the Houſe has proceeded upon, is incomplete and fallacious, I know not what deſcription of men could juſtly refuſe to him perſonally a new and full enquiry.

I would aſk of miniſters themſelves, what would be their feelings, if, after an unſucceſsful undertaking of high truſt and importance, and debarred, by an interdiction, from the preſence of their Sovereign, the means of ſubmitting their conduct to that royal breaſt, where juſtice, and benevolence, and protection to the innocent are ever to be expected, except when truth is perverted or concealed—what would be their feelings if refuſed alſo an appeal to their country? To my brother-officers in parliament I would more particularly apply for ſupport to this amendment, as a common cauſe of the profeſſion: they will conſider the diſcouragement that muſt enſue, and the injury the ſervice muſt ſuffer, if an officer, who is conſcious to have done his beſt, whoſe greateſt enemies pretend not to impute to him any other charges than exceſs of zeal and erroneous judgment, and even theſe charges founded upon a mutilated ſtate of facts—

What is the state of officers, if upon such grounds, and by the artful management of other circumstances, they are disgraced at court, put by, if not inevitably precluded the judgment of a military tribunal, and at last denied the only possible means of justification that remains—a parliamentary investigation of a measure of state with which the rectitude or criminality of their conduct is inseparably blended? To my honourable friends who made the original motion early in the winter, and all who took part in it, I may yet more strenuously address myself, to repair, by the passing this question and amendment, the injury that unintentionally they brought upon me by the then confined mode of proceeding. To all these considerations, Sir, I could join, were it expedient, many more persuasive calls upon the human heart, to take up this proceeding for the sake of an injured individual: but I wave an appeal to private sentiments, and desire the motion to be considered as a call upon the public duty of the house; and, divesting myself, as far as possible, of every personal motive; scorning the pitiful contention, for such comparatively it would be, whether the minister should exonerate himself from *this* error in his instruction, or the general

from

from *that* in his execution; I here in my place as a reprefentative of the nation, require and demand a full and impartial enquiry into the caufes of the mifcarriage of the northern army in an expedition from Canada.

It is a great national object. The crifis of the time emphatically requires it. The exiftence of the Britifh empire depends upon the exertions of the military, and the beft foundation for public fpirit, is public juftice. In addition to the natural animation which as Britons the army poffefs, place before their eyes that fecondary fpring and controller of human actions, reward and punifhment. Let the firft and moft glorious reward, the honeft applaufe of the country be obtained by a fcrutiny into truth for thofe who deferve it: on the contrary, if there has been delinquency, let the fpirit of Manlius prefide in the punifhment.

" The hand of fate is over us, and heaven
" Exacts feverity from all our thoughts."

If there has been difobedience; if unauthorifed by circumftances, if *uncompelled by orders* (for I will never fhrink from that plea) a general has rafhly advanced upon the enemy, and engaged againft infurmountable odds, the difcipline of the ftate fhould ftrike, though it were a favourite fon.

I, Lictor

"*I, Lictor, deliga ad palum.*"

These, Sir, are the means to excite true ambition in your leaders, these are the means to keep them in due restraint; this was the system of the glorious patriot,* whose obsequies you now celebrate, and could his ashes awaken, they would burst their cearments to support it.

<small>Lord Chatham.</small>

As for myself, if I am guilty, I fear I am deeply guilty: an army lost! the sanguine expectation of the kingdom disappointed! a foreign war caused, or the commencement of it accelerated! an effusion of as brave blood as ever run in British veins shed, and the severest family distresses combined with public calamity.—If this mass of miseries be indeed the consequence of my misconduct, vain will be the extenuation I can plead of my personal sufferings, fatigue and hardship, laborious days and sleepless nights, ill health and trying situations; poor and insufficient will be such atonement in the judgment of my country, or perhaps in the eyes of God—yet with this dreadful alternative in view, I provoke a trial—Give me inquiry—I put the interests that hang most emphatically by the heart-strings of man—my fortune—my honour—my head—I had almost said my salvation, upon the test.

But, Sir, it is consolation to me to think that

that I shall be, even in surmise, the only culprit—Whatever fate may attend the general who led the army to Saratoga, their behaviour at that memorable spot must entitle them to the thanks of their country—Sir, it was a calamitous, it was an awful, but it was an honourable hour—During the suspence of the answer from the general of the enemy, to the refusal made by me of complying with the ignominious conditions he had proposed, the countenance of the troops beggars description—a patient fortitude; a sort of stern resignation, that no pencil or language can reach, sat on every brow. I am confident every breast was prepared to devote its last drop of blood rather than suffer a precedent to stand upon the British annals of an ignoble surrender.

Sir, an important subject of enquiry, as I mentioned at my out-set, still remains—the transactions at Cambridge, and the cause of the detention of the troops. If I there have been guilty, let me there also be the only sufferer.

Sir, there is a famous story in antient history, that bears some analogy to my circumstances; and when allusions tend to excite men's minds to exertions of virtue or policy, I shall never think them pedantic or misplaced.

ced.* The event I mean happened in an age when Roman virtue was at its height. It was that wherein Manlius devoted his son and the first Decius devoted himself. A Roman army, shut up by the Samnites at Candium, were obliged to surrender their arms, and to submit to the more ignominious condition of passing under the yoke of the enemy. The consul who had commanded them, proposed in the senate, to break the treaty whereby the army was lost to the state, and to make him in person the expiation, by sending him bound to the enemy to suffer death at their hands. In one point of view the present case extremely differs from the example, because by the treaty at Saratoga the army was saved to the state. It is the non-compliance with public faith that alone can lose it——and here the parallel will hold; if I have been instrumental to the loss of those brave troops *since* the treaty, I am as culpable as if I had lost them *by* the treaty, and ought to be the sacrifice to redeem them. Sir, this reference may appear vain-glorious. It may be doubted whether there exists in these times public

* It had been mentioned in a former debate, that references to ancient history carried sometimes an air of pedantry and were seldom of use.

spirit

spirit seriously to emulate such examples. I perhaps should find myself unequal; but others, who are most ready to judge me so, must at least give credit to one motive for stating the parallel—that I am too conscious of innocence to apprehend there is the least risk of being exposed to the trial.

Sir, I have only to return my sincerest thanks to the house for the patience with which they have endured so long a trespass upon their time, and to join my hearty concurrence with the other gentlemen who have spoken in favour of the amendment.

Jovis, 28°. *die Maii,* 1778.

MR. Hartley moved, "That an humble addrefs be prefented to his majefty to entreat his majefty, that he will be gracioufly pleafed not to prorogue the parliament; but that he will fuffer them to continue fitting, for the purpofe of affifting and forwarding the meafures already taken for the reftoration of peace in America; and that they may be in readinefs, in the prefent critical fituation and profpect of public affairs, to provide for every important event at the earlieft notice."

Sir George Savile feconded the motion. No perfon offering to anfwer, the Speaker was proceeding to put the queftion. General Burgoyne applied to the treafury-bench, to know whether the king's fervants meant to agree to the motion? In which cafe he faid he fhould give the houfe no trouble: that otherwife he thought hemfelf pledged to deliver his fentiments. The call was, "Go on;" and General Burgoyne proceeded in fubftance as follows:

Mr.

Mr. Speaker, I shall not purſue the argument of the honourable gentleman, upon the expediency of parliament being ready fitting to deliberate upon the firſt intelligence that may arrive from your commiſſioners; that argument has already been too ably enforced to require a ſecond: neither, Sir, after ſo long an indulgence as I received in a former debate, ſhall I again preſs upon the attention of the houſe the debt they owe to national juſtice and policy, upon the ſubject of enquiry: though the Generals Howe and Carleton may be expected every day; and it was upon their abſence alone, that the greater part of the houſe ſeemed diſpoſed to poſtpone ſo important and neceſſary a duty. But, Sir, I ſhall reſt ſolely upon a view of the preſent ſtate of this country, as univerſally compulſive upon the underſtanding, in favour of the meaſure propoſed. While an enemy is prepared upon the neighbouring coaſt, and perhaps is at this hour embarking, diffidence, deſpondency, and conſternation, are evident among great part of the people. A more fatal ſymptom prevails among a greater part; a torpid indifference to our impending fate. Men dare not, or will not, look into their deſperate circumſtances. God grant that general panic be not the

the refult of all thefe demonftrations! for panic is incident, upon fome occafions, to thofe who have been moft diftinguifhed for bravery upon others.

The falvation of the country depends upon the confidence of the people in fome part of government. The miniftry have it not; the whole nation fee, or think they fee, their infufficiency. I mean not to apply thefe words grofsly or virulently; there are among them many to whofe perfonal qualities and talents I bear refpect, and to none more than the noble lord in the blue ribband. But talents are relative to times; and it is no reproach to fay, that men well qualified for negotiation, finance, or the fmooth current of government, may be totally unfit for their ftations, when the crifis requires inftant refource, decifive counfel, animating action. That thefe are notoriously wanting, the beft friends of the minifters fhake their heads and confefs. Is there a man of common fenfe and common fpirit in the country, that does not ftand confounded and aghaft at the late fupinenefs? that does not think the heralds ought to have accompanied your coach, Sir, when you carried up the addrefs of the commons; and that the declaration of war at St. James's gate fhould have accompanied

panied the anfwer from the throne? " Be patient," we are told; " France may repent; Spain yet fpeaks us fair,"—Sir, to be patient in our fituation is to be abject: our pufillanimity gives tenfold encreafe to our natural weaknefs. Patience in private life, under affliction or difeafe, the ftrokes of fortune, or the hand of heaven, is a virtue of lovely hue; but political enduring—tamely to fuffer provocation and injury,—the moft wanton infult that ever was offered to a nation,—I mean the meffage of the French ambaffador:

——————————Turn thy complexion there,
Patience, thou young and rofe-lipp'd cherubin,
And there look grim as hell.———

It will be difficult to thofe who are moft converfant in hiftory, and accurate in obfervation, to point out examples, where, after an alarm, the fpirits of men have revived by inaction. This nation is put into the ftate of a garrifon, whofe out-pofts are abandoned, whofe fallies are ftopt, and who are to combat in the body of the place for their laft ftake. I do not fay, that men have not fought defperately in fuch fituations; but then they have been brought to extremity by a progreffion of conflicts, and have feen great examples to raife and
ftimulate

stimulate their public paffions. I know of no great exertions, where the governing counfels have fhewn apprehenfion and terror, and confequent confufion at the outfet. The fuccefs of vigorous meafures to reftore an army after a panic, is almoft invariable; ancient hiftory abounds with examples; in our own time, they are frequent. When General Romanzoff found the Ruffians impreffed with apprehenfions of the Turkifh cavalry, his firft meafure was to lay afide the ufe of chevaux de frize, and to encamp without entrenchments. The revival of the general fpirit of a ftate depends upon the fame principles. We need not look abroad for examples; we have a more ftriking one at home than foreign annals can produce, in that immortal year, 1756, the commencement of the Earl of Chatham's adminiftration. The moft glorious tribute we can pay to his memory, is to follow his example. Let minifters vifit his remains, while yet above ground, and catch wifdom, and vigour, and virtue from the view. Did he keep fleets at Spithead to prevent invafion? Did he fear to truft the internal defence of the nation to her own fons? No, Sir, your navy was employed in offenfive operation in every quarter of the globe; and the nation, fupported by

a juft

a juſt confidence, were ten times ſtronger after the difmiſſion of the Hanoverians and Heſſians than before. Every ſhip became a fleet, every regiment felt itſelf an hoſt.

We have now a brave admiral riding at Spithead, who knows the way to prevent invaſion by ſeeking the enemy at a diſtance. His ſhare of glory in the defeat of Conflans is on the minds of his followers; you cannot gratify him or them more than to give them a ſecond occaſion, and by the ſame means, to ſave their country. The brother of that admiral, a member of this houſe,* bred alſo in the beſt ſchools of his profeſſion, is ſecond in command on ſhore, and ſecond to one who needs no other praiſe than that he was the favourite, † and the friend, and the confidential executor of the arduous plans of the great ſtateſman I alluded to.—Let theſe men be aſſiſted with national ſpirit, and England is not to be ſubdued, while a river or a hill remains; without ſuch ſpirit, another battle of Haſtings may make another conqueſt.

Sir, I repeat that the beſt hope of generating and diffuſing this genuine ſtrength of the mind, to which arms and treaſure are but inadequate ſubſtitutes, depends upon the preſence of parliament, " to provide (according to the

* General Keppel.

† Lord Anſon berſt.

words

words of the motion) for every important event at the earlieſt notice,"—To ſtrengthen the crown, not by adulatory addreſſes, but by ſuch occaſional ſanctions, as would give freſh and extra-energy to its power, pending the emergency that might require it: To ſupport public credit, in union with the city of London, not only by common engagements of faith, but by acts of quick and encouraging efficacy towards individuals, who might nobly riſk their all in the cauſe: but above all, in full numbers and by general continuance, to exhibit themſelves to the world a true repreſentative of a determined people attacked in their vitals;—to prove that they are not to be ſeduced from their duty by the allurements of pleaſure or perſonal intereſt, but have fortitude to await the approach of the enemy, as the Gauls were awaited by the ſenators in Rome; and, if need were, to receive death in theſe ſeats, to give example and fire to their ſurviving countrymen. Sir, a parliament, thus inſpired, (the occaſion, I believe in my conſcience, would give the inſpiration) would ſpread immediate and extenſive veneration and influence.—Faction in this great city, if faction there is, would be no more;—majorities and minorities here would

be

be loft in unanimity for the public fafety;— the King's name, thus fupported, would be in truth a tower of ftrength; and the daring attempts of the enemy would only tend to the prefent glory and future ftability of the ftate.

Sir, thefe are my fincere fentiments; and for this free delivery of them, I doubt not that I fhall read in the morning papers of to-morrow that I have thrown myfelf into the arms of oppofition. I am confcious I never did fo true a fervice to the king and to the country as I do in the part I now take; and whatever may be the idle comments of the day, I truft that with the refpectable part of the public, if the term *oppofition* is to imply blame, it will be applicable only to the rejection of this motion. If the king's minifters take the lead, and exercife their perfuafion for that purpofe, I hold them to be oppofers of national fpirit, oppofers of public virtue, oppofers of the moft efficacious means to fave their country. Sir, I fcorn to take up this language upon fo pitiful a motive as perfonal refentment. Government, whoever are the minifters to conduct it, fhall have my voice when my confcience directs it. That I think myfelf a perfecuted man, I avow;

that I am a marked victim to bear the sins that do not belong to me, I apprehend; but this is not the first time I have stood the frowns of power for parliamentary conduct; and whatever further vengeance may be in store for me, I hope I shall endure it as becomes me. I am aware that in far better times officers have been stript of their preferments for resisting the possessors of that bench.—They cannot take from me an humble competence; they cannot deprive me of a qualification to fit here; they cannot strip me, I trust they cannot, of the confidence of my constituents to seat me here; they cannot strip me——I am sure they cannot——of principle and spirit to do my duty here.

I never was more excited by these motives, and I never can be more, than upon the present occasion to give my vote in support of the motion.

APPEN-

APPENDIX.

Copy of a Letter from General Washington *to Lieutenant General* Burgoyne.

Head-Quarters, Pensylvania,
March 11*th*, 1778.

SIR,

I Was, only two days since, honoured with your very obliging letter of the 11th of February.

Your indulgent opinion of my character, and the polite terms in which you are pleased to express it, are peculiarly flattering; and I take pleasure in the opportunity you have afforded me of assuring you, that, far from suffering the views of national opposition to be imbittered and debased by personal animosity, I am ever ready to do justice to the merit of the gentleman and the soldier; and to esteem, where esteem is due, however the idea of a public enemy may interpose. You will not think it the language of unmeaning ceremony, if I add, that sentiments of personal respect, in the present instance, are reciprocal.

APPENDIX.

Viewing you in the light of an officer contending againſt what I conceive to be the rights of my country, the reverſe of fortune you experienced in the field cannot be unacceptable to me; but, abſtracted from confiderations of national advantage, I can fincerely ſympathize with your feelings, as a ſoldier, the unavoidable difficulties of whoſe fituation forbid his fucceſs; and as a man, whoſe lot combines the calamity of ill health, the anxieties of captivity, and the painful ſenſibility for a reputation, expoſed, where he moſt values it, to the aſſaults of malice and detraction.

As your aid de camp went directly on to Congreſs, the bufineſs of your letter to me had been decided before it came to hand. I am happy that their chearful acquieſcence with your requeſt, prevented the neceſſity of my intervention. And, wiſhing you a fafe and agreeable paſſage, with a perfect reſtoration of your health,

   I have the honour to be,
    Very reſpectfully,
     Sir,
   Your moſt obedient ſervant,
    GEO. WASHINGTON.

NOTE,

APPENDIX.

NOTE, *respecting the First Debate.*

SINCE the substance of the speech has been prepared for the press, it has been observed, in a daily paper, that General Burgoyne stated, that it had been a race between the Congress and him, to engage the Indian nations. It is a mistake, that General Burgoyne made any mention of himself being any ways concerned in any negotiations with the Indians, prior to giving directions for their junction with the army upon Lake Champlain; excepting in the council of the autumn to 1776, in which they were dismissed for that year.

It is true, General Burgoyne did state, in his speech, that there had been a race between the emissaries of the Congress, and the conductors of India affairs on the part of the British government; to engage not only the contiguous, but also the remote nations. This fact might have been proved by Mr. St. Luc le Corne, had he thought proper, as well as by many others.

This part of the Indian subject accidentally escaped the press, by its being omitted in the notes from which the speech was collected.

NOTE,

APPENDIX.

NOTE, *respecting the Second Debate.*

MR. Wedderburne took occasion, after a short argument against the expediency of the motion, to propound *doubts* relative to General Burgoyne's capacity to vote in parliament; and he argued them, at length, with visible preparation, and much learning. He referred, very particularly, to the story of Regulus; and, to make the cases parallel, stated the General as a common prisoner of war (the convention of Saratoga being broke); that, consequently, he was not *sui juris,* but the present property of another power. He insisted, with still less expression of doubt, that the General, under his present obligations, was incapacitated from exercising any office, or bearing arms in this country.

General Burgoyne, in reply, stated the mistake upon which Mr. Wedderburne's argument was in great measure founded, viz. that the convention was *broke,* and that the General was under the usual restrictions of a prisoner of war. The convention was declared by the congress not intended to be broke, on their part; though the execution of it was suspended. The General therefore insisted, that he was under no other obligation, than that

APPEENDIX.

that fpecified in the convention, "Not to serve in America;" and that of his parole, "To return at the demand of the congrefs, and due notice given": that in this country he was free to exercife his rights as a citizen and a foldier; that fhould the enemy land, though his prefent disfavour might preclude him from the command which his rank, and fome experience, might entitle him to, he trufted the king would not refufe his requefi, to take a mufquet in defence of his country. He proceeded to argue, that even upon the fuppofition that Mr. Wedderburne's pofition had been true in its full extent, and that he had been, *directly*, a prifoner of war under parole, he fhould not have been incapacitated from acting in parliament; and in anfwer to the precedents brought from remote ages, he produced one of a prefent member (Lord Frederick Cavendifh) who, when a prifoner to France, after the action at St. Cas, and upon his parole in England, fat and voted in parliament. That noble lord, upon quitting France, had afked, whether any refiraint in that refpect was meant? as he fhould certainly vote for every meafure that could diftrefs the enemy—He was told, that they fhould as foon think of refiraining him from getting a
child,

APPENDIX.

child, left, when it came to maturity, it should do them mischief.

The General proceeded to observe, that the cases, in point of explanation, were precisely the same; for that before he left the army, it had been intimated to him, that there were persons, *in Boston*, who *doubted* whether he should not be restrained by parole from taking any part in parliament, at least, when America was concerned; that he came to an explanation with those entrusted with the sentiments and powers of the congress; and declared, that if such restraint was intended, he would remain and die in that country, rather than return home—The idea was abolished; nay, more, it was expressed, that the friends of the congress conceived rather advantage than injury from the General's presence in parliament; that they wished for peace upon proper terms; that they were persuaded, the General, as a man of humanity, wished the same; that they believed he had honour to speak truth; and that truth would conduce to that desirable end.

After this explanation, Mr. Wedderburne acknowledged no doubts remained upon the General's rights; and the house were unanimous in the same opinion.

FINIS.

Boquhan

SPEECH

OF

GEORGE DALLAS, Esq.

SPEECH

OF

GEORGE DALLAS, Esq.

MEMBER OF THE COMMITTEE APPOINTED BY
THE BRITISH INHABITANTS RESIDING IN
BENGAL, FOR THE PURPOSE OF

PREPARING PETITIONS

TO

HIS MAJESTY

AND BOTH

HOUSES OF PARLIAMENT,

PRAYING REDRESS

AGAINST AN ACT OF PARLIAMENT, &c.

As delivered by him at a Meeting held at the THEATRE, in
CALCUTTA, on the 25th of JULY, 1785.

CALCUTTA, PRINTED.

LONDON: REPRINTED for J. DEBRETT, opposite
Burlington House, Piccadilly.

SPEECH

OF

GEORGE DALLAS, Esq.

Gentlemen,

CONSCIOUS as I feel myself of my own want of importance, unpractised as I am in the arts of public elocution, and surrounded by several whose superior powers might well discourage the temerity of thus challenging your attention, it is not to be wondered at that I should feel myself considerably affected in attempting to address so numerous and respectable a society, and that the agitation inseparable from the novelty of my situation should deprive me of that

calm-

calmness and recollection I could wish to preserve upon so momentous and interesting an occasion.

Assembled as we now are, to deliberate upon measures of the utmost consequence to the future interests of this society, the moment is an awful one, and the call is equally solemn; the eye of the nation will be upon us; and possibly the leaders in this day's debate may have courted a perilous pre-eminence: but I shall never decline the hazard, where the approbation of my own heart, and the applause of the good and wise, may follow the attempt. I am sensible that many, adverting to my youth, and to the superiority of their own claims to the honour I have thus presumptuously assumed, will arraign the propriety of my rushing into public notice, and pressing forward to distinguish myself by an animadversion upon the measures of Government at home. In my own conscious humility of talent and situation, I anticipate, in some measure, the aptitude of their observations; but from your candour and indulgence,

I also

I also derive a confidence which emboldens me to proceed; for there are, Gentlemen, certain occasions when the meanest individual may feel his indignation awakened, and, spirited by a sense of public wrongs, may boldly step forth in the hope of being serviceable to the community, by sedulously labouring to promote their redress. This I humbly apprehend to be one of those; and stimulated by this persuasion, I will venture to expose myself to all the severity of remark. If, in the course of our present deliberations, I should be flattered by your attention, and honoured with your support, I shall then, for the moment, rise in my own estimation, and, protected by your approbation, feel myself shielded from the acrimony of attack.

The importance of the subject on which I am now presuming to address you, a subject which most nearly interests both your honour and your fortunes, does in itself preclude the necessity of farther apology on my part, a consideration which I am confident will find its excuse in every impartial breast, dictated, as it is,

by

by a warm concern for the prefervation of our characters, as men; of our conftitutional and unalienable rights, as Britons.

It is not, I apprehend, neceffary to inform any gentleman prefent, that by the Act of Parliament lately arrived in this fettlement, and paffed in the twenty-fourth year of his prefent Majefty's reign, entitled, " An act for the bet-
" ter regulation and management of the affairs
" of the Eaft-India Company, and of the Bri-
" tifh poffeffions in India; and for eftablifhing
" a Court of Juftice for the more fpeedy and
" effectual trial of perfons accufed of offences
" committed in the Eaft Indies," a new and unheard-of judicature has been eftablifhed in England: a judicature as arbitrary in its powers, as it is illegal in its original principles; tending to deprive us of that ineftimable bleffing, the glory of our conftitution, the right of trial by a jury of our peers. A judicature which daringly violates our great charter, the palladium of our liberties, and feems defigned to extend the iron hand of oppreffion over thofe chiefly

who

who may be so unfortunate as to fall under the stigma of having served the East-India Company.

This act, so generally known by the name of "Mr. Pitt's Bill," and which has excited universal discontent throughout our settlements in India, is one of those bold attempts to violate the purity of our constitution, which have been too often made during the late unhappy fluctuation in our councils: it is true, necessity, the plea of tyrants to palliate every enormity, has been urged in vindication of its birth; but have the united efforts of falsehood, prejudice, and faction (and they have all been exerted) been able to establish its existence to the conviction of one reasonable or impartial mind? I reply, they have not. In proportion, then, as the innovation was glaring and injurious, that necessity which alone could vindicate the principle of this act should have been clear and apparent; and none but the most urgent and self-displayed should have authorised so open a violation of our ancient jurisprudence, or warranted

ranted so odious and humiliating a distinction between ourselves and the rest of our fellow subjects on that island from whence this oppressive act dates its existence. It is by encroachments like these, that our constitution will be ultimately determined; and that, in losing the dignified title of freemen, we shall cease to be considered as a great and respectable people, and forfeit the envy of surrounding nations.

Were the Minister to say to me, Sir, what are your objections to my bill? I would tell him, Sir, I object to it upon solid and unanswerable grounds—I would tell him, that it is ill fitted to remedy the evil it is designed to eradicate; that the violence of its principle must destroy the effect that it was intended to produce; and that, in alienating our affections from the parent state, it must ultimately endanger the security of the British possessions in the East—I would tell him, that it wantonly deprives us of those rights, inherent in us, as subjects of the British empire; and that no class of men should

be

be disfranchised of their privileges, without an adequate proof being exhibited of their delinquency to sanctify so painful a proscription—I would tell him, that such is the opinion of one of the brightest characters that illumines the present age, I mean the Earl of Mansfield, whose superior wisdom all admire, and whose extensive knowledge all respect. This venerable and enlightened sage, in arguing against the Cricklade Bill, in the House of Lords, on the 13th of May, 1782, (which had for its object to deprive the electors of their privileges) armed with the powers of eloquence and truth, particularly said, " That the House were not " competent to punish a community indiscri-" minately, without evidence being produced " at their bar, amounting to a conviction of " guilt; that supposition was an illegal plea to " warrant the infliction of pains and penalties." Lord Thurlow, as celebrated for his wisdom as for the unvaried manliness of his conduct, was also of a similar opinion, and forcibly cautioned the House against " violating rights made " venerable by time, and sanctified by the ap-
" pro-

" probation of our anceftors." With authorities like thefe to produce, I would tell him, I hefitate not to combat the principal of his bill in all its parts, and to exclaim againft the tyranny of its intent—I would tell him, in oppofition to it, we have many acts of the legiflature to produce, which have ever been held facred until now, and which our anceftors wifely defigned as a fence againft the predatory inroads of unreftrained ambition, or the lawlefs invafions of unbridled power. Firft, the Conftitutions of Clarendon, in the time of Henry the Second; fecondly, Magna Charta, in the reign of King John; thirdly, the Petition of Rights, in the reign of Charles the Firft; and, laftly, the Bill of Rights, upon the acceffion of William and Mary. With refpect to Magna Charta, that noble pillar of our freedom, it was confirmed thirty feveral times by the three eftates, and even fecured by a law, (the forty-fourth of Edward the Third) which pofitively declared, " That
" no ftatute which fhould be afterwards enact-
" ed in contradiction to any article of that
" charter fhould ever have any force or vali-
" dity."

"dity." And is not this act enacted in opposition to that law, and in violation of that charter? And should it, then, possess force or validity? Where is the necessity of making laws, if they are to be trampled upon by the very people whom the nation delegate to frame them? That law has never been repealed. If, then, it is now to be considered as an unrevoked deed of the state, am I not warranted in saying, that even the law of the land authorizes us to reprobate the provisions of this act, which unconstitutionally and illegally trench upon our honour and our fortunes; for that law must be first repealed, before this act can be justly said to possess that constitutional legality which should bind us to yield it obedience. In the Bill of Rights delivered by the Lords and Commons, on the 16th of February, 1689, to the Prince and Princess of Orange, are these memorable words: " And they do claim, demand, and " insist, upon all and singular the premises, as " their undoubted rights and liberties." And the Act of Parliament itself, (1. W. & M. stat. 2. c. 2.) specially recognizes, " All and sin-
" gular

" gular the rights and liberties, afferted and
" claimed, in the faid declaration, to be free,
" ancient, and indubitable rights of the people
" of this kingdom." And are we not fubjects
of that kingdom? Are we not, by this act, deprived of thofe rights? Are we not cut off from
the enjoyment of thofe privileges, which at the
period of that glorious Revolution were defigned to be a national bleffing for us all? I
therefore call this ftatute, an act of power againſt
the ancient law of the land; violent in its operation; illegal in its principle; and calculated
to brand, and irritate, by adding infult to injury,
and gilding oppreffion with the forms of juftice.

Such, Gentlemen, are my objections to the
general principle of this act. Many others, of
equal force, will, doubtlefs, occur to your own
imaginations. I will now proceed to urge a few
others, which more immediately affect your private interefts, by pointing out fuch parts of the
act as appear to me particularly hoftile to them.

By

By the fifty-fifth claufe of this act, all the Company's fervants are required, within two months after their arrival in England, to deliver in, to certain officers of Government, inventories of their whole real and perfonal eftates. Having fo done, by the fixty-firft claufe, incitements, and rewards to a capital amount, are liberally held forth to all informers; and, as if this benign mode of collecting evidence againft thefe oriental plunderers, thefe prejudged delinquents, were not fufficient to facilitate its acquifition, by the feventy-fifth claufe, the father, the brother, the fon, the bofom friend, is to be compelled, by the terror of heavy penalties, to violate the ties of friendfhip, and to turn the accufer of thofe with whom he may ftand connected in the deareft and moft confidential relations of life.

By the fifty-fixth claufe.—For the fpace of three years after his return to his native land, the devoted Eaft Indian is to ftand in a predicament unheard of in our hiftory, and hitherto unexperienced by any Britifh fubject, holding his eftate almoft at the mercy of the Minifter,

to

to whom, if he is obnoxious by any parliamentary oppofition, a door is opened for bending the laws to the purpofes of private vengeance.

If, during that fpace of time, any accufations are lodged againft him, he becomes fubjected to all the miferies of imprifonment; during which he is to be excluded from the ufe of his eftate; and, after all, by the fixty-fixth claufe, he is to fubmit his honour and his fortune to the award of a tribunal, not cafually nominated from among his countrymen in general, but felected from a particular defcription of men, confifting of a mixture of officers of the Crown, and hereditary nobles, and members of the Houfe of Commons, with this invidious exception, in the feventieth claufe, that no perfon who has ferved the Company can be a member thereof; although, from that circumftance alone, he might reafonably be fuppofed (where equality of ability prevailed) to be in poffeffion of fuperior qualifications to entitle him to this proof of confidence from his country. Neither, in the courfe of the profecution, is this tribunal

tribunal confined to thofe modes of proceeding which are cuftomary in all other cafes of criminal jurifdiction. It is not to the refpectability of its members we object; the moft prejudiced muft admit the probability that a fuperior rectitude of conduct and generofity of principle will influence their proceedings; becaufe juftice and liberality are the attributes of minds enlightened by fcience and enlarged by education. It is the inftitution itfelf, and the authority it affumes, which we reprobate, as oppofite to the genius of the Conftitution, and calculated to deftroy the beauty of its fabric. Every innovation upon its foundation is dangerous, and fhould be guardedly watched; for let it be remembered, with exulting pride, that the Conftitution of Great Britain is a bleffing not common to all, but peculiarly intailed upon the pofterity of Englifhmen; which they are bound, by every obligation binding upon fociety, to tranfmit to their defcendants in the fame pure and inviolate manner in which it was bequeathed to them by their anceftors, many of whom bled, and died, to permanate its fuperftructure,

C and

and to give it a stability beyond the accidents of time.

That guarded care with which our excellent laws protect the life and property of the meanest subject, has provided with respect to even the most notorious criminal, that he shall be tried upon the oath of his accuser, delivered face to face in an open court, so as to afford him every fair opportunity to invalidate his testimony. This has for ages been established as a fundamental maxim in our jurisprudence; but here, by the eightieth clause, " All writings which " shall have been transmitted from the East " Indies to the Court of Directors of the said " United Company, by their officers or servants " resident in the East Indies, may be admitted " to be offered in evidence ;" so that the persecuted prisoner, having no opportunity of seeing or cross-examining his accuser, is placed in the same predicament with the unhappy criminal who stands before the secret tribunal at Venice, or the bench of the Holy Office at Lisbon; and this is particularly alarming from the known and

proverbial

proverbial indifference with which the natives of this country will confent to perjure themfelves, if they can, by this means, gratify refentment, acquire patronage, or obtain pecuniary advantage.

I know it will be afferted that the guilty alone will have any caufe to dread the excercife of this new judicial authority; but let no man fuppofe that the pureft innocence will avail (as the matter at prefent ftands) to protect him from incurring all the penalties of the blackeft guilt. At any period within the allotted fpace of time after the return of a Company's fervant to Europe, fhould the moft profligate and abandoned villain, with a view to the gratification of malice, or the fruition of reward, think proper to prefer an accufation againft him, it refts at the arbitrary option of the Court of Exchequer to imprifon his perfon, and to place the whole of his fortune in a ftate of temporary fequeftration, and in this fituation he is to remain, if they deem it expedient, until fuch evidence may be procured from India as may be fufficient either to acquit him, or to substantiate the charge. By the fifty-seventh clause he is disabled from alleviating his miseries by an enlargement upon bail, as in all other cases, (I believe) except those of felony or treason. The act, though it cherishes perfidy, affords no redress against false information. No specific time is limited, as in the cases of general jail delivery, for the virtual acquittal of the accused for want of evidence; and the charge once made, and admitted by the Court of Exchequer, he may continue to languish for years within his dungeon, torn from his family, doomed in lonely anguish to breathe a wretched existence — all the blossoms of his hope blighted! — all the happiness of his life obstructed and destroyed!

The principles upon which this jurisdiction is established, are equally illegal and absurd, and, in many points, directly contradictory to the spirit of those laws which form the bulwark of our freedom.

In every other instance, innocence is supposed until conviction; but here the idea is totally reversed, and assumed guilt precedes accusation.

In every other instance, the highest authority in the state dare not attempt forcibly, or unfairly, to procure evidence against a suspected person; but here, before there is even room for suspicion, we are compelled to furnish matter for prosecution against ourselves.

Even in cases of notorious criminality, the culprit who is arraigned at the bar of his country, so far from being necessitated to answer interrogatories tending to criminate himself, (as this act binds us to do) is particularly cautioned to avoid a confession of his guilt; and should he plead guilty when put upon his defence, his Judges are the first to advise him to retract his declaration. An avowal of culpability thus obtained, can only be compared to a confession wrung by the force of torture. Indeed the latter mode would leave the accused an option of preserving his property for the benefit of his family,

family, by a patient fubmiffion to the agony of pain; whereas the former, by an awful appeal to his confcience, and the irrefiftable force of a religious obligation, compels him to be the unhappy inftrument of his own deftruction. This argument, I admit, will only apply to the fituation of the guilty; but even criminals have rights which equity and humanity refpect.

How different the fentiments of a Committee of the Britifh Senate once were, I will now proceed to fhew.

In the year 1781 Commiffioners were appointed by Parliament to examine, take, and ftate the public accounts of the kingdom. In the month of June, 1782, they delivered in their firft Report; in which (after forcibly ftating the difficulties to which they are expofed in the purfuit of evidence to complete their inveftigation) they fay, " By what means then are " we to detect (if fuch there have been) pecu-
" lation, fraud, or mifapplication? for we ad-
" mit no charge againft perfons abroad, who
" have

" have no opportunity of being heard in their
" own defence; and we are cautious that our
" examination does not lead to self-accusation."

These were the manly, generous effusions of liberal minds, who scorned to bend to persecution, or even to detect misconduct by the perpetration of injustice. But what was the language of the honourable framer of this act himself, when a Minister of unprecedented talents fell from his office in the attempt to introduce another of a tendency less injurious to the rights of individuals, and the interests of society? He said, " Let the honourable gentleman beware, " that in attempting to protect the natives of " India in their rights, he does not violate those " of his countrymen." How forcibly do these words recoil upon himself! how immediately do they apply to his own act, which not merely violates, but directly destroys those rights! In these times, a consistency of conduct, in political life, is a phenomenon rarely to be met with. Men's opinions are too apt to veer upon the triumphs of party, or the disappointments of

aspiring

aspiring expectation; and those Spartan sentiments which delude the unsuspicious, and favour the purposes of the day in the career to station, too often vanish from the statesman's mind in the hour of successful ambition. He then discerns the difference between the theory and the practice of power, and dazzled by the charms of his situation, exultingly vindicates the apostacy of his principles, by exclaiming to his opponents, *Non sum qualis eram!* " *Tempora* " *mutantur et nos mutamur in illis.*"

But if any farther authority were necessary in proof of the illegality of this act, I need only refer you to the Protest of the dissenting Lords for a full exposition of its fatal aim; a protest which does honour to their feelings as men, adds lustre to their characters as senators, and registers them upon the records of their country the illustrious guardians of liberty, and the generous protectors of the oppressed.

To concentrate, therefore, all the injurious tendencies of this arbitrary act,

This

This novel act deprives us of our right of trial by a conftitutional jury:

This novel act deprives us of our participation in the ineftimable act of Habeas Corpus:

This novel act deprives us of our option, and compels us to appear as evidence againft our deareft friends. It, therefore, loofens the bands of fociety, extinguifhes the firft affections of the heart, and tends to convert the neareft relations of life to fnares of difhonour and deftruction:

This novel act is ftained with illiberality, and pregnant with defpotifm. It taints the effence of the Conftitution; it poifons the fource of freedom; it deftroys the foundation of thofe liberties which are at once the pride and glory of our country:

And, finally, it introduces an idea which even the Minifter, in the plentitude of his power, and the precipitation of his projects, hath

hath not dared to avow — that by entering into the fervice of the Eaft-India Company, we have relinquifhed all our moſt valuable privileges as members of the Britifh empire.

If thefe are grievances, it is fufficient to ſtate the fact; it is impoffible to err in the comment, that they demand redrefs: for certainly this nefarious act can be viewed in no other light than as a libel upon the fervice in general, and upon all others who may have been attracted to the country by a fpirit of commercial enterprife; and if we fubmit to it *fub filentio*, our filence will doubtlefs be confidered as an acquiefcence in the juſtice of its afperfion. It, therefore, behoves us to exert every juſt and conftitutional means to promote its repeal, and to vindicate our characters to the world from the unmerited obloquy to which it dooms them; for what will be the inevitable refult of our patient acquiefcence but an implication of our culpability? Will not pofterity confider, that in our criminality originated this wound to the Conftitution, and that our vices forged the firft link of

flavery's

slavery's chain? Will they not devote us to deathless execration? Will they not consign us to never-dying infamy? It is then that the irritated historian of these times shall glowingly record our baseness upon the unperishable page of history, and awaken the indignation of future generations against us! It is then that he shall imprint upon the tablet of their memory this painful tale — that, at such a period, there existed a race of British subjects in India, whose rapacity was so unbounded, whose cruelty was so unparalleled, and whose offences were so deeply enormous, that even the common law of the land, hitherto found adequate to the trial and punishment of a murderer, was deemed insufficient for the conviction of these more flagitious delinquents; and that, in order to bring their offences within the pail of punishment, it was necessary to violate *Magna Charta*, and to convulse that glorious fabric of British freedom which has long been the applauding theme of admiring ages! It is then that we shall be loaded with the bitterest curses of nations unborn in ages to come!

But

But what will be the confequence of governing thefe diftant countries upon fuch narrow and oppreffive principles? Many, loathing the ingratitude of their countrymen, will expatriate themfelves for ever, and become attached to thefe climes, whilft others will emigrate into foreign countries to live beneath the protection of milder laws. That is no country to me that does not cherifh, fofter, and protect me in all my native rights, in my honeft fame—my liberty, and fortune! Here the beautiful apoftrophe of Mr. Addifon, in his epiftle to Lord Halifax, rufhes upon my mind with captivating force, and charms me to repeat it.

O Liberty, thou goddefs heavenly bright!
Profufe of blifs, and pregnant with delight,
Eternal pleafures in thy prefence reign,
And fmiling plenty leads thy wanton train
Eas'd of her load, fubjection grows more light,
And poverty looks chearful in thy fight;
Thou mak'ft the gloomy face of nature gay,
Giv'ft beauty to the fun, and pleafure to the day.

Independently,

Independently, then, of the tie of family connection, what is it that renders our native country peculiarly dear to us, but the blessing of living under a free government? Deprive us of that enjoyment, and there are few countries in Europe which do not offer superior comforts; for if, upon our return to Great Britain, we become cultivators of the soil, one half of the produce of our estates will be swallowed up in a variety of taxes, to support that pressure of national distress under which the state has been long sinking. But this is not the case in any other country to which we may retire. Therefore, unless the exceptionable parts of this act are repealed, England will inevitably sustain a considerable loss of subjects, and of wealth, at a period when most she has occasion for the support of both to aid in reviving her faded honours, and to lighten the burden of her unweildy debt. How much, then, does it become the wisdom and equity of Administration to reflect soberly and dispassionately upon these circumstances, and, by redressing our grievances, to guard against the probability of their happening! Faction has too long usurped

the

the reins of Government; but now, that in degrading her country, her triumph has been complete, it is time that milder reason should re-assume her gentle sway. Whither shall we fly to avoid oppression, in the event of the continuation of this new and odious power, can never be the question of a moment; for o'er the wide range of Europe, see foreign liberality extended to shield us from these intemperate gusts of ministerial persecution! There unreviled by faction, and unexposed to the capricious frown of authority, we shall tranquilly enjoy our estates; and, viewing at a distance the increasing gales of national contention, we may calmly bid defiance to their turbulency and force!

It might, Gentlemen, have been expected, that the institution of a tribunal, the nature of which is utterly subversive of every idea of civil liberty to those upon whom its despotic powers are meant to be exercised, subversive of the hereditary freedom and chartered rights of Englishmen, would, on the very first proposal of it in Parliament, have met with that determined and
effectual

effectual oppofition which fo alarming a meafure deferved, and that its authors, in wounding the conftitution, would have been expofed to the refentment of an infulted nation. But the minds of men in England were prepared for the event; their feelings were irritated by the artful and captivating declamation of popular fpeakers, their pity was awakened by the fabulous recital of imaginary diftrefs, and their judgements were warped by the intemperance of public debate, which, at that period, generally diffufed itfelf throughout the nation. Every bafe art to which malevolence could have recourfe was adopted to calumniate and revile us; and it was during the tumultuous phrenzy which enfued upon the triumph of paffion over reafon, that the nation were deluded into a meafure as injurious to our rights as it is fatally dangerous to their own—a meafure that, in the cooler moment of returning reafon, muft appear to them fraught with impending danger, and ftrikingly calculated to produce the downfall of the Conftitution. For the fame arguments which have been ufed by the Miniftry, in the prefent inftance, will equally apply

ply to every diſtant part of their dominions; and in this is eſtabliſhed a precedent on which any daring and profligate Adminiſtration may, at ſome future period, found the neceſſity of a ſimilar mode of judicature for the detection of guilt, and the puniſhment of offences in the other dependencies of the empire; and thus will become confirmed a ſyſtem of legiſlative deſpotiſm which will, in a ſhort time, pierce the Conſtitution to its vitals. The moment that ſuch inquiſitorial courts are tolerated, and their proceedings ſo generally admitted of by Britons, the inſtant that ſuch tribunals ſhall thus become, and be regarded as a component part of the Conſtitution, farewel to our boaſted freedom! to that birthright, and to thoſe privileges which give us our proper rank in the ſcale of nations! The whole glorious fabric will at once diſapear, and leave nor a trace behind it, except the ſad remembrance, that Britiſh liberty had once exiſted!

And ſhall we be the firſt, who ſervilely bending to the yoke, who quietly acquieſcing in the
arbitrary

arbitrary difpenfation of an ambitious Minifter, and an oppreffive fenate, being to overthrow the freedom of our native foil, and tamely wear the galling chain of defpotifm ? No ! I truft, that the fpirit which we have inherited from our anceftors will ftill continue to hold its influence in our minds, and that we fhall be able to evince to our deluded countrymen, and to the world at large, that the relaxing influence of the climate has not fo far debilitated our hearts, or weakened our underftandings, as to induce us to permit any power on earth to encroach upon our rights as men, and as Englifhmen, in paffive filence ; or that we are fo loft to every fenfe of honour, to every regard for perfonal dignity, as to ftand with patience before a tribunal where our characters are to be put to the rack—where dark informers beckoned by the hand of power, with an interefted malignity, and a perjury heedlefs, becaufe fecure, may, at any time, lay proftrate the honour of our lives, and ftrip us of the produce of our labours—and where we are to be dependent upon the mercy of a court whofe jurifdiction ftands counter to the ordinances of our anceftors, and whofe judgement every other Englifhman would feel himfelf impelled by that inborn fpirit of freedom which fuperfedes all law, to fcorn and reject! Rather than degrade ourfelves fo low, we ought to relinquifh our national attachment, and obliterate from our minds every early prepoffeffion in favour of a country that has expofed us to fuch contumely! Tell me, Gentlemen, fhall the people of England, bleft with every advantage of climate, fociety of friends, the mutual interchange of family affection, trample thus wantonly upon thofe who, by the facrifice of every fond tie, of every dear connection, have given an empire to the native country? Who, with often the lofs of health, and, at beft, by a long and painful refidence in a climate uncongenial to their conftitutions, have accumulated a moderate competency as a fhelter for the evening of their day; fhall they, like felons, be dragged before fuch an inquifition? Shall the winter of a life, wafted in the fervice of their country, be unfeelingly rendered a feafon of joylefs exiftence? No! perifh the idea! vanifh a thought fo repugnant to

the

the feelings of a British mind! Is this the descendant of the illustrious PITT? Is this the youth whom nature graced with ripened talents in the morn of life? Is this the asserter of his country's cause? Is this the guardian genius of her sacred rights? O! venerable shade of immortal CHATHAM! How would thy patriot bosom, warmed by freedom's flame, now glow with generous indignation, could'st thou but view thy favourite son, whom nature kindly destined to emulate thy virtue, and share thy deathless fame, thus turnish the infancy of his career! Look down, bright spirit! and behold him seated on the eminence of that power, which once thy virtues radiated, now sporting with the happiness of millions, and stabbing the freedom of his country! Look down, divine emanation of unrivalled goodness! and through the immensity of all-created space, swift let that towering eagle eye of thine dart its indignant frown to recal him into glory's arms! swift let it flash to his recollection the curse that waits the man

"Who owes his greatness to his country's ruin!"

But,

But, Gentlemen, the opinion at prefent entertained of us at home is fuch, that fo far from our being confidered as entitled to a common participation in the conftitutional rights of Briton, we are fcarcely looked upon as deferving of the name of men. Neither has the injurious light in which we are beheld originated in any cafual prejudice, or malicious biafs againſt us in the hearts of our countrymen—it is the fatal refult of a concerted plan, of a deliberate defign.

A confiderable time hath elapfed fince many fucceffive Minifters of the Crown, anxious to fecure every mode of corruption which might place the will of the national fenate at their command, have purfued every method that the wiles of political management could devife, to transfer the valuable and extenfive patronage of the Eaſt into their own hands. But they were repeatedly baffled in all their attempts by that wife jealoufy with which the nation at large have, at all times, watched and guarded againft every new addition to their power. At length, however, they fell upon a method which appeared likely to anfwer

fwer their end, (among a people whofe feelings are even keenly awake to every idea of tyranny and oppreffion;) and they hoped to ftrike with fuccefs at the Company, through the reputations of their fervants.

In purfuance of this virtuous defign, the moft laboured reprefentations were held forth of the enormities committed by thofe of every rank who were employed in the management of our newly acquired empire in the Eaft. The needy adherents of a venal Adminiftration, anxious to participate in the wealth of India, filled the trumpet of calumny in every quarter. Inflamed by malice, and rankling with envy, they difperfed among the credulous multitude dreadful details of imaginary maffacres, and difmal ftories of ideal depredations, committed by the Britifh in the Eaft, which had no exiftence in truth, but were folely the exuberant phantoms of their own difturbed imaginations. Nay, even fome of the moft eloquent orators in the Britifh fenate (whofe abilities are obfcured by the violence of their paffions, and whofe principles are tarnifhed

by

by their zeal for profecution) were not afhamed to give thefe improbable falfehoods their public fanction, and to diffeminate them to the world in lofty rhapfodies of alternate mifreprefentation, and acrimonious invective. The idle tales exceeded even the fiction of romance, or the authenticated cruelties which fober hiftory relates to have difgraced the dark ages before civilization had improved the heart, or meliorated the human mind. No longer, Gentlemen, may we credit the recorded enormities, which hiftory pictures to our view, of the ceafelefs maffacres which marked the conquefts of Fernandez Cortes in South America, and ftained the character of his nation! No longer may we confider them but as the interefted tales of malice fabricated to obfcure the fame of its conqueror, and tarnifh the luftre of his actions, fince in a more enlightened age fimilar cruelties are attributed to ourfelves, and bafe affertions forged abroad to vilify the glory of a conqueft, as illuftrious from its unprecedented brilliancy, as for the humanity which marked its complection! A conqueft which evidently arofe from the neceffity of our

own

own situation in vindication of the national honour, and not from an ambitious avidity for dominion, or an uncontrolable defire for riches—witnefs, to the truth of this, yon dudgeon ftill exifting! Witnefs, this monument*, which yet records the barbarous deed which roufed us to revenge! Witnefs, the unavailing fighs of thofe who are yet alive to mourn the maffacre of their families, and to execrate the tyrant who gave them to defpair!

Thefe cruel arts, however ridiculous they may appear to us, whofe fituation gives us an opportunity to know, to judge, and to feel, have been crowned with fuccefs to the fulleft extent of their wifhes. The grofs and illiberal flander which has been fo profufely lavifhed upon us all has been attended with fuch effects to the name and character of the fervice in general, that to have wafted the flower of life in India, to have encountered for a long feries of years the rigours of an adverfe climate, the pangs of illnefs, and the

---

* Pointing to each of thofe objects near the theatre.

anxious

anxious folicitude of voluntary banifhment, is now confidered only as reflective of infamy and difgrace. In vain do we undergo all this! In vain have examples been fhewn by the Europeans of this country of extenfive benevolence, of princely difintereftednefs, to which no fociety of men on earth can produce fuperior proofs! In vain, ye intrepid defenders of your country's rights, have ye fmothered the rifing flame of rebellion, or taught the haughty Mahratta to dread the weight of the Britifh arms! In vain, ye gallant faviours of the Carnatic, have ye fuftained toils, and difplayed exertions which would have done honour to the Roman name! In vain, ye unfortunate prifoners of a ruffian defpot, have ye endured a painful captivity, embittered by every fuffering which inventive cruelty could frame! Each laurelled foldier is involved in the general accufation, and afferted to be blackened by the crimes which are faid to contaminate the whole! How injurious and infulting! Where, yes, where is the incentive to emulation? Where is the fpring to valour, if you are to be thus traduced after the ceafelefs perils you have fo nobly
         braved?

braved? Hear me, ye veteran followers of lamented Coote! Let me appeal to that free spirit which dignifies the human mind, and to those quick feelings which are the inseparable ornaments of military breasts. If arms be your profession, is not honour your pursuit? Surely danger is the soldier's joy, honour his mistress, and glory his delight. Will you not then recoil at this wanton attempt to taint its purity? Are you not tremblingly alive to every assault upon your fame?

> Who steals my purse, steals trash;
> 'Twas something — nothing:
> 'Twas mine, 'tis his, and has been slave to thousands;
> But he who filches from me my good name,
> Robs me of that which not enriches him,
> But makes me poor indeed!
>
>   SHAKESPEARE.

Say then, shall this oppressive act lay all your honours in the dust, and rob you of that wreathe which fame has destined to reward your toils, and bids, when dead, still blossom o'er your tombs, and wake to memory the recollection of your virtues?

If this be the case, then proſtrate your colours at the ſhrine of deſpotiſm; it is time you ſhould muffle your drums, and beat the dead march over your expiring liberties! In every ſociety there are good and bad men; for as virtue is the brighteſt ornament of humanity, ſo vice is its darkeſt infirmity; but the latter are doubtleſs few, compared with the former. How cruel and unjuſt, then, that the depravity of a ſmall number ſhould ſtigmatize the remaining virtuous with unmerited ignominy, and that the ſuppoſed miſconduct of one or two ſhould involve a whole claſs of reſpectable people in the ſame indiſcriminate maſs of general delinquency! Such, however, is our caſe; for we are now in a meaſure proſcribed by our country, and recorded infamous to the world. All Europe are taught to view us in the light of miſcreants, no longer deſerving of national favour, unworthy of being governed by thoſe laws which never had a partial diſtinction for their object, and unentitled to a participation in thoſe conſtitutional rights which we have hitherto confidered as a protective barrier for the whole! But, gentlemen, it

was

was neceffary that thofe, whofe factious fpirit kindled the flames of war, and whofe mad ambition has torn an empire from their injured country, fhould endeavour to conceal her bleeding wrongs, and ward off her vengeance, by turning the torrent of national odium from themfelves to make it fall upon the heads of thofe whofe gallantry and fpirit have preferved, with ftubborn firmnefs, their remaining kingdoms in the Eaft! Little will it avail us to affert our innocence at prefent; delufion muft triumph for a while, as the great body of the people feem to have imbibed the prejudice of a faction againft us; but there is a period when its film fhall be removed from the eyes of the public, and afperfion be fubdued, by a full conviction of our wrongs; the virulence of contending parties will then fubfide, the mift of prepoffeffion difperfe of itfelf, and popular rancour yield to more generous and charitable fentiments. We fhall then receive that juftice we have a right to expect from a nation hitherto renowned for its liberality and wifdom, and the lie of the day will be configned to its perifhable exiftence. In the

interim

interim let us devote these insidious arts to the contempt they deserve, and their authors to the reprobation they are destined to receive; for minds that are conscious of their own integrity will rise superior to the attacks of malevolence, and display themselves invulnerable by the shafts of calumny! *Mens conscia sibi recti vim contumeliæ aspernat.*

However much it may have been the fashion of the day to brand us with such opprobious invectives, and to represent us with Bobadil bombasticity, as the " destroyers of thirty millions of " people by famine and the sword," yet I trust it will evidently appear that no conquest was ever effected wherein a greater attention was paid in the outset to the calls of humanity, or a more liberal regard observed on its subsequent completion to the rights of individuals. That the country has been impoverished in its resources, since we became its possessors, may probably be the case; but this is in some measure the common situation of all subjugated provinces, and was the anticipated consequence of our progress by

the

the eye of wifdom. Was it not peculiarly the fate of the Roman acquifitions in Afia? Is not defolation unhappily, to a certain degree, the natural effect of conqueft? Where is the conquered country that boafts of its increafed advantages by reduction, or flourifhes beneath the yoke of fubjection? A mild and vigilant Adminiftration, the members of which are animated to exertion by principles of patriotifm, will doubtlefs ftrengthen and extend the happinefs of the people, and the profperity of the country, over which it prefides; but this is not the cafe in conquered dominions, where the fame enthufiaftic principle feldom influences the human mind: and hence it is, that a delegated government, far diftant from the controling power, muft ever be expofed to a variety of diforders in its internal fyftem, detrimental to the country it governs, as well from the unfteadinefs of its principle, as from the occafional mifapplication of its powers. Thofe caufes therefore, which operated to impair the Company's poffeffions, exifted morally in the nature of things, and would have been equally, if not

more

more forcibly felt, if the sovereignty of those countries had devolved to any other European power; but even if they had owed their origin to an opposite source, it is not the less an act of injustice to make us the objects of punishment who were not the perpetrators of guilt: the truth, however, is, there is little reproach to be cast upon the conduct of individuals, for there is a tide in the affairs of human life which neither the exertion of industry can repel, or the efforts of wisdom subdue. Providence has wisely limited the bounds of earthly prosperity; and kingdoms, however flourishing, are destined to experience the transitory fate of every sublunary substance. Nations, like the favourites of fortune, have each their day: the Romans had theirs, and we have seen ours. *Sic transit gloria mundi!* Rome sunk beneath the burden of her conquests, and the ancient mistress of the world exhibits in her fall a melancholy picture of dethroned ambition, enslaved by bigotry, and subdued by arms. Britain, exalted by her heroes to the summit of imperial grandeur, already waves beneath the pressure of her glories, and

displays

displays in the magnanimity of her efforts to uphold them; an immortalizing testimony of the brilliancy of her career. It is now for America to rise into consequence, and branck into a boundless empire that possibly may level others, until by some singular revolutions, or, perhaps, by the magnitude of her own conquests, she falls a victim to adversity herself, and some new triumphant and tyrannic power raises the fabric of despotism upon freedom's ruins.

I have now, gentlemen, laid before you the fatal effects with which the power of this despotic authority, this new oriental court of star chamber, may be attended to your private interests; but the immediate and personal injuries to which you are subjected by it, are not the only considerations which should rouze your attention. To every man who possesses the smallest portion of public virtue, the welfare of his country will be of some concern to every man who hopes within her parental arms to find a repose for the evening of life, her freedom will be dear! To preserve that welfare inviolate,

and

and to guard that freedom from the baneful blaſt of tyranny, ſhould be the exertion of every Brition, however diſtant from his native ſhore. I will therefore treſpaſs upon your kind indulgence but a very little time longer, for the purpoſe of ſuggeſting a few ideas on the ſubject of the petitions which may probably be the reſult of this day's meeting, and which I now humbly move a Committee may be appointed to prepare. It is true we have been ſeverely wronged, but we have yet the happineſs to reflect, that our complaints are not without a remedy. Under the preſſure of accumulated injuries an appeal ſtill lies to a Sovereign, whoſe enlarged benevolence comprehends every portion of his wide extended empire. His Majeſty is the father of his People, and in thoſe royal virtues which ſo eminently adorn his Throne, we muſt confide for protection and redreſs. There is no ſupport to which we can ſo pleaſingly have recourſe; and I am perſuaded there is none in which we can repoſe ſo juſt a confidence. Let us therefore beware of intemperate zeal, and of meaſures dictated by too ſtrong a ſenſe of the injuries we ſuffer. What

Engliſhman

Englishman who now hears me but would blush for his country, if she were capable of basely yielding to his threats that which she denied to his just reprefentation? The calm, steady voice of reason, will lull to silence the vain clamours of faction, and the rancorous hiffings of envy; and unbar the avenues to returning justice! Let our conduct therefore be marked by temper and moderation. Let us owe to the equity of the State a redress which irascibility can never obtain, but which it will be the pride of a generous people to bestow upon our humble request.

I have ventured, gentlemen, to step forth upon the present occasion, under a conviction, that the sentiments which I entertain, and have expressed, upon the important subject which has this day convened us, (as far as relates to the principle and effect of this act) will be honoured with the approbation of most of my auditors. I was sensible that a business of this kind only required to be introduced to your notice; and that a spirit of unanimous indignation would mark its infancy. This I have united in doing, with an ability inadequate to the task I have assumed, but with a zeal for your interests, and an attachment to the community, that admits of no superiority, and compensates for a deficiency of talents. I am sanguine in my hopes, that the united solicitations of so respectable a colony will not be disregarded by the Legislature at home. I am warm in my wishes, that the neighbouring presidencies, equally injured with ourselves, will be animated by our resolves of this day to imitate our glorious example. It is my prayer, that those hopes may neither prove delusive, nor these wishes remain ungratified! In the awful calamity which has recently befallen the empire, we have seen that the spirit of an Englishman is not of that ductile texture which readily yields to oppression, and that when the powers of despair are awakened, they are superior to danger, and tower above difficulty. I therefore firmly trust, that a candid avowal of our feelings, in a respectful representation to Parliament, will meet with a favourable reception from the nation at large, and be productive of

the

the happiest effect to ourselves, by restoring us again to the bosom of our country. No, gentlemen, you will not assert your rights in vain! You will not long continue in a state of disgraceful separation from the rest of your countrymen! I feel the firmest assurance of success! I already anticipate the day of triumph which shall assuredly succeed to this day of dejection! a day devoted to rapture, and to the mutual heart-felt congratulations which shall mark the bright æra of our restoration to those rights we were destined to inherit: it is then that detraction will be immolated at the shrine of candour, and that it will cease to be a crime to have risen to an honourable independence! To complete the delightful picture of returning justice, good will, and benevolence, nothing is wanted, but that the same hand which has inflicted the wound should, like the hero's spear of old, be stretched forth to administer the remedy, and ensure the cure. Yes, the descendant of the illustrious Chatham shall be among the foremost converts to truth, reason, and liberal sentiment! He is their hereditary votary; no man ever rose more honourably to power, or became more defervedly intrufted with the confidence of his countrymen: if his genius and his eloquence have excited their admiration, the purity of his moral character has equally attracted the tribute of their efteem; and though fafcinated for a while by the fpells of faction, and deluded by the mifts of prejudice, thefe will not long have power to detain his footfteps in the mazy paths of error: he will again become worthy of the great name he bears; again ftand forth the terror, not the abettor of defpotifm; and having burft his own bonds afunder, he will fly with repentant feelings to unbind the ignominious fetters which, in the hour of national delirium, he inconfiderately forged for you. *O! die fortunate!* Let its pleafing expectation fubdue every angry emotion, and rivet our affections to the State which protects us. And whilft it obvioufly veils the paft, let it chearfully gliften upon our minds as a dawning ray of benignity to tinge the horizon of our hopes, and to infpirit us to look forward to that aufpicious moment, when our grievances will be redreffed by a liberal and enlightened nation,

tion, when perfecution fhall yield to juftice, and faction be filenced by truth! Happy moment! It will be for ever dear to recollection! Gratitude fhall fondly dwell upon its exiftence, our children fhall venerate its birth, and pofterity applaud the exertions which produced it! May we all live to fee it! To blefs that gracious Monarch from whofe bounty it is to flow! And to hail, with tranfport, the immortal day, which, in reftoring us to the rights of citizens and men, fhall form an illuftrious epoch in the hiftory of our times, and be for ever rendered memorable in the annals of our country.

THE END.

BOOKS printed for J. DEBRETT, oppofite Burlington Houfe, Piccadilly.

THE PARLIAMENTARY REGISTER, No. XV. of the laft, being the fecond Seffion of the fixteenth Parliament of Great Britain. Containing an accurate, full, and impartial Account of all the Debates of the laft Seffion, collated with the Notes and Papers of feveral Gentlemen, who have very obligingly communicated the fame.

☞ At the defire of feveral Perfons of diftinguifhed Abilities and Rank, this Work was undertaken. The favourable Reception it has met with during the whole of the two laft Parliaments, not only demands the moft grateful Acknowledgements of the Editors, but encourages them to a Continuation of the fame through the prefent Parliament. For this Purpofe, and to prevent Mifreprefentation, they beg leave again to folicit the Affiftance of their former Friends, and every other Gentleman. A ftrict Attention will be paid to all their Commands, and Favours; nor will any Affiduity or Care be wanting to preferve that Truth and Accuracy, for which this Work has hitherto been diftinguifhed.

The PARLIAMENTARY REGISTER, of the former Seffion complete, being the Firft of the prefent Parliament. Containing, amongft a great Number of interefting Debates, the Debates on Mr. Pitt's India Bill; on the affairs of the Eaft-India Company; on the Parliamentary Reform; on the Weftminfter Election; the Report at length of the Privy Council, concerning the Intercourfe between the Continent of America and the Weft-India Iflands, which is no where elfe printed for fale, &c. &c. &c. in two vols. Price 15s. half bound and lettered.

The PARLIAMENTARY REGISTER of the laft Parliament, complete, viz. from 1782 to 1784, in Fourteen Volumes. Price 5l. 8s. half bound.

The PARLIAMENTARY REGISTER of the former Parliament, from 1774 to 1780, in feventeen Volumes. Price 6l. 6s. half bound and lettered.

The

Books printed for J. DEBRETT.

The REMEMBRANCER; or IMPARTIAL REPOSITORY of PUBLIC EVENTS. The American War gave rise to this Work in 1775. Every authentic Paper relative to that War, as also with France and Spain, whether published in England or America, by the British Ministry, or the American Congress, are all carefully inserted in this Work. The Letters of the several Commanding Officers, Addresses, Resolutions of the various Committees, Conventions, &c. To these have been prefixed at the Desire of many Persons, a Collection of authentic Papers respecting the Dispute with America before the Commencement of Hostilities, from the Resolutions which gave rise to the Stamp Act in 1764, to the Battle of Lexington in 1775. Complete Sets of this valuable and interesting Work may be had of the Publisher in Seventeen Volumes. Price Six Guineas half bound and lettered.

₊ Those Gentlemen who are in want of any particular Numbers to complete their Sets, are earnestly intreated to order them as speedily as possible.

An ASYLUM for FUGITIVE PIECES, in Prose and Verse, not in any other Collection; with several Pieces never before published; including the CRITIQUES on the ROLLIAD, revised; the PROBATIONARY ODES for the LAUREATSHIP; Lord G——M's DIARY; Lord M——E on Eloquence; and several Jeu des Esprits, written by Persons of Fashion, on many late Public Topics, intended as a Supplement to the above Work. A new Edition. Price 4s. sewed.

OBSERVATIONS on the MANUFACTURES, TRADE, and PRESENT STATE of IRELAND. By JOHN LORD SHEFFIELD. Third Edition. Price 7s. in Boards.

‡‡‡ This Work includes the important Question relative to the OPENING the PORTS of GREAT BRITAIN to the MANUFACTURES of IRELAND, and also to the COLONIAL and FOREIGN Produce from that Kingdom.

A COL-

Books printed for J. DEBRETT.

A COLLECTION of the MOST ESTEEMED POLITICAL TRACTS which were printed during the Years 1781, 1782, 1783, 1784, and 1785, in 8 vols. Price 2l. 12s. 6d. half bound and lettered. ⁂ In this Collection are contained, among many other valuable Tracts, the Earl of Stair's Confiderations; Lieutenant Tomlinfon's Letter on the State of the Navy; Mr. Northcote's Obfervations on the Nature of Civil Liberty; Lord Beauchamp's Letter to the Belfaft Volunteers; Letters to Lord Beauchamp, in anfwer to the above; The prefent Hour; Earl of Abingdon's Speech on Irifh Affairs; Word at Parting; Lord Chancellor Weft, on Creating Peers; Sir Henry Clinton's Narrative of his conduct in America; Earl Cornwallis's Anfwer; Sir Henry Clinton's Reply to the Anfwer; Debates on the Peace; Mr. Pitt's Speech in Defence of the Peace; Letters to the Earl of Shelburne on the Peace; Thoughts on the Peace; Mr Sinclair's Lucubrations; Hint to a Patriot Parliament; Speech in the Affembly of St. Chriftopher's; Sir Henry Clinton to the Commiffiones of Public Accounts; Mr. Deane's Addrefs to the United States of America; Abbé Mabley's Remarks on the American Conftitutions; Refolutions of the laft Houfe of Commons on the late Grand Conftitutional Queftion; True State of the late Important Queftion; Letter to Sir Thomas Broughton; Free Parliaments; Fox and Pitt's Speeches on the Weftminfter Scrutiny; Three Letters to the People of England; Maffere's Inquiry into the Extent and Powers of Juries, Key to the Parliamentary Debates, Reply to the Treafury Pamphlet; Authentic Statement of the Report of the Privy Council on the Irifh Propofitions; Mr. Fox's Speech, May 12, 1785; Heads of Mr. Fox's Speech, May 23, 1785, with a Lift of the Minority; Candid Review of Mr. Pitt's Twenty Refolutions; Letter from an Irifh Gentleman in London, &c. &c.

A COLLECTION of the moft efteemed EAST-INDIA TRACTS which were printed during the Years 1780, 1781, 1782, 1783, and 1784. In 6 vols. price 2l. 2s. half bound and lettered.

APPENDIX.

Containing the Proceedings of the Meeting held at the Theatre in Calcutta, on the 25th of July, 1785, to take into Confideration an Act, &c.

AT a meeting of the Britiſh inhabitants of Calcutta, held at the theatre on Monday the 25th of July, in purſuance of a public ſummons by the High Sheriff, at the requeſt of the Grand Jury, on the 15th of June laſt, for the purpoſe of taking into conſideration the propriety and neceſſity of a petition on certain parts of an act of the 24th of His preſent Majeſty, entitled, " An act for the better " regulation of the affairs of the Eaſt-India " Company, and of the Britiſh poſſeſſions " in India, and for eſtabliſhing a Court of " Judicature, for the more ſpeedy and effec- " tual trial of perſons accuſed of offences " committed in the Eaſt Indies."

PHILIP YONGE, Eſq; the Sheriff, opened the buſineſs of the day, in the following addreſs:

GENTLEMEN,

This meeting has been convened by me at the requeſt of the very reſpectable body of gentlemen who compoſed the laſt Grand Jury, contained in the following letter:

H To

To Ppilip Yongi, Esq.
Sheriff of the Town of Calcutta.

Sir,

By defire of the Grand Jury, I am to requeſt you will be pleafed to convene a meeting of the Britiſh inhabitants of Calcutta, at the Old Court Houſe, or any other convenient place, on Monday the 25th of July next, to take into confideration the propriety and neceffity of a petition on certain parts of the act of the 24th of His Majeſty, entitled, " An act for the better
" regulation of the affairs of the Eaſt-India
" Company, and of the Britiſh poſſeſſions in
" India, and for eſtabliſhing a Court of Judica-
" ture for the more ſpeedy and effectual trial
" of perſons accuſed of offences committed in
" the Eaſt Indies."

I have the honour to be, &c.

C. Purling,
Foreman.

Grand Jury Room,
Calcutta, June 13, 1785.

Feeling, gentlemen the neceffity of a public appeal, I moſt chearfully complied with the requeſt of the Grand Jury, and I am ſure, their wiſhes muſt be fully gratified, at ſeeing ſo large and reſpectable a number of their fellow citizens attend their call, and I have no doubt, gentlemen, but your reſolutions this day, by their moderation and firmneſs, will do honour to them and to yourſelves.

Charles

Charles Purling, Esq. was then unanimously called to the chair, when he addressed the meeting in the following speech:

Permit me, gentlemen, to return you my unfeigned thanks for the honour you have conferred upon me. The more unsought the distinction, the more I am impressed with the obligation to exert my poor share of abilities for the general good, in the pursuit of which I am persuaded, I shall have the ready support, concurrence, and approbation of every one who stiles himself an Englishman.

The numerous assembly of respectable characters whom I observe, assure me, they are well apprised that no trivial matter has now called us together.

It may however be expected, that the individual of this society who has stood forward to convene a meeting for the consideration of a solemn appeal to our Sovereign, or the Legislature of our country, may be induced to open the subject to them. Any less important occasion could not have impelled me to have undertaken a task, to which I feel myself so very unequal; and if I sue for favour, gentlemen, it is not from an apprehension of not obtaining it from your liberality, but because I fear there will be but too much room for indulgence.

The mode adopted for convening the British inhabitants of Calcutta, was esteemed the most constitutional, and therefore the most ad-

viseable.

viseable. The subject of our intended deliberation was declared to be the propriety and necessity of a petition against certain parts of the late act of Parliament, for the better regulation and management of the East-India Company's affairs.

The introduction of a tribunal of justice, solely for the trial of Indians; the deprivation of that invaluable, that blessed birthright, the judgement of our peers; and the several provisions, which form a system of judicature totally different from that by which the whole empire is governed, are a novelty in our constitution, an evil to the nation at large, and a grievance, disgrace, and indignity, to Indians in particular, whose reputations have received a death-stroke which no human exertion can remedy, recall, or obliterate; however the repeal of this offensive, this criminating act may avert the injuries which impend over our fortunes and our families.

By the passing of this act we stand prejudged, in as much as it sets forth, that the detection and punishment of crimes committed in India, requires different laws, and severer than those which already operate over the whole body of British subjects. This presumption criminates, because it distinguishes. We all know, that the law supposes crimes; but we also know, that it does not attach crimes to particular men or particular bodies of men.

This law provides penalties and pains hitherto unknown (and I scarce think any one will say nay

nay when I add) unproportioned to the offences they are intended to check and punish.

It establishes an extraordinary and an alarming innovation in the constitution of our country, which the supporter of the bill was bold enough to avow, and the representatives of a free people were supine enough to admit.

It deprives the British-born subject who has resided a few years in India, of the rights and privileges enjoyed by the rest of his countrymen.

It exposes him to the malevolence of any man whom he may accidentally offend, during the three years of probation, or may have offended before he left India.

It renders him a marked and branded being among those with whom he is obliged to associate on his return to his native country.

It erects a partial, unjust, and odious distinction between the King's and the Company's servants, though both are employed in India, and equally liable to the same frailties and temptations.

It involves the innocent with the guilty in one common destruction : nay,

It spreads in its contagious blast, ruin to the infant and the unborn.

Prejudice and crimination are stamped on its forehead. The very approach of the monster, its ghastly and horrible appearance, without waiting for its destructive effects, urges our resort to the first principle of nature, self preservation; and every manly, resolute, deliberate,

rate, and legal oppofition, which it is in our power at this diftance to exert for its extirpation, is loudly called forth.

The delufion, malevolence, and prejudice of the times, and the ready attention paid to all tales in crimination of Indians, feem to have been our bane and misfortune.

The ftory of Almas Ally Khawn * brings but too ferious reflections to my mind, however it may have excited the gibe and the joke in the metropolis of our country. It has ferved to convince me, that even improbable ftories have been greedily caught at, and have added to the mifchief which mifreprefentation and a total exaggeration of facts had originated. But allowing even that Almas Ally Khawn had met with a merited punifhment from his Sovereign, for default of revenue, treafon, and rebellion; and a hufband and a father had been cut off from an unfortunate family, ftill we find that his eftates were faid to be untouched. That

* Extract from the inftructions given by Mr. HASTINGS to Mr. Briftow, dated October 23, 1782, relative to *Almas Ally Khawn*. Vide *Parliametary Debates*, vol. xvi. page 409.
" If any engagement fhall actually fubfift between them,
" at the time you have charge of the refidency, it muft,
" however exceptionable, be faithfully obferved; but if
" he has been guilty of any criminal offence to the Nabob
" his mafter, for which no immunity is provided in the
" engagement, or he fhall break any one of the conditions
" of it, I do moft ftrictly enjoin you, and it muft be your
" fpecial care, to endeavour either by *force* or *furprife* to
" fecure his perfon and bring him to juftice; I mean that
" you urge the Nabob, on due conviction to punifh him
" with *death*.

family,

family, therefore, whose pathetic complaints have been exhibited in our newspapers, would have been left in a far more eligible condition, than our wives and children will be, when any of us, under the restrictions now prescribed, and for an act which never was a crime till this law made it so, shall, after furnishing suspicion against himself, and answering interrogatories upon oath, be shut up in prison, have his whole fortune and property attached, perhaps confiscated; be subject to a tedious process to extend the imprisonment and seizure to years, and entirely uncertain that they will not last for ever. Deprived of their prop. and support, and spoiled of the just expectations which the law of reason and humanity has decreed to the weaker and more helpless part of the creation, and has rendered the natural and inherent right of the offspring of all mankind, and of our offspring, till the passing of this bill, our families must either turn themselves for a hard-earned subsistance to menial employs, which our situations in life would have protected them from, had we never visited these climes, or be reduced to a state still more humiliating, of pinching, but silent penury and want, poverty stricken with shame, and shrinking from the eye of the world.

In short, the virulence, cruelty, and persecution, with which Indians are from henceforward to be pursued, and at the very period in which

laws

laws have been made to check peculation, and to curb oppreſſion, extortion, and injuſtice, will far ſurpaſs what has even been ſuſpected of them, however far ſuſpicion may have gone — and will even exceed the ſeverity, if it had been inflicted by the advice of an Engliſh gentleman, on Almas Ally Khawn.]

I cannot urge more, gentlemen, than that our liberties, as Britiſh ſubjects, perhaps the preſent form of our admired and excellent conſtitution; our fortunes as individuals, our happineſs as huſbands and parents, the future maintenance of our wives and children, and the dependence of thoſe who have not yet ſeen the light, are all involved in a proper and ſpirited exertion for the repeal of this ill-adviſed, this ill-omened act,

None more powerful motives, no objects of greater importance can exiſt to induce unanimity; and I ſanguinely hope, that diverſity of opinion will not prevail to obſtruct our honeſt, temperate, and lawful endeavours for the accompliſhment of ſo deſirable an end.

The following RESOLUTIONS *were then propoſed, and unanimouſly agreed to.*

I. Reſolved—That His Majeſty's ſubjects in the Eaſt Indies are entitled to the protection and ſupport of the laws of England, in common with the other ſubjects of the realm.

II. Re-

II. Resolved—That so much of the act of the 24th of His present Majesty, chap. xxv. entitled, " An act for the better regulation and " management of the affairs of the East-India " Company, and of the British possessions in " India, and for establishing a Court of Judica- " ture, for the more speedy and effectual trial " of persons accused of offences committed in " the East Indies," as compels the servants of the East-India Company, upon their return to Great Britain, to deliver in upon oath, an inventory of their whole property, under penalties of excessive severity, is grievous and oppressive to the servants of the said Company, and repugnant to the constitution of our country.

III. Resolved — That the erection of a new tribunal by the said act, for the special purpose of trying offences, charged to have been committed in the East Indies; a tribunal unrestrained by the settled rules of law, and subject to no appeal; and the depriving them of their undoubted birthright, the trial by jury, are violations of the Great Charter of our liberties, and infringements of the most sacred principles of the British constitution.

IV. Resolved — That the said act, by exposing of His Majesty's subjects residing under this presidency, to be sent forcibly to England, and there to be tried for offences committed or charged to be committed by them within these
provin-

provinces, is highly dangerous to the fecrity of their perfons and fortunes.

V. Refolved — That it is injurious to the fervants of the United Company, to be fubjected by the faid act of Parliament to be difmiffed from their employments in the Eaft-Indies, or to be recalled at the pleafure of the Crown, which is in other words, at the will of the Minifter.

VI. Refolved — That the provifion of the faid act of Parliament, which enacts, that all writings which fhall have been tranfmitted from the Eaft Indies to the Court of Directors, by their officers or fervants refident in the Eaft-Indies, in the ufual courfe of their correfpondence with the faid Court of Directors, may be admitted by the Commiffioners to be offered in evidence, and fhall not be deemed inadmiffible or incompetent, is fubverfive of the eftablifhed rules of evidence, and manifeftly dangerous to His Majefty's fubjects returning from this country to Great Britain.

VII. Refolved — That it is therefore becoming and highly expedient for His Majefty's fubjects in thefe provinces to endeavour, by all legal and conftitutional means, to obtain a repeal of fuch claufes in the faid act of Parliament as impofe thefe and other hardfhips upon them. And that for the purpofe of obtaining fuch repeal, petitions, humbly laying our grievances before His Majefty and the two Houfe

of

of Parliament, are adviseable, necessary, and proper.

VIII. Resolved — That a Committee of fifteen gentlemen, selected from the inhabitants of Calcutta, be appointed to prepare petitions to His Majesty and the two Houses of Parliament, and to correspond with the inland stations subordinate to this government, and with the other presidencies in India. And that it be recommended to them to take all such measures as they shall judge necessary for transmitting the said petitions to Europe, and for promoting and obtaining an effectual redress to His Majesty's subjects in India. And that the said Committee be empowered to fill up vacancies as they may happen in the course of time.

IX. Resolved — That as considerable expence must be unavoidably incurred by our endeavours to obtain redress of our grievances, a subscription shall be opened by the Committee who shall be elected by this Assembly; and that as soon as the petition shall be ready for signature, a book shall be produced for the said subscription, to the end, that every man may have the opportunity of promoting, by voluntary sacrifice of a small share of his property, that security of the whole which is the grand object of our petitions.

X. Resolved — That all subscriptions be received, whether in specie or in paper, and that the amount subscribed, shall be paid by each subscriber to such person or persons as the said Committee, when elected, shall appoint to receive the same.

XI. Resolved—That this assembly do authorize the said Committee to dispose of and expend the whole, or any part of the sums of money so paid, in such manner as shall appear to them best calculated for the general benefit of the cause for which they were subscribed.

XII. Resolved — That Mr. Charles Purling be a member of the Committee, and that he be requested to propose fourteen other gentlemen to the meeting for their approval.

XIII. Resolved — That the following gentlemen are elected for the purposes mentioned in the foregoing resolutions, viz.

PATRICK DUFF,	T. H. DAVIES,
CHARLES PURLING,	J. EVELYN,
PETER MURRAY,	J. CHURCH,
H. VANSITTART,	HERBERT LLOYD,
WM. COWPER,	GEORGH DALLAS,
WM. SCOTT,	JOHN BRISTOW,
JONN DUNCAN,	AND
JOHN MURRAY,	PHI. YONGE, Esqrs.

XIV. Resolved — That this assembly of the British inhabitants of Calcutta, having the most perfect confidence and trust in the uprightness, integrity, and abilities of the Committee chosen

for

for the conduct and management of their interest, and for the protection and defence of their rights, as subjects of Great Britain, do, in in order to give vigour and efficacy to their acts, and to free them from future trouble, embarrassment, and obstruction, delegate to them full authority; and do express a plenary reliance on them for the exercise of it; -and do pledge to them the concurrence and support of the said assembly in the fullest manner possible, to all measures they shall legally adopt, for obtaining a repeal of the oppressive parts of the aforesaid act of Parliament.

XV. Resolved — That the thanks of this meeting be given to the Grand Jury, for having convened a legal and constitutional meeting of the British subjects in this settlement, for the purpose of petitioning His Majesty, and the two Houses of Parliament, for redress of those heavy grievances imposed on them by the before-mentioned act of the Legislature.

XVI. Resolved — That the thanks of this meeting be given to Philip Yonge, Esq. the High Sheriff, for his patriotic conduct in calling the assembly at the request of the Grand Jury.

XVII. Resolved — That the thanks of this meetting be given to Charles Purling, Esq. for the great precision, candour, and regularity, with which he has conducted the business of the day.

XVIII. Re-

XVIII. Resolved —That the above resolutions be printed and made public.

RESOLUTIONS *framed the 13th, and agreed to on the 17th of March,* 1785, *by the* Officers *of the* Third Brigade, *stationed at* Cawnpore.

THE general voice of the gentlemen at this station, taking into consideration the most proper mode of obtaining a repeal of the clauses of Mr. Pitt's India bill, which, under the unjust, illiberal plea of delinquency on our parts, constitutes the New Court of Judicature,

The following heads are recommended to the perusal of the gentlemen at large, and if approved of, their signatures are requested.

I. That as Britons, we are entitled to the protection and support of the ancient and established laws of England, in common with the other subjects of the realm.

II. That the inventory required from the servants of the Honourable East-India Company, and the New Court of Judicature constituted by Mr. Pitt's bill for the trial of delinquents, are contrary to the laws and customs of England, insomuch, that it compels, under very severe penalties, men born free, to give evidence against themselves, and deprives the subject of the inestimable blessing, and his birthright, Trial by his peers.

III. That it is the duty of every subject to

support,

support the laws, and by every legal and honest endeavour, to prevent innovations in the constitution.

IV. That we do most solemnly believe the New Court of Judicature, constituted by Mr. Pitt's bill, to be contrary to the constitution.

We farther resolve—That so soon as the several opinions of the gentlemen at this station be obtained, we will elect by ballot a Committee to correspond with the other Committees at the several stations, and aid and assist their good endeavours.

Resolved likewise — That when called upon, we will chearfully subscribe what proportionate sums of money may be requisite in support of this our just cause.

N. B. The above resolutions were subscribed by the gentlemen present at this meeting, and afterwards by circulation, and at the subsequent meeting on the 17th March, 1785, by about 150.

It was also agreed at this meeting, that a general meeting of those gentlemen who may be willing to sign the accompanying resolutions, be requested on Thursday next, the 17th inst. at Alcock's Tope, to ballot for a Committee to conduct the business.

The mode of ballot proposed is, that each subscriber shall bring or send a list of twenty names, and from a majority of votes thus given, thirteen or more gentlemen may be returned as a Committee.

The

The following Protest *being alluded to in Mr. Dallas's speech, page* 24, *we have subjoined the following correct copy from the* Parliamentary Register, vol. xvi. page 64.

August 9, 1784.

THE *East-India Regulation Bill* was read the third time: moved, "That the bill with the "amendments do pass."

The question being put thereupon, it was resolved in the affirmative.

Dissentient,

Because we think the principle of the bill false, unjust, and unconstitutional — *False*, in as much as it provides no effectual remedy for the evils it affects to cure — *unjust*, as it indiscriminately compels all persons returning from India to furnish the means of accusation against *themselves* — and *unconstitutional*, because it establishes a New Criminal Court of Judicature, in which the admission of incompetent evidence is expressly directed, and the subject is unnecessarily deprived of his most inestimable birthright, *a trial by jury.*

PORTLAND,
CHOLMONDELEY,
CARLISLE,
DEVONSHIRE,
NORTHINGTON.

F I N I S.

THE
SPEECH

OF A

SCOTS WEAVER.

[Price One Shilling and Sixpence.]

THE

SPEECH

OF A

SCOTS WEAVER:

DEDICATED TO

RICHARD GLOVER, Esq.

LONDON:
Printed for W. NICOLL, at No. 51, in
St. Paul's Church-yard. MDCCLXXIV.

SPEECH

RICHARD GLOVER, Esq.

TO you, Sir, I addreſs the following ſheets; becauſe to you alone I owe the ſubject matter of them.

Much did I regret that my abſence from town prevented me from hearing the diſplay of your eloquence at the bar of the Houſe of Commons; but my loſs has been amply made up, by your ſubſequent Publication.—There you have fully obviated all the doubts I had conceived, as to the nature of your harangue. —I thought you had been flattered by the partiality of your friends: But I am now convinced, *That you really believe it is for the intereſt of Great Britain to*

DEDICATION.

encourage German linens rather than our own:—That the Author of Leonidas alone underſtands Scotch affairs; and that not one of a million and a half of people in that country knows any thing of the matter:—That the Scots, by carrying from England into their own country half a million of gold in exchange for paper, ruined their linen manufactory:—That the king of Pruſſia will deſtroy our woollen manufactures, ſhould we tax the Sileſia linens; although by his edict long ſince promulgated, he has totally prohibited the importation of them into his dominions: And many other propoſitions of *equal truth and importance.*

I can now, Sir, ſee the reaſon why the Scotch nation, acute and ingenious

as you allow them to be, had such difficulty in being convinced *by your arguments* that Nine was more than Five:—
And although your speech supplied me with some melancholy thoughts; yet these were soon banished by the pleasing reflections I made, on the happiness you must enjoy in the internal consciousness of your own wisdom and importance.—
" The frog is charmed with her own
" song."——Far be it from me, Sir, even to wish, that my sentiments should impress you with other feelings; on the contrary, I hope that my attempt to answer your elaborate oration, will but confirm you in your present opinion.—
The poets well know, that pleasing dreams are as good as realities, whilst they last.—That you may continue to live until these happy effusions of imagination

nation cease, is my wish; if so, there will be no more occasion to insure your life.

I am, respectfully,

Sir,

Your most humble and obedient Servant,

THERMOPILÆ.

ADVERTISEMENT.

THE following sheets are the work of a Scots manufacturer, now in the country of England.

The publisher having submitted them to the inspection of a gentleman of known abilities, was assured by him, that they contained matter of much national importance; he therefore gives them to the public without further apology. They appear in the form of a Speech at the bar of the House of Commons; why the author has chosen this mode, we cannot take upon us to determine.

THE

SPEECH, &c.

I Agree with Mr. Glover, that the queſtion now before this Honourable Houſe is of the higheſt national importance.

The ſtrength and power of Great Britain depends on the number of her people; and theſe numbers depend on the full employment that can be given them. If by peſtilence, famine, or the ſword, one half of our people were cut off, whilſt we preſerve the means and inſtruments of employment, the void would immediately fill up. On the contrary, however great our numbers may be, if the means of employing them be wanting, they muſt waſte and decay, and finally ſink down to the number only required for the different occupations in the ſtate.

To illuftrate this propofition by a common and familiar example. If a field will maintain precifely twenty fheep, and if each fheep brings forth annually one lamb, it is evident that you may kill twenty every year, and the fame number will ftill remain: but fuppofing that you kill none; then the fheep will either never produce, or they will die, or they will leap the fence: for by the hypothefis, the field can only maintain twenty.

In like manner, if our pafture fail, our numbers will diminifh; enrich the pafture, and they will encreafe. This is a fimple view of the rife, progrefs, and decay of nations.—Let us apply it to the cafe in hand.

The linen manufacturers of England, Scotland, and Ireland, are now at your bar, complaining that their trade is ruined. They have made out their propofition, by proving that their prices are

are fallen within thefe two years from fifteen to twenty-five *per cent.* that the quantities manufactured are diminifhed near ten millions of yards *per annum*; that above one hundred thoufand people, who were induftrious manufacturers, are now deftitute of employment and of bread; and laftly, that many thoufands have from neceffity left their habitations, to feek, in America, that fubfiftence which their own country could not afford them. Thefe are facts undifputed on all fides: they fpeak to the hearts of a Britifh fenate, more than the thundering eloquence of a Demofthenes.

If our people want bread, and emigrate abroad, every landholder in Britain muft feel the confequence; the demand for the produce of the foil muft leffen; the price muft of courfe fall; rents muft diminifh; or the tenant muft abandon his farm, and even his country. In a word, to trace the fatal confequences of this event, would be no lefs painful to me, me, than to this honourable houſe, who, I am perſuaded, ſee them in their full extent; and ſeeing, will remove what muſt otherwiſe deſtroy this nation.

Permit me now, Sir, with that diffidence which becomes a private man, to point out what appears to me the real ſource of our grievance. This will be beſt done, by conſidering the cauſe.

Mr. Glover has entertained you with a long hiſtory of Scots circulation; in the courſe of which, 600,000 l. of gold was carried from England, in exchange for Scots paper. This ſhall afterwards be conſidered; but as he imputes the preſent ſtate of the linen manufacture to this cauſe, I will now endeavour to ſhew how far he is miſtaken.

1ſt. The decay of the linen manufacture preceded even the inſtitution of the Air Bank. The weaver has been loſing by his buſineſs for many years. So ſoon as as Germany was reſtored to tranquillity, after the late war, and the people were re-eſtabliſhed in their manufactures, the goods imported from thence became cheaper than they could be made here, at home; and this has gone on increaſing gradually and progreſſively, ſo that now they have obtained a general preference. The Britiſh and Iriſh manufacturers were not, however, immediately diſcouraged; they had gained money during the war; they continued their trade in hopes of better days; and it was only after heavy and repeated loſſes, that they began, in 1769 and 1770, to diminiſh their trade. Now the decreaſe in 1772 could not ariſe from the convulſion felt in the mercantile ſyſtem in the courſe of that year, becauſe a piece of linen from the flax takes two years to ſpin, weave, and bleach, before it comes to market; and the decline had taken place three years before that period. Wherefore the decreaſe was ſo far from being occaſioned, even in Scotland, by

the

the misfortunes of 1772, that it actually begun at the very period of 1769 and 1770, when there ought to have been an encreafe of this commodity, by the facility which prevailed at that time, of obtaining money in the courfe of circulation.

2dly. The manufacturing counties of England and Ireland feel the decay of the linen manufacture in a ftill higher degree than Scotland; yet, Scotland has hardly any commercial connection with them; none that can effect this queftion. Here then is an effect much greater than the caufe; a Scots circulation which has deprived England and Ireland of their linen manufactures, although neither of them had the moft diftant connexion with that country; yet they are both more affected than Scotland itfelf.

But let us attend to what muft have been the natural effect of the circulation in Scotland.

Mr.

Mr. Glover says the Scots obtained from England 600,000 l. of gold and silver, in exchange for their paper. None of this money is yet repaid. A great accession of money will account for an encrease of trade and manufactures; it will account for high prices; but with Mr. Glover only, will it account for a prodigious decrease, and a great fall in the value of any article of commerce. The rest of the world are yet left to seek the cause; let us now try if we can discover it.

Great-Britain pays in gross, about twelve millions yearly, in taxes; or, about fifty shillings yearly, for every living soul in the island. Ireland is also greatly taxed. She maintains an army and civil establishment, more expensive than any nation in Europe, in proportion to the numbers of her people. Germany, after profiting by the millions spent by Great-Britain in the late war, enjoys perfect tranquillity. Tho' articles of luxury, in some districts, and the soil itself, be taxed, the subsistence of the labourer is no where taxed. He can live and support his family for sixpence per day, over all Germany; in Great-Britain and Ireland, he can barely do it for nine pence per day. It will appear a paradox, but it is neverthelefs true, that this circumstance confidered, labour and manufactures are cheaper in Britain than in any other European country. The superior capitals, the skill of our people, and the invention of machinery, has, in some degree, compensated for our heavy taxes in all our manufactures; and in those where machinery can be employed to the greatest advantage, they fully make up for the dearnefs of labour. Unhappily, Sir, the linen manufacture either admits lefs of this than the hardware; or at least, has been lefs the subject of invention. So far however seems certain, that deducting taxes, our labour is as cheap, as in any other European nation.

It

It has been already stated, that every living soul in Great-Britain is taxed, on an average, fifty shillings. As the families of labourers, one with another, consist of four people; this would make ten pounds in taxes, on every labourer. This, it may be said, is placing the taxes of a weaver on the footing of those paid by an opulent merchant, or a great peer of the realm. A difference there will be; but much smaller than is commonly imagined. The richest man in Great-Britain eats no more than a peasant; he can drink no more; he requires no more stuff to clothe him *;

---

* It is not meant here to say that a rich man buys no more clothes than a poor man; but that he can wear no more. For supposing him to buy six shirts a year; he can only put on one at a time; when the year is out, he either sells them to another wearer, or gives them to his servants, and they become a part of their wages, and it is only the difference between the first value and the latter that can be imputed to him. This is the true state of the matter as to the taxes paid by the individual.

he may sleep longer, but can occupy no more space in a bed, nor more blankets to cover him.—He keeps, however, forty servants; he drinks claret, and entertains company; all these involve taxes. —True, but on whom? The servant pays his own taxes, in the same sense as the labourer. His maintainance is part of the wages of his service. Whether a great man gives twenty pound, in the name of board, or thirty pound, in the name of board and wages, it makes no sort of difference; the servant's labour is what pays his maintainance, and consequently his taxes, although the price of his labour goes from his master's pocket. Or, which is the same thing, the servant's wages are enhanced by the taxes, as much as the labourer's.—A guest at a gentleman's table may be considered in the same point of view. He gives his time to his host, in exchange for his venison and claret; and, in many cases, the purchase is dear. Thus, viewing taxes as they affect labour, every man's taxes will be reduced to the con-

sumption

sumption of himself and his immediate dependants, his wife and children. But the labourer drinks no claret. He drinks, however, porter : he works harder, and will drink more ; and many a coalheaver in London pays more taxes on the liquor he consumes, than the richest duke in England. I will, after all, admit that the rich man pays more taxes than the labourer; although the disproportion is not great. But supposing every idle, or rich man in Great-Britain, to pay double the taxes on his consumption that a labourer does; yet, unless it be said that more than a fifth of our people do not labour, this would only diminish the taxes paid by the labourer one fifth. In place of ten pounds per annum, or fifty shillings per head, which has been shewn to be the average rate of taxation, he would only pay forty shillings per head, or eight pounds per annum. But this is above one half of the wages of a labourer, or manufacturer, taken on an average, throughout

Great-Britain. We may therefore lay it down as an inconteſtible fact, that the labourer, or manufacturer of Great-Britain is taxed more than half the amount of the wages he draws. If, therefore, the German manufacturer had equal ſkill and machinery, he could afford his goods, excluſive of the raw materials, at half the price of the Britiſh tradeſman.

Here, then, is a cauſe, that muſt operate in giving foreign linens a preference in every market in the world, where they can be brought on equal terms. But the competition is perfectly on equal terms with regard to all America, and to every country but Great-Britain. For although there be a freight from Germany to Britain, this is compenſated fully by the freight of the raw material, flax uſed in the Britiſh manufactures; and the duties on foreign linens being drawn back at exportation, both manufactures ſtand equally at their prime
coſt

cost when sent from hence to any part of the world.

Having thus found the cause, which lies deep in the very foundation of the British government; a cause which will operate in all times, and in all places, where a competition arises between the manufacturer of a country heavily taxed and one that pays few or none;—Let us in the next place look out for the remedy.

Here, Sir, I will agree with Mr. Glover, that it would be better to give up manufactures in which we struggle against foreigners on unequal terms, provided we can give our people bread by a more profitable industry.—If the gentlemen of the woollen manufacture will find employment for the poor linen weavers in their business, no-body will say that the linen branch ought, in that case, to be an object of peculiar attention to government. — But let the experiment be tried.

tried. Set but 50,000 of the people now unemployed in the linen branch, to weave woollens, which they could learn to do in three months; What would be the confequence? We all know there are at prefent as many hands employed as the woollen trade demands.—Encreafe them; then would the clamour be irrefiftable, that the woollen manufactory is ruined.—Neverthelefs, in this cafe, more woollen goods than ever would be at firft wrought up. But no demand being made for the increafed quantity, prices would fall, and the quantity would gradually fink down to the demand of the market; you would then have in the place of humble petitions from Ireland and Scotland, 50,000 woollen weavers at your door.—Their arguments would no doubt awaken the attention, and move the feelings of this Houfe.

The experiment has been already tried with regard to the filk.—Some London mercers employed the weavers in Paifley, a manufacturing town in Scotland, to weave

weave silk gauzes; they soon reduced the prices 30 *per Cent.* and drove Spitalfields out of the trade.—This was the real occasion of the disturbances in London, which we all remember.

The same reasoning will apply to the hardware manufactures.

This question, however, naturally arises; How comes it that the woollen and hardware manufactures go on successfully, both which must be equally affected by our taxes, whilst the linen manufacturers are teizing the legislature, year after year, for bounties on their own linens, and duties on foreign linens? The answer is obvious.—The two first enjoy a compleat monopoly, both of the home consumption and the exportation to America.—Let the same experiment be tried with the linen, for seven years, and there will be found no occasion for bounties.—Parliament will be no more troubled with applications. This single

measure

meafure would, in an inftant, raife the linen trade to a magnitude and importance equal, perhaps fuperior, to the woollen manufacture, great and important as that now is.—If there be, therefore, no means of employing our people in other branches of bufinefs, and if the linen manufacture cannot employ them without parliamentary protection; they muft either receive that fupport, which will enable them to fubfift in Britain; or they muft and will emigrate. The effects of emigration, with regard to the intereft of every man who enjoys any portion of the foil in Great Britain or Ireland, has already been noticed.—They are fo manifeft that they will hardly be denied, even by Mr. Glover.—He has accordingly thought himfelf obliged to account for thefe emigrations, by making them folely proceed from the rapacious difpofitions of the landlords, in raifing their rents beyond what their tenants can pay.— It ftands however in proof before this honourable houfe, that many thoufand weavers,

weavers, with their families and inftruments, have gone to America within thefe few years; all people who held no lands, and could not be affected by the rife of rents.

It will at the fame time be admitted that fome tenants and labourers have alfo gone abroad; but whatever clamour may have been raifed againft landlords, the caufe of thefe emigrations, when traced, will be found to arife in a great meafure, if not entirely, from the decay of the linen manufactures.—For it is very well known that the fpinning is carried on by the families of the farmer and labourer: So that whilft the manufactures go on profperoufly, he can pay a good rent to the landlord by the aid of his family, who are fpinning within doors, while he is employed in the field; but when that refource fails, his affairs muft go to wreck: And thus, Sir, the emigration of this clafs of people is, by fair deduction, as imputable to the decay of the

D manu-

manufactures, as that of the weaver himfelf.

The queſtion now, Sir, is, what natural and proper remedy can be applied to this diſorder?—Bounties have been propoſed.—I confeſs; ſeveral difficulties occur to this plan.—Firſt, Bounties, as hitherto given, go only to exportation; whereas, we ſhall ſhew hereafter, that the firſt and natural object of every country ſhould be to ſupply the demand at home.—Secondly, Bounties are the mother of taxes. You can only give encouragement in this way, by firſt impoſing a tax to pay it, which tends to the increaſe of wages, and conſequently, to raiſe the price of manufacturing labour. —Thirdly, The bounty is only giving money to America, by ſelling linens ſo much cheaper than they could otherwiſe get them: It is, therefore, an abſurd policy; as it is ſupplying them with the produce of Britiſh taxes, in the price of linens, at the very time that it is found

neceſ-

neceſſary to tax them for the ſupport of government.—I will therefore lay aſide this plan entirely, and beg leave, in anſwer to the queſtion, to ſay, that the natural and proper remedy is this—Lay on ſuch a duty upon foreign linens as will enable thoſe of the Britiſh and Iriſh manufacture to find a preference in our home conſumption; and when the foreign linens ſhall, by this means, be entirely excluded from ſale here, and the quantity of our own increaſed ſo much as to enable us to participate in the exportation trade; then lay on ſuch duties upon the foreign linens ſhipped from hence for foreign parts, as will ſecure our linen a preference; and finally, when our quantity equals both the home and foreign demand, prohibit all German and other foreign linens whatſoever.

Three objections, from Mr. Glover, occur to this meaſure.

The first is, that forcing a trade by legiflative authority, is mifapplying the national induftry, and rendering it unprofitable; it is like rearing exotics in hot-beds, which can never thrive and profper, fo as to be beneficial to the country; but the moment they are abandoned, they will wither and decay: Whereas, by confining our culture to the natural production of our foil, no artificial aids will be neceffary; we will, on the contrary, be able, by the furplus of our native produce, to acquire fuch articles in exchange, on cheaper terms than we can rear them.

I readily admit the principle of this objection, were this country on a footing with the reft of the world in point of taxation. But, until this be the cafe, which can only be by throwing the whole national taxes upon the foil, or its produce, we muft either renounce every manufacture whatever, or compenfate, by the favour of legiflature, the heavy burden

burden now impofed upon us. I have already obferved, that it is by the means now propofed and no other, that our woollen and hardware manufactures have been created.—Both have been raifed from no very diftant period to their prefent magnitude and importance, entirely by the active and repeated interpofition of parliament in their favour: So that although they were reared and nurfed in a hot-bed, they are now hardy and vigorous, and can contend on equal terms with all the reft of Europe, without any particular favour from the public, as is evident from the large quantities fent to different European markets under the difadvantage of both freight and foreign taxation.—Here then are cafes in point.—All theoretical reafoning is liable to uncertainty; but experience, the guide of all wife men, can hardly deceive us. —It were eafy, by comparing the ftate of the woollen manufacture in the days of James and Charles the Ift, and the hardware fo late as Queen Anne's time, with

the

the state of these two manufactures now, to shew what will be the consequences of a similar conduct with regard to the linen; but it would be injurious to the wisdom of this honourable house to suppose such a detail necessary.

The first object with every state is to secure its own independence, by rearing and cultivating within itself, whatever is necessary for its existence, defence, or convenience. Few articles are now more necessary than linen. If, by prohibiting or taxing foreign linens, the consumption of Great Britain was secured to our own manufactures, we might pay, in the beginning, 1 *d.* or 2 *d.* per yard higher than we do at present; but the whole price paid to Germany, &c. would be saved; no money would go out of the country; and the landlord, the tenant, and every man interested in the prosperity of Britain, would feel the benefit by an increased population and a consequential demand for their respective

articles

articles of produce. Even this inconvenience would soon be removed; for the competition between the various manufacturers in Britain and Ireland, would early operate, and prices would fall lower than ever.—That this would follow, is not only evident from the hiſtory of the woollen and Birmingham manufactures, but from the linen itſelf, which, in conſequence of the paſt encouragement it has received, is now cheaper and better than ever.—I do not talk of the late ruinous fall of the prices, owing to the competition with Germany; but I affirm, and it will hardly be denied, that regularly and progreſſively as the manufacturers have increaſed in practical ſkill and experience, the goods have been improved and brought cheaper to market. —It may indeed be ſafely averred, that in ten years time, under the advantages of an excluſive market for our own linens for home conſumption, we would be cheaper ſupplied, than by foreign linens at preſent.

When

When the increased state of our linen trade will admit of our supplying the American market, or of participating in it by taxing foreign linens; the advantages to Britain are equally obvious. What do we gain by sending seven millions of yards of foreign linen to America? The freight, and profit of the merchant.—But if we export our own linen, the whole price is a net increase of the national capital. That is, if Great Britain gains 400,000*l.* a year by exporting foreign linens, it would gain, by exporting British or Irish linens, two millions.—And this is allowing the merchant for his profit and freight 20 *per cent.* which Mr. Glover will acknowledge is a very ample allowance.

It may be said, that the American would pay dearer for his linen than at present. This will doubtless be the case; until, by the continued exertions of the rival manufacturers, which would naturally result from such encouragement, they

they were enabled by fuperior fkill and machinery to compenfate the weight of our taxes.—This is, in a great meafure, the cafe with the woollen, and it is entirely fo with the hardware manufactures at prefent.—But fuppofing this fhould never be the cafe with the linen. It will be only and folely a tax upon America; a tax which her warmeft advocates admit your right of impofing; and which, confidering the difficulties that are likely to occur in taxing her more directly, is but juft and equitable. —It will have this further advantage of every other tax, that there will be no charge of collection, and every fhilling produced thereby, will come clear to the benefit of this country.

It has been faid that we ought not to encourage manufactures for internal trade. " *Traffic between fubject and fub-* " *ject cannot be productive of any national* " *wealth; and it is only by exporting* " *produce and manufactures that wealth*
" *is*

"*is received* *." From what school Mr. Glover has learnt this doctrine, I will not pretend to conjecture; for the honour of Scotland, I hope, it was not there; I will presume it to be a specimen of his "*common sense*," which that country is so totally devoid of; may they ever remain so!—In that country the opinion is, that the foreign trade of this and of every great nation is trifling, both in point of extent and advantage to the state and the individual, when compared with its internal trade.—The whole capital employed in foreign trade by this opulent and commercial country, is not equal to one year's expence during the late war; nay, it does not exceed the amount of one year's grofs taxes at this moment.—For the truth of this I appeal to the accounts of exports and imports, in viewing which, I defire only attention to this circumstance—That the exports and imports are carried on by one and the

---

* Mr. Glover's speech, p. 32.

the fame capital; the goods brought into Britain being either returns for the goods fent out, or the goods fent out returns for thofe brought in, bullion included; fo that only one of them can be put to account, and I leave Mr. Glover his choice of either.

If it be then a certain and undeniable fact, that the whole foreign trade of Great Britain does not employ a capital of 12 millions, and the utmoft ftretch of invention cannot make it greater; and were this the only fource of wealth, or did it indeed bear any proportion to the wealth of the nation; How could we levy 12 millions of grofs taxes yearly, which is our prefent fituation, although there be not more than 10 millions of net revenue? How could we have carried on a war at an expence of, from 12 to 18 millions yearly, for feven years together? I fhall leave Mr. Glover to reconcile this to his fyftem, and will now endeavour to explain it by mine.

Great-Britain contains above five millions of people: Thefe people fubfift at an expence of, at leaft, eight pounds per head. Here is then an internal trade of at leaft forty millions yearly. But how does this enrich?—I anfwer, the riches of a country confift in the riches of the individuals in that country; and if thefe will increafe without foreign trade, the country will grow richer.—If Mr. Glover has land to the amount of 1000 l. a year, he will either cultivate it himfelf, or leafe it to tenants. In either cafe, the produce will be at leaft three times the rent. Here is a clear increafe of capital, although there be no foreign trade. If Mr. Glover rents his lands, and fpends only 500 l. a year, he will be clearly richer without foreign trade. If the tenants can pay their rents, live and fave 500 l. they will alfo grow richer.—The fame reafoning will apply to every rank in life; to every profeffion and trade that can exift in a country.—Mr. Glover wears a good coat, a wig, and a fword,

when

when he attends this honourable houfe.—If his barber, taylor and fword-cutler can live by their bufinefs and fave 10l. yearly, apiece; although neither wigs, cloaths, nor fwords are exported, they will grow richer: But as the wealth of a country confifts in the accumulated wealth of the individuals, the country itfelf muft grow richer; and all this, without foreign trade.—I will add further, that this will equally happen (though not fo rapidly) if there were not a piece of coin, or bullion, in Great Britain.—For example, Mr. Glover may have invefted, at fome time, his whole capital on German linen; Was he poorer on that account? It is juft fo with the nation; it is the ftock of induftry and commodities that form the national wealth.—How trivial a part of our capital confifts in coin, has appeared by the late experiments made on the gold.

The next objection is, the influence that any difcouragement given to the
German

German linens here, might have on the fale of Britifh woollens in Germany.

The alarm has been founded, and the quiet and eafy woollen manufacturers have been artificially made parties in this queftion. They deferve a hearing, and are entitled to every preference compatible with the good of the ftate, where there arifes a competition of intereft. But I will beg leave to afk one queftion. Germany was, until lately, the great ftaple for hardware; Was the woollen manufacture hurt by the eftablifhment of the Britifh hardware, which is now, though but a modern acquifition, fold over all the four quarters of the globe, and in very large quantities to Germany itfelf? It can neither be faid that it was, nor would the argument be admitted if it had; becaufe the lofs of a woollen trade to the extent of even half a million [*], the full amount of

---

[*] I am aware of Mr. Glover's affertion, that although the exports to Germany be but half a million;

of all our exportations to that country by Mr. Glover's eftimate, would not juftify the giving up a manufacture by which the nation acquires feveral millions yearly. Yet, the hardware manufacture enjoys a monopoly againft Germany and all the world; not only of the confumption of Great-Britain, but of all America.

The argument, if it means any thing, means that foreign princes and ftates will prohibit, or difcourage the importation of our woollens, if we tax their linens.

---

million; yet, a great part of what we fend to Holland goes from thence to Germany, to four times that amount.—I doubt the fact; but were it admitted to its full extent, it does not affect my argument. In the firft place, I have allowed the whole exports as if they were of woollens; whereas woollens form but a fmall part of them.— 2dly. What paffes through Holland to Germany goes there as Dutch, not as Englifh goods: And a total prohibition of Britifh goods to Germany would only force the whole in place of a part to pafs through Holland.

linens. That at prefent they encourage the one, in confideration of the benefit they derive from the other. Now it will hardly be difputed, that the individual, every where, will buy his coat or fhirt where he can get it cheapeft. The queftion is only then with regard to ftates; and here I will beg Mr. Glover to point out any other country or ftate in Europe, which has ever confidered taxation in any point of view but for the purpofe of revenue, except France a very little, and perhaps of late Pruffia, in fome inftances; and it happens unfortunately for this argument, that our woollens are prohibited in both thefe countries. The maxims that prevail in all nations, appear fimply thefe; to confider what the prince or ftate wants; and, 2dly, what is the eafieft way of levying the taxes neceffary for fupplying thefe wants. It would be a difappointment to moft princes, if our goods were not carried into their country, becaufe they would be deprived of a fubject of taxation.

Money taxes, although of all others, perhaps, the easiest and best, occasion discontents and murmurs; it is frequently impossible to raise them in the most despotic governments. But a tax on goods is submitted to by the merchant, because he knows the buyer must pay him, with his profits on the tax itself, in the price of the goods. The poor consumer again is deceived. He thinks he is only paying for his coat, when he is perhaps paying, under that name, the hire of a soldier to fasten his own chains. Let any man reflect what murmurs the house and window tax occasioned, trivial as they are, and the ease with which the malt, soap, and candle taxes were submitted to, and he will see the force of this observation. Our woollens and hardware will find a market wherever they can be sent better and cheaper than from other countries. Princes will tax them according to their wants or conveniencies; but always so as not to disappoint the end of taxation, the raising of revenue,

But it is said, the king of Pruffia has the command of the great rivers, and if we disoblige him, by taxing the Silesia linens, he will prevent all trade with Germany. Were this plea to have weight, I beg to know where it would stop? If he can ruin our woollen trade in consequence of our laying additional duties on his Silesia linen, he is equally able to do it unless we take off the duties that now exist. Nay, he may insist on a bounty on the importation of his linens, and that they shall have a preference to our own. If our trade depends on the will of any prince or power on earth, we are no more a free people, but subject to the arbitrary dictates of others. Thank God! this is not the case; altho' his Pruffian majesty does possess places on most of the great rivers, he is so far from having the command of the German trade, that he can supply very few

few places in his own dominions without paſſing thro' other ſtates, by whom he is ſurrounded on every ſide. This complicated ſituation occaſions an arrangement among the different princes and ſtates whoſe dominions lie on the great rivers; the reſult of which is, mutual conceſſions and rates of taxation, ſuited to their reſpective ſituations and dependencies; theſe no ſingle prince can break through, without quarrelling with all the reſt. The wiſe and beneficent Governor of the univerſe has ſet bounds to the power of princes; he ſays to them as to the ocean, " Thus far ſhall " you go, and no farther." And with regard to the ſea coaſt, we may add, that four Engliſh frigates would effectually block up every communication that prince has with the ſea. It would be trifling to follow the argument further; we have experience to determine the queſtion. We were in open hoſtility with this prince during a great part of the war before laſt; would any civil

regu-

regulation excite his animosity so much as the support we gave to the Empress-Queen during that period? Is he of that mild and gentle temper, as to submit to injuries, when he can repel them? Did his heart ever refuse to execute, what his head could dictate for the annoyance of his enemies? Yet, what loss or injury did our woollen manufactures receive by our contention with that prince? But it is truly contemptible to talk of his resentment for regulating the internal policy of Great-Britain, according to its own interest; when there is not an injury in his power that our woollen manufactures do not sustain at this moment, even to a total prohibition of the importation of them into his dominions.

The law of God, and the policy of all nations, justify retaliation; and had our woollen manufacturers petitioned for a prohibition of Silesia linens, they would have acted with propriety, and would have deserved regard. Several instances can be be shewn of similar conduct by our legislature; to repeat them would be idle; the book of rates is in every body's hands.

We may, on the whole of this matter, safely assume, that our woollen trade can never be hurt, but will, on the contrary, be benefited by encouraging the linen; and although the clamour and artifice of some interested Hamburgh merchants have misled the woollen counties upon the present occasion, they will soon see and feel their own interest.

Mr. Glover's third objection falls now under consideration, *viz.* that encreasing the taxes on foreign linens, will encourage smuggling.

He has discovered, and says he has proof, that there is at present one smuggling company in Scotland; and he is greatly alarmed that if the duties on foreign linens be increased, smuggling
will

will become general, and the poor linen weaver ruined by the large quantities the ſmugglers will import, and the low prices at which he will ſell his goods. It were well for both Scotland and England that there were but one ſmuggling company in either; but unfortunately, until the minds and morals of men are mended, deſperate and diſhoneſt men will be found in every country where the duties are high, to run all hazards in attempts to earn a profit: But if it will be any ſatisfaction to Mr. Glover, I will inform him that there is more ſmuggling in one month, in the river Thames, than in all Scotland, in one year; and that in the very article of German linens. Conſiderable dealers have been known to enter their goods under wrong denominations, for the ſake of paying an inferior duty, and have thereby added the guilt of perjury to that of ſmuggling. But how does this agree with the reſt of his arguments? for, if additional duties will increaſe the importation of German
linens,

linens, then, whether they are smuggled or not, is of no confequence to our German friends. The woollen manufacturers could have no reafon to complain; and our good ally the king of Pruffia would have no caufe for wrecking his vengeance on us. We might ftill hope that he might content himfelf with prohibiting our woollens in his own dominions, without barring our trade to Germany altogether.

That increafed duties have a natural and neceffary tendency to promote fmuggling is undoubted; this, however, was never heard of as a reafon for abftaining to levy any tax which policy required. Brandy pays a duty of eight fhillings per gallon, and the original value of the fpirit is frequently under one fhilling per gallon; and yet very large fums of duty are annually paid, and brandy keeps up at a price that will afford this duty. Smugglers do not carry on their bufinefs from principles of patriotifm, to fupply the market cheap; they do it for their own profit, and fell as dear, allowing for the risk of the buyer, as the fair trader. The hazard of fmuggling is however fuch, that notwithftanding the profits they get by faving the duties, hardly an inftance occurs of any man in Great-Britain having carried it to any height, without being ruined. None indeed but people of defperate fortunes will engage in a bufinefs, where every failure of fuccefs, by forfeiture of the capital, involves in it the ruin of the adventurer.

If the principle be once admitted, that it is the intereft of Great-Britain to encourage our own manufactures, rather than the German; I would be glad to know how it is to be done but by duties on the latter. The wifdom of the Irifh, in the invention of ftamps for their linens, has indeed fuggefted a means of preventing fmuggling in that article beyond what can be contrived in almoft

any

any other. Let every piece of linen be ſtamped, at importation, with the rate of duty paid; this will not only protect the fair trader, but will enable every man who chuſes, to detect any frauds at importation by entering under wrong denominations.

Having now, I hope, fully anſwered Mr. Glover's objections, as far as they deſerve that name; I would here conclude, and leave all his invectives with regard to Scots projects, lunacy and circulation, entirely unnoticed, had I not heard that well meaning though ill informed men have been miſled by them. I will therefore beg your indulgence to make a few obſervations upon this ſubject.

The buſineſs of the Bank of England, and that of all banking ſocieties in Britain, is entirely of one and the ſame nature. It conſiſts in receiving depoſits of money, to lie at the command of the proprietors,

proprietors, and in iffuing notes which circulate as money. Thefe two things are the only foundation of profit; and the profit is got, by lending their notes and the money fo depofited, in the way of difcount on bonds or bills. From this it is evident none of them can draw any profit but by extending thefe loans beyond the fum of actual cafh neceffary to anfwer the demands that may be made on them, and confequently all fuch banks are expofed to injury and liable to ftop payment by any fudden fhock or difcredit. Witnefs the year 1745, with regard to the Bank of England; and 1772, with regard to the Air Bank.

The word Circulation is applied in various fenfes: like Patriotifm it is fometimes put for what is moft advantageous and beneficial in a free country; and fometimes for what is a moft pernicious evil to the ftate. The circulation of the Bank of England notes, Mr. Glover will

will acknowledge, is advantageous; but that of the Scots Air Bank, is hurtful; yet both are founded on the fame bafis, viz. extending their credit upon fecurities to a greater amount than they have gold or filver to anfwer at the time. Mr. Glover will I fuppofe allow, at leaft no man but himfelf will difpute, that were the Bank of England to have a demand made for all her notes in the circle at any one time, a much greater void would be found there, than in the Air Bank, when fuch an experiment was tried.

But the Air Bank drew bills on London to fupport their credit. So did the Bank of England on Holland, during the reigns of both William and Anne; and it is believed fince that time; tho' there be no fuch direct evidence of the facts in latter times, as the writers of the former periods afford us. What is then the ground of clamour againft the Bank of Air? That will beft appear
from

from a short account of its institution and history.

Scotland had long enjoyed two public Banks; but their capitals amounted only to about 100,000 l. each; a sum too small to be generally and universally useful. Other inferior banks had in the course of time been established; and a set of public spirited noblemen and gentlemen, observing the increase of trade and manufactures, in different places, by means of these little local Banks, judged that a more extensive company, with a capital and credit suited to the necessities of all, would be of like general advantage to the whole country. About one hundred and fifty men, chiefly of rank and fortune, did accordingly institute a Bank, and subscribed about 160,000 l. for beginning the business, binding at same time their whole fortunes, to the extent of about six millions, in security for the engagements of the company. This was the Bank of Air.

Air.—The management of this fociety, like all others, fell into the hands of four or five people, whofe local refidence, leifure and inclination, admitted of regular attendance. Thofe gentlemen, who were unacquainted with trade, attended more to the general principle of their inftitution, the encouragement of the agriculture and trade of Scotland, than to the natural flow progrefs of a circulation of notes. They lent fafter than they could get their notes to circulate through the country. The confequence of which was, That they fupplied the void by their credit with the London bankers, and in June 1772, they had 350,000 l. of bills running on London.

The Bank of England had found the fame diftrefs, for fome years, in a leffer degree; for though I will not aver that they had much increafed the fum of their notes during that period, becaufe I have not fufficient evidence of the fact;

fact; yet, it will be allowed, they had not diminished the extent of their dealings, and the same sum that they had formerly circulated, could not continue to float in the country; because every trading town in England has of late years got a bank, which sends forth its notes in its own corner, and thus occupies in part, the ground formerly possessed by the Bank.——To make this more plain, I beg leave to observe, that a certain sum of money is necessary for circulating the trade of every country; and whether that sum consist of gold, silver, or paper, it makes no difference, (provided the credit of the paper be fully supported) as far as it is employed for the purpose of internal commerce. But, as the precious metals are the only common monies used in Europe, where any country is possessed of more current money than answers the purpose of its internal commerce, the surplus of coin and precious metals will immediately be exported. Let me put

put the cafe of a market being overstocked with any other commodity, and it will ſtrike every man that this muſt be the conſequence : For the owner of that commodity will immediately caſt about and export what is above the demand to ſome other market where it is more in requeſt. The great misfortune of this ſubject is the perplexity with which it has been treated by moſt writers, who have conceived money to be ſomething different from any other commodity or article of trade, whereas it ſhould be conſidered intirely in the ſame point of view. Gold and ſilver are no articles of conſumption, nor do they produce any profit, but in ſo far as they are employed in exchange or barter for other commodities, therefore no man keeps them but as vehicles or machines for acquiring other articles, they being univerſally admitted as equivalents for and repreſentations of all other commodities; wherefore the quantity of theſe precious metals is limited in every country to its

uſe

ufe and wants in this way, fo that the moment the quantity exceeds what is neceffary for circulating the commerce of any country, the furplus will be exported to other countries for commodities of more real ufe, and where the demand is greater. But paper being confined to the country where it can command gold and filver, whenever there is a fuperabundance of it, the paper muft remain in circulation, whilft the gold and filver, not being in demand more than to circulate the paper, will be carried off. As foon as this comes to be the cafe, the exchange turns againft that country, becaufe no man will carry away the metals whilft he can get bills as cheap to anfwer his purpofe abroad; nor will any man export gold but for a profit, which profit he makes by felling his bill on Holland or France at a high exchange for the amount of the gold fo carried off. What was the reafon that, previous to the calamities of 1772, gold was at 4 l. 2 s. per ounce, and

filver

silver at 5 s. 8 d. per ounce? The principles juſt now explained will enable us to anſwer this queſtion. The reaſon was, that the quantity of paper money was greater than what anſwered the internal purpoſes of the country, for which reaſon the metals were continually ſeeking a market abroad, where they were in demand, and where the paper ceaſed to be a commodity, and by this conſtant exportation they became ſcarce and dear. As a further proof of this we may obſerve, that the exchange was againſt Britain with all Europe at the time that the gold and ſilver was ſo dear and ſcarce; whereas had this ſcarcity ariſen from a want of money, the exchange would have been in her favour. For whenever the Bank diminiſhed the circulation of notes, as we ſhall immediately relate, ſo as to make money ſcarce for the purpoſe of internal commerce, gold and ſilver became plentier than ever, the prices of both fell, and the foreign exchanges

changes have been ever since in our favour.

The Bank of England then finding it necessary to lessen the circulation of her notes, fixed upon the Scots paper as the first object for this purpose, and in June, 1772, took at once the resolution of refusing every Scots bill. What their reason was for this undistinguished rejection, no private man has a title to ask.—No man can believe that humour, passion, or resentment could enter into this measure; far less will it be supposed that any jealousy of the Scots manufactures, or predilection for the German, could operate. The mischief, however, was great; a run immediately was made on the Air Bank; their whole notes were brought in against them; and their debt to England was, by paying off their notes in Scotland, increased to 600,000 *l.* in a few months.—This measure of the Bank of England could not arise from any doubt of the security, because that
would

would imply an ignorance which cannot be presumed in such a respectable society; and the world is, by this time, perfectly convinced, that there never were grounds for any suspicion on this head; the Air Bank having given superabundant landed security for every shilling of debt contracted by them.—The stop of discounts at the Bank with regard to Scots bills was general; and the effect was proportioned to the cause. The almost unlimited facility with which all Scots bills had been discounted until the 20th of June, 1772, had led the London correspondents of that country to rely on the discount of the bills sent them from Scotland for their payments. The sudden and unforeseen stop of all discounts did therefore occasion four or five of them to cease making payments. But all or most of them have since gone on and satisfied every engagement.—This violent operation did not however relieve the Bank of England, until, by diminishing still greatly the other channels of her discounts,

counts, her notes in the circle were reduced to the fum that was barely neceſſary for the accommodation of the public; fince which, gold and filver have funk down to the coinage prices; and this will always be the cafe whilſt the currency of the country, whether coin or paper, is no more than fufficient for the purpofes of internal commerce.—The diſtreſs in Scotland was, however, great, in confequence of the ſtop of the Air Bank. A general diffidence and difcredit took place over the whole country; and nothing can fhew the true fituation of things there in a clearer point of view, than that amidſt all this great and general diſtreſs, only five houfes ſtopt; and of thefe the principal and greater part have paid or fatisfied their creditors by fecurities.—Let me not be mifunderſtood.—I do not under this aſſertion include the failure of a banking houfe in London, although one of four partners happened to be a Scotſman; neither do I include the confequences of that failure, although they ruined

three

three houses, two in London, and one in Scotland, because they were previous to the stopping of discounts by the Bank; and as well might the Dutch impute to England the failure of the Cliffords of Amsterdam, because they are English subjects, as to impute the convulsions in Scotland to the failure of that banking house, with whom they had no other connection than that one of the partners was from that country.—But Mr. Glover has avoided to particularize the transactions of private men, and he did it wisely; first, because such kind of discussions, unless for important and public benefit, is indecent, and even unjust, and the man who attempts it, should himself be above all reproach.—The principles and motives of conduct in individuals are latent and unknown, and from ignorance in this particular, many a man has suffered censure when he deserved applause.—I will also inform Mr. Glover, if he does not know it,—That there were men involved in these affairs,

who

who ſtand high in the opinion of thoſe who know them, and of their country in general, both as to worth and abilities, and who, if they choſe to enter the liſts upon this occaſion, would ſoon make it unneceſſary for either of us to attempt the illuſtration of this ſubject.

I will now conclude what I have to ſay on this head by one aſſertion, which Mr. Glover may deny if he can.—That in the whole of the bad affairs, within theſe two years paſt, ariſing from whatever cauſe, whether from misfortune or miſ‑ conduct either of individuals or of publick bodies, all England cannot aſcertain a loſs of 10,000 l. by Scotland.

Let not men be impoſed on by words; a circulation of 600,000 l. has a mighty found.—A Bank in Air, was wit in the mouths of thoſe who uſed the word.— But mighty as the ſum of 600,000 l. may found when applied to Scotland— Mr. Glover knows of a ſingle houſe in

a very

a very different quarter, which failed within thefe eighteen months, and whofe fingle circulation was equal to this fum, three-fourths of which are loft.—Did this excite any clamour againſt Holland? Yet the lofs to England by that fingle houfe is greater, I will venture to maintain, than has been loft by all Scotland fince the Union.

I will not examine the principles upon which Mr. Glover was pleafed to lay open in this houfe, any information he may have received from the Bank of Air, either by perufing their books or papers, or in private converfations with the managers. But I would afk, upon what principle is a whole country to be arraigned, for the error or mifconduct of four or five men? Was the Englifh nation ever reproached for the grofs abufes committed by individuals in the South-Sea year? Are the great yearly and daily bankruptcies with which our Gazette is filled, owing to the imprudence or mif-

fortune

fortune of individuals, confidered as a reflection on the nation?——One thing muft have occurred to Mr. Glover in examining the affairs of the Air Bank, which is fingular, though exactly true, that amongft the immenfe fums lent out by, and due to that company, there is nothing owing by the linen dealers or manufacturers of Scotland. The managers of that fociety were landed men, and the farmers and improvers of land were, they thought, the moft ufeful citizens, and were as fuch fupported by them. With what grounds can it then be faid, that the linen manufacture was injured by the Air Bank? or for what purpofe was it introduced into this queftion, unlefs to fhew Mr. Glover's great importance?

To conclude: If this houfe fhall be fatisfied that the linen manufacture fuffers greatly from the interference of the German goods—If you are fatisfied that the home trade is of more confequence than the

the foreign to this nation; that our own manufactures deserve encouragement rather than those of foreigners; that the distress of the linen trade proceeds from the weight of parliamentary taxes, and that it is therefore a duty of the legislature to support our manufactures under this pressure; we shall humbly hope for relief. If this relief is only to be obtained by additional taxes on the foreign linens, I hope parliament will not be deterred from imposing them, either by groundless apprehensions of resentment from German princes, or the bugbear idea of encouraging smuggling; but will consider the importance of enabling the industrious weaver to gain his subsistence at home, and not reduce him to the necessity of emigrating to America. The woollen manufacture was gained to Britain by the oppression of the government of Spain; let us not lose the linen by a similar conduct.

FINIS.

www.ingramcontent.com/pod-product-compliance
Lightning Source LLC
Chambersburg PA
CBHW050846300426
44111CB00010B/1146